Global Deals

Marketing and Managing
Across Cultural Frontiers

Michael Hick

Skyward Publishing
Dallas, Texas

**Michael Hick** is an internationally known keynote speaker and seminar leader. He makes presentations to Fortune 1000 companies, non-profit organizations and government agencies worldwide. He is Director of Global Business Initiatives, a Houston based consulting firm developing International Business skills for managers and assisting companies throughout the world in their global expansion strategies.

Testimonials

"Michael Hick's highly readable *Global Deals* is an essential book for every business leader who even thinks about doing business overseas. All managers who catch international flights should have a copy of *Global Deals* in their briefcase."

Tony Alessandra, Ph.D.,
Author, *The Platinum Rule* and *Charisma*

"We do business in 20 languages and 35 countries. This book is a powerful, practical, insightful guide to building relationships, increasing sales, and boosting revenues for us and for any global company."

Brian Tracy, Author, Speaker,
CEO Brian Tracy International

"Michael Hick has written a fabulous book which shares the wisdom he has acquired during a lifetime of international business transactions. If you've been successful in international business, this book will hone your skills. If you've been frustrated by attempts at international business, this book will set you straight. Don't leave home without it!"

Roger Dawson,
Author, *Secrets of Power Negotiation*

"This is a compelling book! *Global Deals* is a book we have all needed for quite some time. In this age where cultural differences sometimes spawn hatred and resentment, it is refreshing to know that a little cultural understanding can lead to some very good deals. Michael Hick has written a book which is not only highly useful and financially rewarding to readers, but it is also a very enjoyable read! Filled with stories and real-life examples, you will love this book!"

Jim Cathcart, Author, *The Acorn Principle*
and *The Eight Competencies of Relationship Selling*

"If you travel to other places, work with others who do, deal with people who come from other places, or simply want to better understand what the 'global business environment' really means, this is a book you'll want to read–twice. Getting from 'hearing what they said' to 'knowing what they meant' is the key to getting things done. Michael Hick shows you the way."

Warren Evens, Founding Chairman of the International Federation of Professional Speakers, 5000+members in 27 countries

"The same wit and charm that has taken Michael Hick from Russian to Australia can be found in his new book *Global Deals*. A hard-nosed and practical businessman, Michael can show you the hidden rules that get international deals done and long-term overseas business relationships formed."

Bernard Hale Zick, Author, *Negotiating Paradox–How to Get More By Giving More* and *Power Marketing for Consultants*

"Understanding why the world's culture groups think and act the way they do and applying that knowledge to negotiating, selling and managing is immensely important for every manager who intends to be competitive in today's business world. *Global Deals* explains the skills we need to thrive in the new global economy, where doing day-to-day business across cultural and political frontiers is rapidly becoming a way of life."

Daniel Burrus, Author, *Technotrends*

"In a relatively short time, we've moved from doing business with our neighbors to doing business with people we may never meet in places we may never go–in languages we don't speak. This is all part of the increasingly rapid globalization of our economy. With different cultures come different rules of engagement. Read and apply what you learn in this engaging book and speed your journey toward global success."

Roger E. Herman, CSP, CMC, FIMC, APF, Strategic Business Futurist, Author, *Impending Crisis*

"Michael Hick inspires thought, insights, and profound knowledge. He knows that going global is a mindset first, a series of strategies next, and the courage to do business creatively. This book is a mind expander and, thus, a business expander."

Hank Moore, Author, *The High Cost of Doing Nothing*

"This is a must-read book for any leader who wants to understand and pursue global opportunities for business and commerce. Practical. Useful. Substantive."

Nido R. Qubein, Chairman, Great Harvest Bread Co.
Founder National Speakers Foundation

"Thinking global is an essential mindset for any executive whose responsibilities include planning for the future. *Global Deals* provides a solid foundation and proven methodologies for making that mindset a reality in the way a company conducts business. Don't just read it! Study it, refer to it regularly, and don't lend it out!"

George Morrisey
Author, Morrisey on Planning, Series

"*Global Deals* is an engagingly written practical guideline that is a must for those seeking to acquire new skills as international negotiators or those seeking to expand their knowledge about doing business internationally. Michael Hick writes in a persuasive, easy to read and to the point, eloquent style that manages to balance motivational intent with practical applications. It is the kind of work that can be easily read in one sitting and then revisited as a reference manual."

Juan C. Perez, Ph.D., Executive Director, International Initiatives
Houston Community College System

Publisher: Skyward Publishing, Inc.
             17440 N. Dallas Parkway
             Suite 111
             Dallas, Texas 75287
             Phone: 972-490-8988
             E-mail: skyward@semo.net
             Website: http://www.skywardpublishing.com

Library of Congress Cataloging-in-Publication Data

Hick, Michael.
    Global Deals: Marketing and Managing Across Cultural
    Frontiers / by Michael Hick.
    p. cm.
    Includes bibliographical references.
    ISBN 1-881554-30-9
    1. International business enterprises—Management—
    Cross-cultural studies. 2. Export marketing—Cross-
    cultural studies. 3. Sales management—Cross-cultural
    studies. 4. Negotiation in business—Cross-cultural studies.
    5. Intercultural communication. I Title.

HD62.4 .H533 2002
658.8'48—dc21   2002010517

Printed in the United States of America

Table of Contents

Acknowledgments

I could never have completed this book without the technical help of numerous people, particularly my wife Bernice McElwain-Hick. Others who were helped were Maralyn Bernard in the editing process and Annette Lavine who has a published author's sense for good copy. All are talented unsung heroes.

My thanks to countless friends in the National Speakers Association who taught me how to write a book and not give up, particularly Tony Alessandra, the late Art Berg, Dianna Booher, Dan Burrus, Tim Connor, George Morrisey, Alan Weiss, Dottie Walters, Somers White, and Thom Winninger, all highly successful authors.

Then my thanks to Skyward's Jim Harris and Shirleen Sando, who believed in the book, and Barney Zick who showed me how to get it done.

Global Deals

Marketing and Managing Across Cultural Frontiers

Introduction

As I walked into my office after the usual early morning physical assault of the London underground, the phone rang. Tokyo on the line, Mr. Hick," I was told.

"Hello. Michael Hick here," I answered. In the mid-1970s, international calls were not of the clear, sharp clarity they are today, and what I heard next, through the phone static, was a representative of a large Japanese insurance company with a proposal for our firm. The group wanted to bring an overseas underwriting branch to London and have our firm manage it. They wished to commence as soon as possible in the new year. Could I meet them somewhere on neutral ground to put it together? "What about Hawaii in ten days?"

"Certainly," I responded, breathless with excitement. I looked out of my office window at the wet roofs of the city of London under a late November sky and said, "I'll be there."

"Lucky bugger," complained my colleague, Tony. "Getting away from this bloody place for a few days before Christmas. Some people have all the luck."

* * *

Ensconced at the Hilton Hawaiian Village, Oahu, I looked out over the tropical blue Pacific. London seemed a lifetime away. My technical assistant, Tom Kerr, and I had met the group from Tokyo at a nearby Japanese hotel where they were staying. There were five of them. The leader, Ozo, was not the one I had spoken to on the phone. He did all the talking; the others listened very respectfully at a distance. In fact, I'm not sure to this day whether any of them even spoke English. Ozo suggested that we rest for a day after our long flight.

"Fine with us," I said as I thought of lounging in the pool and spreading out on the silver sand beach.

"Tomorrow we will all take a tour of the island and get to know our environment," Ozo said.

"Fine," I again replied, remembering that he was the client.

The odd thing was that Ozo was not on the tour the next day. A couple of brand-new Japanese chaps turned up. One had the American Express Card; the other spoke the English.

On the morning of our third day there, Ozo called, saying, "Sorry I could not come on the tour, but I had some business to do." That stirred up my work-ethic conscience.

"When are we going to begin our discussions, Ozo?" I inquired.

"Today, this afternoon. We will meet at 3:30 and then have dinner."

I had no sooner put the phone down than it rang again. My boss was calling from London. "Just calling to see how it's all going."

"Fine, just fine," I responded, not mentioning the magnificent weather, swimming, island tours, or the good food. Our afternoon meeting was remarkable by the fact that, apart from Ozo, we had met none of the other five Japanese in the room. Dinner was spectacular, but little seemed to be moving on the negotiations. Tom Kerr, my practical conscience, grumbled, "Bloody waste of time if you ask me."

The following two days were the weekend, so we went shopping and down to the beach. I was getting entirely too much suntan for London criticism.

Sunday night the phone rang. It wasn't Ozo; it was my wife calling from England. "When are you coming home? Don't you realize that Christmas is only ten days away?"

"Heavens, I hadn't thought about Christmas!"

This time I called Ozo at his hotel. "Sorry, Mr. Ozo has been called back to Tokyo," I was told. "He will be back tomorrow. Meantime, I, Mr. Tanaka, will take our meeting."

"Mr. Tanaka, we have to be back in London by Friday; we need to have an agreement signed by then, please." Another weekend away would be death by Christmas pudding.

That evening the boss called again. His voice was like a dentist's drill. "No excuse. I've got this deal in next year's budget. Bring it home or else!"

Ozo was a day late coming back to Hawaii. I was getting fed up with blue skies and silver sand. Confronting him, I said, "Ozo, we've got to have an agreement early tomorrow—we are leaving on the afternoon plane."

"No problem. I will have an agreement ready for your signature and will pick you up at your hotel for the airport."

Wedged between four Japanese gentlemen in a wild drive to the airport, I signed a deal that was not as good for us as we had hoped. The Japanese side constantly wanted to amend and fine-tune the contract. It had a short life and led to many misunderstandings, mostly culture based.

If only I had done my homework on the techniques of negotiating with the Japanese, I might have done a better deal.

If I had realized that we were working on their time-table, that I should have agreed on an outcome with them first, that they work in groups, that developing the relationship was primary, and that they do not celebrate Christmas in the same way that we do, things would have gone more smoothly.

I might have succeeded in negotiating a better deal for my company if I had understood that, for the Japanese, a signed contract is only the beginning and that they like to adjust and amend it as time changes the conditions.

* * *

The challenge of building overseas business, with its massive opportunities, will confront every manager seeking to break into new markets. The trade routes of those having done this are littered with gravestones of failures, broken deals, collapsed companies, frustration, regrets, and huge amounts of wasted money. Understanding a few basic principles and learning some new skills can avoid many problems. Like any new business venture, pushing your business into international activity is a management skill that can be learned and developed.

These chapters will give you some answers to your overseas business expansion and assist you in navigating the torrid and confused streets of culture differences. To the uninitiated, trying to drive in these conditions is asking for trouble: crazy drivers come from every direction; pedestrians, caring not for their own safety, step into the road; taxis blare out and rickshaws dodge between the trucks; the noise, the smell, and the pollution are overwhelming to the visitor. We call it culture shock.

Since September 11, 2001, we recognize how little we know about the way the rest of the world thinks and acts. Cross-culture shock turns into cross-culture catastrophe, which, despite global communication, often encourages the ancient prejudices, antagonisms, arrogance, and envy associated with cross-culture incompetence and upon which war feasts itself. The global manager's world is not always a safe place, but it has always attracted the entrepreneurial adventurer willing to take business and personal risks. This book is about risk-reduction by becoming world-savvy.

During previous periods of globalization (there have been many in man's history), there was always one cultural force attempting to dominate all others by believing that theirs was the right way. Victorian entrepreneurs believed that their mission was to civilize the savage and the wars of the western world were wars of culture control, just as the first war of the twenty-first century turns out to be a war of culture collision.

Today's globalization process is different, not only because there is a ferocious anti-movement against a perception that America dominates the world economy, the world financial institutions, the United Nations, and the deeply influential pop culture, but also because we are dealing with a very different world from the one our Victorian ancestors lived in. Two massive factors, unknown to people one hundred years ago, have swept the world and changed it forever: the technology of the Internet and the technology of travel. These practical tools, combined with the belief in self-determination and cultural independence, have created the paradox of all connected, yet all different. Included in this equation is the fact that as cultures become more subject to globalization (or Americanization as some call it), they become more attached to, and protective of, their root culture. The spirit of fundamentalism grows from this.

Globalization isn't going away anytime soon. Certainly for the foreseeable future, managers must operate in its whirlpool and construct deals that will hopefully stay together in the wild waters of cultural mix, confusion, and collision.

Getting along with others is a life lesson that we start experiencing at a very early age. We soon learn that tolerance is a virtue; however, many of us take prejudices, judgments, and enmities to the grave, particularly when they relate to opinions about people who are not like us.

We may have harbored some of these hang-ups for years. Some are developed from the company we keep; some we obtain from experience, and some we just invent as we move through life. Whatever the cause, the effect can be devastating–particularly when it comes to business.

This book gives advice on how to avoid unnecessary collisions when driving your business through the chaotic streets of the world's cultural differences.

1

Going for the Global Gold

Standing in front of me in the queue at London's Gatwick airport was a man of fifty or so waiting to check in for the same flight to Houston. When it came his turn, the security officer asked him, "Sir, where is your office located?"

"Right here," replied the passenger, indicating his Compaq laptop carrying case. He was perfectly serious.

"Mmm," said the security officer, struggling to fill in the right box on his questionnaire, "maybe we need to update this form."

Working conditions and methods are moving much faster than the bureaucracies and systems that traditionally formed the framework for business. Suddenly, we are *living* global, and all our institutions, governments, and agencies have been left standing, while struggling to cope with a world that has burst the banks of their control and flooded their power base.

Meanwhile, corporations are looking around at the new environment and eagerly reaching out to grasp the opportunities unfolding before their very eyes in this Aladdin's cave of surprises. Global expansion is a major priority for business and will remain so for the foreseeable future.

International diversity of business risk and production is seen as the only way to avoid the consequences of overwhelming local competition. The global marketplace is the largest and potentially the most rewarding opportunity that businesses face as we begin a new century. It was not always this way. Global opportunity has been with us before, but at that time, the rules were different.

Near View Mirror

In 1885 the English city of Birmingham was a hive of activity. Engineering enterprises were springing up all over this grimy town, and families were pouring into the area from the countryside in search of work and wealth. Rampant free enterprise was on the go and fortunes were being made in half a lifetime, something unheard of in the English social system. Huge houses for the nouveau riche were built in the Warwickshire countryside away from the smoking chimneys, and *iron kings* became masters of men and machines as they fed the avaricious demand of the industrial revolution. In a short few decades, Britain changed from being nothing-but-picture-postcard pastoral to the major industrial nation in the world. Nothing had changed the world up to that point like the industrial revolution changed it in the nineteenth century. No longer would civilized, or even semi-civilized, man live in a purely agricultural society, for in that period, the known world was networked with a web of rail tracks, and towns and cities grew like mushrooms after a warm dew-filled night.

Within a matter of a few years, it was clear to the iron kings, the cotton kings, and the textile kings that they could not feed their huge manufactories from business derived solely from Britain. After all, Britain was of limited size and population. Perhaps there would be some maintenance, the occasional bridge to build, or some new factory to equip, but the heady days of vertical growth were over. Profits would plummet, dreaded bankruptcy would loom, and social disgrace and poverty were just around the corner. Not only that, but it was getting increasingly difficult to make big profits in England. Legislation against the employment of children and safety controls of dangerous machinery were drawing the attention of Parliament.

Never to be outdone, the kings of industry were, if nothing else, resourceful. The men who had originated the steam engine, the locomotive, the blast furnace, the spinning machine, and a thousand other brilliant inventions would not be held back in their quest to keep the chimneys smoking. What about doing business abroad?

The very idea must have conjured fearful thoughts in the broad chests of these John Bull Englishmen. The world was a different and more difficult place in those days, full of people *not like us*. Where would our John Bulls go? Certainly not to Europe. The only two countries in continental Europe that might be interested in English products were either competitors or political enemies.

France had always been at loggerheads with England and the old enmities take generations to die; after all, 1885 was only seventy years after Waterloo. *You could never trust the French, and they can't speak "king's" English.*

What about Germany? In 1885 the Germans were in the throes of their own industrial, political, and geographic revolution as Bismarck was hammering out his steel agenda on the anvil of central Europe. These Mr. Bulls would certainly not be popular there and, besides, *those Germans shout too much.*

In the last decades of the nineteenth century, Britain was building its empire from Singapore to Saskatchewan, from Calcutta to Cape Town. At midday on Tuesday, June 22, 1897, Queen Victoria of England–Defender of the Faith, Empress of India, Ruler of the British Dominions beyond the Seas–entered St. Paul's Cathedral to thank God for the greatest empire the world had ever seen. At that moment, she could claim that she ruled over no less than half a billion subjects. This was the high point of British influence across the globe with the hackneyed claim: "The sun never sets on the British Empire." That bold, imperial statement may have been geographically correct, but even as the noble queen took her seat with the highest in the empire, her control over this disparate collection of nations and races was starting to crack. Wars against the Sudanese, Zulus, Boers, Afghanis, and Maoris were taking place, or about to take place, as Britons made their political, religious, and cultural presence felt.

Our intrepid John Bull character, however, believed that, protected by the greatest navy on the seven seas, he could work his business acumen anywhere in Victoria's realm. Between 1880 and 1900 the worth of Britain's machine tool exports doubled to $40,000,000, which equals $4 billion in today's currency. These iron kings sold mining machinery, dredging gear, and stone crushing machines to Australia, lumbering plants and saw mills to Canada, fire tenders and locomotives to China, Singapore and India, lighthouse machinery to New Zealand, printing equipment to the United States, and steam cranes and drilling equipment to South Africa. They built dams, canals, and rail and road systems through impassable jungles and over endless deserts. British-built ships sailed these cargoes over the world's oceans; British banks financed the trade; Lloyd's of London insured the venture, and British culture ruled.

These entrepreneurs, from a variety of cultures, equipped the planet with railroad lines, bridges, telegraphs, and steam ships, and, in a short three or four decades, changed the way the world lived as it moved from an agrarian into an industrial economy. This was the age of the amateur, the age when creative ingenuity dominated science and people of little or no formal education were making extraordinary constructions, discoveries, and inventions. Sheer adventure pushed the boundaries of human capabilities and nothing was normal again. They looked just like us, except for side-whiskers and stovepipe hats.

Scot on the Rocks

Scotsman Alexander M. Ross built the first iron bridge across the St. Lawrence River at Victoria in 1859. It carried the Canadian Pacific Railway over a point on the river two miles wide where the torrent ran at 2,500 cubic feet per second. Observing engineers said that the bridge would topple under the blocked ice of the first winter. Not only did the masonry piers and the iron rail bed withstand the test of that first winter, but also, many years later, it was found to be easier to reuse them to support a new road bridge rather than dismantle them and rebuild another system. Ross had little formal education, was working in a totally different environment, and was from a foreign culture.

Gold Cooker

South Africa owes its position as the world's major gold producer to another Scot, amateur chemist J. S. MacArthur. In 1889 the South African gold mining industry had come to a halt. Only three years after the rush had begun, the miners met an immovable problem. Their gold-bearing seams hit a pyretic zone, and they could not extract enough gold from the pyrites to make the effort worthwhile. Their property was put up for sale, businesses went bankrupt, and miners left the country. A year later, in 1890, along came MacArthur, who arrived in Johannesburg with an idea. Why not use his special cyanide process to get rid of the pyrite? The miners were skeptical as they watched him with his pipes and vats, and they grumbled about the acrid smell. However, all that changed when an almost perfect gold ingot emerged from MacArthur's little portable furnace. He had saved the economy of an entire country.

MacArthur's invention, along with the development of hundreds of others during that prolific age of discovery, changed a geographic wilderness into a country fit for modern families.

Nowhere else was change more prevalent than in the United States where, in the space of fifty years, a continent was tamed by the might of industrial invention and production.

We sometimes talk as if change were a phenomenon of our times. Not so. Consider the upheaval of the period we are discussing. This was major change. Agrarian people moved from basic farming to machine tools, from mule back to railroad track, from sail to ocean steamer, and from field to city.

The population commotion that occurred in European cities 150 years ago is now happening, without hesitation, throughout the rest of the world. Consider Tehran. At the time of the Islamic revolution, 45 percent of the population of Iran lived in cities. Today it is 63 percent and rising. When the Shah was overthrown in 1979, there were 5 million people living in Tehran. Since the revolution, the population of the Tehran/Karaj conurbation has grown to approximately 8.5 million.

Surfing the Steel Web

The massive changes and threats to culture stability in the nineteenth century were taking place not only among the comparatively educated Europeans and North Americans but across the swamps of Bengal and the Jungles of Madras, over the peaks of Peru and the pampas of Argentina, through the ravines of the Rift valley, along the steppes of Tsarist Russia, and in the deserts of Sudan. Within a generation, this new type of web–a web of steam and steel–surrounded the world. The entrepreneurs spreading their promise of wealth and prosperity were there–*surfing* this early day web connecting traditional and cultural boundaries–*surfing* for opportunity at every bend of the river.

This great age of three or four generations ago, filled with global expansion, was not, therefore, dissimilar to our own. It is our *near view* mirror.

American business has always been conscious of competition. It is the bedrock of the antitrust concept; it is regarded as the natural law of consumer interest; and it is part of the inherent freedom endowed to the United States citizen. The opportunities presented to a start-up business in the later years of the last century must have been awesome: a great expanding country with no apparent limitations, thousands of fresh immigrants coming in to man the factories, a prosperous customer base, all anxious to improve their living standards. Banks and institutions were, as well, ready to lend, and there was negligible taxation. It must have seemed like a dream world, although on closer inspection that was certainly not the case. Economic cycles weren't a new phenomenon when they hit our fledgling business, and the damage they did was awful. Vast numbers of men were put out of work with devastating social consequences. In some cases, it destroyed the social fabric of an entire town.

King Capital

Businessmen of that period were not renowned for their social conscience or cultural empathy. Capital was king and people were expendable. Thousands of businesses went bankrupt in their early years. Fortunes were lost, and brilliant inventions and ideas were swept away in the winds of economic turmoil. But the profound ability of entrepreneurs, coupled with the spirit of America, enabled the overturned to be uprighted, the failures to become successful. Few nations have the deep cultural instinct to start again, despite all odds. Few national cultures have the willingness to forgive failure like America.

It has been said that since World War II American business moves into major expansion every twenty years. In the 1950s companies broke out from their local city marketplace and became regional; in the 1970s they became national; and in the '90s they became international. Seeking new markets, moving away from local competition, following the customer–whatever the reason, it only applied to firms having the financial resources, having a product or service that could be duplicated, and having the owner/management urge to step into unknown territory. These essentials were rarely present together, so in the '70s only a handful of firms made the leap into the international void. Now, thirty years later, it's different. Everybody, yes, everybody, can go for the *global gold*. Modern technology has seen to that.

Why Go Global?

Why should you go global? Well, it should not be just because your customers have already gone global, although that could be as good a reason as any. But, much more important, going international is a frontier that has all the wonderful unknowns, including the most unusual learning experiences you could wish for and some of the best return on investment you could hope for–providing you follow the new rules which apply to doing business overseas compared to doing business in hometown, U.S.A.

"How many more times do we have to reduce our

prices?" "What more must we have to do to service this account in order to keep it?" " We get squeezed from both sides–they think you can get blood out of a turnip?" Regardless of the business you're in, you've heard this before, over and over again. And there's only one promise: it's going to get worse.

Most business is on a roller coaster of *Cheaper, Faster, Better!* As we know, on a roller coaster, we can't all sit in the front seat. And that's precisely what happened to hometown, U.S.A.

Wal-Mart arrived!

Our competitors are already over there!

Every minute of every day (and night), businesses do business overseas. Our competitors are already there making deals, making money, and building alliances. Time after time people at home wonder why their tried and trusted relationships, built over many years, become disturbed by influences from abroad. Simple. Overseas business often becomes more progressive and competitive, worldlier than the business at home. Managers with overseas experience are at the cutting edge of competitive challenges, and they often introduce wider perspectives to the equation. The relationships are often deeper, due to shared entrepreneurial challenges and foreign adventures, as well as from the culture mix brought into the organization. Can you really afford for your competitors to make deals with your customers just because you haven't left your familiar territory?

Lost Energy

Houston-born and raised Jack Skinner got a job with a local insurance agency. He soon found that he had the best of both worlds. He could keep company with his childhood and college buddies and, at the same time, keep in close touch with the roller coaster, boom 'n' bust oil business he'd grown up around. He landed a prime account–a local-based oil well equipment-engineering firm, Danford Engineering–where an old school friend was company comptroller.

Danford's set up an independent subsidiary in the United Kingdom to better service their North Sea accounts. The U.K. firm prospered and fared better than the Houston company during the downturns of the oil business. Tim Collins, the English managing director, became the star performer in the group. Suddenly, he was appointed global CEO of Danford's, which by now was selling in thirty countries and manufacturing in six.

In an age of global expansion, Danford's had to keep up, and global service of insurance was just part of the jigsaw Tim Collins had to manage. But he gave Jack Skinner a fair hearing. "Can you service Danford's business in the United Kingdom, Australia, South Africa, and the Middle East?" he needed to know.

Jack had to say that he was unable to do that. His knowledge was limited to local markets; he had no global understanding of his profession. This was not what Tim Collins wanted to hear. He turned to a friend at global insurance broker Marsh who could offer service in all his locations.

The Jack Skinner story is happening every day around the world. Local-based companies are not keeping up with global-based customers.

Service industries have recognized the need for global presence for a number of years, and this has previously been the province of the big firms. Large-sized firms of insurance brokers, attorneys, accountants, advertising agencies, architects, and others have set up offices and relationships with representative firms of similar style and quality. Today, however, trade and professional associations are establishing a presence overseas. They are working with local interests, putting alliances together, and helping to create long-term relationships so that their smaller members can benefit from global coverage and the input of foreign business and experience.

Qualcomm's Quandary

Global competition has been rife for years in the world of high tech. Consider Qualcomm. This innovative, San Diego-based telecommunications company believed that nothing could prevent it from becoming the world leader in cellular phone technology. Then along came LM Ericsson, the Swedish mobile phone giant. Using a lethal combination of organized competition and government regulation, Ericsson almost kneecapped Qualcomm by devising a new standard for the next generation of cellular telephones based on, but not compatible with, Qualcomm's technology. Ericsson then used its well-connected network with European regulators and got the standards changed to align with its own standards. In short, Qualcomm was caught off guard when the Swedes used their culture-specific relationships with European regulators to give them competitive advantage.

Next Ericsson recruited the support of Nokia of Finland, Siemens of Germany, and Nippon Telegraph and Telephone of Japan. This combined group then placed the new standards before the United Nations rule-setting body on telecommunications. All's fair in love, war, and business–a perfect example of culture collision. The fourteen-year-old Qualcomm could have been frozen out of world markets by this carefully planned strategy, based on Swedish understanding and ability to negotiate with government regulators. Qualcomm fought back. Using every weapon in the armory, they filed intellectual property lawsuits on an international scale and sought assistance from the U.S. Department of Commerce to counteract the European regulatory action. What could be more laced with American culture than that?

Cultural-driven strategies have been used for centuries to defeat competition. Qualcomm, a free-rolling entrepreneurial business, was not used to competing on the turf of a giant north European organization the size of some governments and, in many ways, run like a government. It became evident that the tough world of high stakes and high tech was not for the fainthearted or for those overly impressed with the excellence of their own product. Qualcomm realized, after some immense pain and expense, that their big competitor was very active in global strategic warfare, using every fiber of its cultural instincts to gain victory.

Regulators rarely understand the extremes of world competition and are often criticized for taking action against consumer interests, particularly when the powerful persuasion of politically connected corporations is brought to bear.

Your domestic competitors are already working in the global market and can attack your prize accounts, using every available weapon including those of their cultural connection. In these days of commercial chaos and constantly moving targets, we have little or no idea from where the attack may come. One thing is for sure: few of the original rules apply. Try to figure out their next move by asking, "Where are they coming from?"

Innovate or Die!

The connection between culture mix and innovation is becoming a well-appreciated reality.

In July 1995, having completed substantial study and research, the Australian Manufacturing Council held a groundbreaking seminar with some of the most successful, and not so successful, firms in Australia. The intention of the study was to discover the reasons and methodology for innovation in business. Large firms, small companies, overseas-owned companies, and independent operations as wide-ranging as manufacturers of data communications equipment, horticultural products, software, and protective clothing were all included.

The major conclusion developed from the study and seminar was that international business and creativity were closely intertwined. Those firms of any size doing global business were leaders in the innovation process. The final report said that government policy, which aims to enhance both exporting and innovativeness, is mutually reinforcing. Push on one, and the economy also gets the advantage of the other. Encouraging firms to export might well be the single best measure for stimulating innovation.

By the same token, innovative firms are more likely to export. Constantly pitching your product, service, and price against the best in the world keeps you right on the mark where innovation is a permanent part of the picture. The pressure on your business to improve is balanced by your enhanced capacity to deliver. The cycle of innovation is driven by continuously looking outward.

This capacity is provided by access to a constant flow of new customers, employees, and associates with different attitudes, background, belief systems, and priorities–in other words, people of cultural variety. "Of all the variables we examined," said the Australian Manufacturing Council's report, "in terms of both practices and outcomes, that which differentiates innovative firms from the rest is exporting. Innovative firms can compete against the best in the world."

Fishing in International Waters

Casting your net into global waters, charting its depths, its reefs, and safe havens, provides a whole new supply of trade routes and contacts that feed your business. Realize that international traders are a close-knit lot and that it's important to know how to become part of the family.

* * *

Five hours after the Air India flight for New Delhi was due to leave Heathrow Airport, London, I was still waiting in the Maharaja Lounge. The great thing about travel hold-ups is that they give you the chance to practice all those restraints you learned about in management seminars and conferences. They also allow you to enter a special world of bonding with other people in the same misery.

As it happened, one of my traveling companions was a member of a major Manchester textile manufacturing family. With over one hundred years of experience in blanket manufacturing, his company had developed markets throughout the Indian subcontinent. He was on a sales trip to the region to show both new and existing agents his blanket samples and to unscramble some alliances that appeared to have wrecked. "Culture collision?" I asked.

"Yes, you can say that," he replied. "Our people have been jumping out of the fifth story of our mill trying to work with some of these people. I don't understand it. I have more friends in India than I have at home. I get on with them just fine."

"It's the same old story," I said. "The boss shakes hands, says the right things, and moves on, leaving the day-to-day operators to work with the other day-to-day people, without either of them having the slightest idea how to deal with all the cultural nuances which are buried in the relationship."

We see this every week as international mergers and acquisitions are agreed by handshake at a high publicity event, only to hear later of the deal running into serious operating problems due to cross-culture collisions. Examples are: Daimler/Chrysler, AOL/Time Warner, Disney/Europe, and Yahoo/Amazon United Kingdom.

No international deal will survive if the operators are not fully aware of cross-culture issues that will impact such basic principles as understanding, confidence, and trust.

Midnight Meetings

I recently flew business class from Sydney to London on Air Malaysia, with a five-hour holdover at the new Kuala Lumpur International Airport. They certainly know how to look after business passengers. The Malaysian Airlines Golden Lounge for first-class and business-class passengers is the largest waiting lounge in the world. With more than 4,000 square meters of space, it's larger than a football field! It has a fully equipped 24-hour business center and an audiovisual studio area. It has slumberettes, a mini-gym, showers, sauna, a coffee bistro, a computer games corner, a world-class restaurant, and a children's nursery and rumpus room.

A Frenchman, a Japanese, a Singaporean, and I, a British-Expatriate-American en route to London, hung out together in the middle of the night during the holdover. All four of us spoke English and, with our antennae up, could immediately tell that each one was a savvy world traveler. As clear representatives of extreme diverse cultures, we interacted in a type of global culture outside of our own: a culture of international business, of unspoken understanding, of mature respect and courtesy toward each other. As we discussed everything from the condition of Asian business to our favorite New York restaurants, we enjoyed each other's company for the diversity of the moment and the interesting viewpoints of people one doesn't meet every day.

Thanks to the exotic surroundings and the excellent facilities that allowed us to talk without interruptions, we will probably never forget where we met or what we discussed. Each encounter with someone from another culture group is an education in itself. It broadens the mind, titillates the adventuresome spirit, and takes us on vicarious journeys to places that we might otherwise never see. This type of fortuitous encounter takes place every minute around the world. From the long bar at Raffles Hotel Singapore to the Admirals Club at JFK, business people from multiple cultures interact and react. Deals are born every second. The multi-million dollar question is "Can they stay together? Can they stand the test of cross-culture interaction and continuation?"

Small Is Big!

Big developed countries have a problem. By having a large domestic market, they don't need to export in the same way as a small-developed country. Look at the numbers.

The United States exports only 12% of its gross domestic product, compared to the Netherlands, which exports 54%, and the United Kingdom, which exports 29%.

Even a medium-sized country like Germany, which exports 23% of its GDP, appreciates the importance of world trade. Taiwan does a thumping 48%, and Cote d'Ivoire exports a bumper 43% of its gross domestic product.

Of course, it is true to say that since the United States has the world's largest economy with a GDP of approximately $8 billion, exporting 12% represents a substantial number by any calculations. However, its biggest trading partners are Canada (23%), Japan (16%) and Mexico (8%), followed by the United Kingdom at 5%.

It is arguable that trade with Canada and Mexico is almost like domestic business. For example, it is difficult to say how much trade with Mexico involves the Maquiladoras program, whereby huge amounts of products are trucked across the border for assembly and finishing and, in many cases, are then shipped overseas from Mexico to the end-user country.

Japan's trade imbalances with the United States have been a perennial problem. A good deal of Japanese export trade has grown as a result of trade agreements and continual pressure by successive U.S. governments, so again, these numbers are somewhat artificial and do not represent the real self-developed export trade of American business.

This indicates that there is room for improvement if the United States is to be regarded as a true global trading nation.

Fortune 500 companies have generated almost 85% of the export activity from the United States. This number will dramatically change in the next few years to the point where over 50% of America's exports will be generated by companies with revenues of less than $100 million, and this will represent over 20% of the U.S. gross domestic product. That is the fundamental revolution that will take place in American business over the next two decades and the one that will effectively change the way the world works.

The *American way*, economically and culturally, will be the most significant impact on the cultures, attitudes and lifestyles of mankind in this century.

The New Frontier

The remarkable opportunities for increasing business through international expansion can only be understood by getting out there and getting on with it. There are, of course, horror stories of firms and individuals encountering serious problems when they go global. Certainly doing business in the international marketplace is not for the faint-hearted. In many ways it can be compared to the courageous westerly migrations or to the colonization of the New World. This is the new frontier of business, and we are all players in the game because the globalization of business is leading to the confrontation of cultures and lifestyles. These social upheavals are causing considerable difficulty and anger as people believe and fear the disappearance of their culture and the homogenizing of mankind.

Wrecking McDonald's and tearing down the golden arches won't stop the onward urge of international business, but it does make us stop and think about the outcome of a world gone global and the consequences of shifting standards brought about by the imposition of another dramatically different culture. It seems that young people the world over buy into certain aspects of the American way–fast food, casual clothes, and entertainment, for example. Their parents despair at this trend, seeing it as a denial of their national culture. The fact is that these youngsters are not just buying the *Big Mac*; they are buying into the American experience–its freedoms, its attitudes, and its forward thinking. For example, Young Rostof, a fluent English-speaking student, cycled up to me on the sidewalk in Minsk and asked, "Do you have anything from America?" We rummaged in the luggage for a Houston Astros tee shirt.

"It will be his most treasured possession," said our Russian lawyer guide. "For him it is like touching the hem of America."

Doing Business with America

Yes, believe it or not, the world wants to do business with America and Americans, but many Americans find that difficult to accept. For a country renowned for its self-confidence, America is often surprisingly insecure about its international popularity, particularly in the shadow of current events when the media fills the vulnerable mind–numbed by the tragedy of September 11–with the belief that America is not admired, but hated. Not so. The fact is that most of the world wants to do business with America–

restricted, of course, to the countries we also want to do business with. But American entrepreneurship and easy forgiveness constantly push the boundary of possibility to find ways in which we can do business even with previous enemies. Japan and Germany showed that was possible a few short years after World War II.

* * *

Valentina Kroshcov taught Russian history to seventh grade children in Communist Soviet Union. As a party worker, she rose rapidly through the ranks. In 1989 she was asked to visit the United States on a government-sponsored mission. "It was the biggest learning experience of my life," she said. " I had been raised to believe that all Americans were bad people and did I get a shock! Everyone was wonderful–the country was beautiful."

After the fall of Communism, Valentina got a job with the Russian Peace Foundation, and now she spends her time working with visiting groups of Americans who assist the Russian people with social improvement projects.

Pushing the envelope to do business wherever business is to be found is the American way. We must, however, experience common sense along the way. America's greatest historian, Barbara Tuchman, put it best:

> We cannot mould the non-western world to our desires nor require its acceptance of our concepts of political freedom and representative government. It is too late in history to export to the nations of Asia and Africa, with unschooled and undernourished populations in the billions, the democracy that evolved in the west over a thousand years of slow, small-scale experience from the Saxon village moot to the Bill of Rights. They have not had time to learn it, and history is not going to give them time. Meanwhile we live on the same globe. The better part of valor is to spend it learning to

live with differences, however hostile, unless and until we can find another planet.

This book helps the reader learn to work with the differences, to do profitable deals, and make a difference to the world at large.

2

Getting a Global Mindset

A firm's mindset shapes all its perceptions. How it thinks of its employees, its market, its customers, and its product largely determines how the business relates itself to its competitors and the world around it. It follows that a company's mindset, therefore, has a major influence on corporate strategies: what investments it will make and where, what it will do to implement them, and what outcomes it seeks.

Success in the Mindset

Mindset is committed attitude. It determines the character and personality of the company, its potential in its industry, and its perceptions of the future.

Mindset refers to the filters through which we, as individuals and organizations, perceive and make sense of the world. We are all selective in what we observe, and we process these observations in different ways through our filters. We develop these filters through experiential learning, and they are modified in accordance with our willingness to change, to abandon our preset attitudes and prejudices, and to learn and utilize new influential material.

Just how important is mindset? It is vital to the success of any business seeking global presence to review its mindset to determine whether some attitude changes need to be made before proceeding with that huge commitment.

Ikea Idea

Ikea, the Swedish furniture retailer, rushed into overseas activity in the mid-1980s. Without checking its mindset regarding international expansion, the company entered the United States in the belief that its Swedish products, methods, and culture would be acceptable to the American buyer. Ikea soon discovered that the American customer was not looking for a Swedish experience, but rather for good prices, quality, and service with some Scandinavian panache. Ikea did some fast footwork and shook up its business from top to bottom. Major management and attitude changes took place. Ikea emerged from this Cultural Revolution a vibrant, determined business, ready to take on the world with a global mindset.

CEO's Challenge

At the end of the 1990s, approximately 300 American chief executive officers were surveyed in a Baldrige Award Foundation initiative. They were asked to name the most important challenge they had to face in the near future. They named "the ability to think globally" as the most pressing. It is interesting that they put aside more practical issues, such as cost cutting, strategic planning, and employee retention in favor of an attitude-based one. Rethinking corporate mindset is not new to CEOs who must do this regularly, but retooling corporate mindset to think globally is a whole different project.

Global mindset depends on two vital principles: open-mindedness and inquisitiveness. It thrives in a transparent, communicating environment where there are no ceilings, closed doors, or secrets. It matures in an atmosphere of respect and appreciation for the individual talents and skills of all people. It lasts when leaders realize that the world is home and, that as an individual human, one is only as good or as worthwhile as any other individual human on the planet.

Getting our head around this concept is a major step. Perhaps the astronauts seeing Earth from space get the idea faster than most. They have often stated that when they look at our fragile, blue sphere in the dark abyss of the universe, they get an overwhelming feeling of awe and are never the same again. What a way to get a global mindset! But most of us have to get the concept right here in our own backyard.

Global mindset is not simply an extension of the international mindset that appreciates the need to export, that is, to be represented overseas. To think global requires a quantum leap. It has unique dimensions and perspectives.

The global mindset is able to comprehend a specific business and a particular industry in global terms. It is also able to understand market sectors and functions on a global basis rather than one country or region at a time. The appreciation of global competition, global customer trend, and economic issues are all part of the makeup of a global mindset.

An organization with a global mindset operates on the premise that cultures can be different without being better or worse than each other. It operates in the belief that diversity is a fact of life, that value systems vary, that there are different standards of behavior and different assumptions regarding reality –Vijay Govindarajan and Anil K Gupta, "Success Is All in the Mindset," *The Complete MBA Companion in Global Business.* "Financial Times" Pitman, 1999.

Global mindsets not only appreciate that diversity of cultures exists, but they also understand why they exist and why people of differing cultures think and act the way they do.

Small Power

People living in smaller countries have a better chance of getting a global mindset than those living in larger ones. That is, of course, a general statement. I have met hundreds of people in the United Kingdom who never want to even think of another country, let alone visit one. And I know of numerous Americans who are extremely world savvy and have been to almost every country on earth. Many Australian young people have backpacked their way through some of the most remote mountain passes in the world. So, if you live in a small country, an island, or a landlocked principality, and you can afford to travel, it isn't far to the border. Furthermore, much of the news we read, view, or listen to is about places other than our own.

The past of smaller countries shows that they embarked on overseas trade early in their history. Cramped for room and lack of territory for entrepreneurs, coupled with the necessity to feed their people, led to the need to travel. They discovered new lands often bigger than their own, built navies, and went into business. Global mindset became part of the character of these people. Some grew up perhaps knowing more about the world as a whole than about their own country.

It's not as easy for Americans and others who have been raised with wide horizons around them. "Enough to explore here," they say, "without going off to some far-flung place at the ends of the earth." Seeing beyond their horizons and traveling great distances overseas–perhaps overlooking the opportunities here at home–require a certain amount of imagination, determination, and guts. Getting a global mindset for them is an act of courage. We know plenty of business leaders who have taken the necessary steps. Many have led their companies into a state of global mindset and become the most respected companies in the world. It is clear that a determined change of attitude from ethnocentric to global mindset is the most pertinent decision a business and its leaders can achieve to assure survival in this century.

Ethnocentric Mindset

Most people are born with an ethnocentric or domestic mindset. It takes experience, travel, and study to grow into a global mindset. If an individual decides to take the step and has the opportunity to gather the experience needed to make the transition, the change can be achieved relatively quickly. But let us first understand what we mean by an ethnocentric mindset.

For the businessperson with an ethnocentric mindset, all reference points come from one single culture or commercial environment. Whenever they are faced with an unfamiliar problem, they tend to fall back on their own domestic experience as this is their only point of reference.

We often read and hear of cultural and behavior faux pas committed by travelers. It seems to be a favorite issue for the press. The following section was taken from *The*

Wall Street Journal, 15 August 2000.

"Companies Go Global But Many Managers Just Don't Travel Well"

When more than 400 managers from around the world gathered at an executive training seminar at IMD, the business school in Lausanne, Switzerland . . . the Europeans, who were the bulk of the participants, spoke disparagingly of American businessmen. Among their chief put-downs: Americans are provincial, ignorant of world affairs, uncouth and too materialistic . . . even the most educated don't speak any language besides English, don't know how to drink or eat properly, don't know anything about European history, let alone geography . . . one manager visiting the United States was surprised to learn how few of them have traveled abroad and how personally non-global they are.

U.S. executives have to meet their foreign colleagues halfway–by getting acquainted about European culture and not assuming the American way is always the best.

Manager's Misunderstanding

It is reported that between 30 and 40 percent of American managers run into cross-culture collisions. The figure is probably much higher. We all collide with culture misunderstanding in some way at some time in our international transaction interface. Some managers adapt to alternative culture easily and, like a chameleon, they are able to assume the local color without too much difficulty. Others cling desperately to the comfort of their traditional habits and refuse to budge from the beliefs they were raised with. Such is an ethnocentric mindset.

Test Your Global Mindset

Do you have a personal global mindset? Does your organization have a global mindset?

Before we move too much further into the subject of global mindsets, let's check our concepts about getting into international business. Test your global mindset potential by answering the following questions.

	Yes	Maybe	No
1. Are you motivated to do international work?			
2. For more money?			
3. For career advancement?			
4. To enjoy a comfortable lifestyle?			
5. To escape a difficult work situation at home?			
6. To save, or escape from, a personal relationship?			
7. To experience a different lifestyle?			
8. To become more internationally and culturally aware?			
9. To show foreigners how to run a business?			
10. Because the company tells me I have to go?			
11. Because I am excited by living overseas?			
12. Because I love new experiences and adventures?			

How did you score? If you are motivated to work overseas primarily for money, career advancement, or to escape the difficulties at home or in the work environment, then there is much to be done to achieve a global mindset. If, on the other hand, you scored positively on the side of curiosity, experience, and excitement at the prospect of an overseas opportunity, then you are well on the way to developing a global mindset.

Do you have a global mindset in business?

- When you interact with other people of differing cultures, do you give them equal status along with people of your own culture?

- Are you keen to have substantial input from people outside your culture?

- Are you just as keen to accept their views and suggestions as those given by people from your own culture?

- Do you make an effort to build culturally diverse teams?

- Are you sensitive to the creativity that diverse cultures can produce when they work together?

- Are you excited about being in close contact with a different culture?

- Do you like to study alternative cultures, their history, language, religion, and traditions?

- Are you keen to train your international work force in cross-culture competencies?

Does your organization have a global mindset?

- Are all customers given equal consideration regardless of national origins?

- Are you a leader in exploring emerging market opportunities?

- Do you recruit people by choosing the best available, anywhere in the world regardless of nationality?

- Are you building your brand not only a regional basis but also on a global basis?

- Does every employee, from anywhere in the world, have the same opportunity for advancement in the organization?

- Do you know every major competitor throughout the world, the way they work, and what they sell?

- Do you see the world as if it were one huge domestic market?

- Would you be prepared to locate your headquarters anywhere in the world on the basis that it would be the best location for global management and development?

How did you come out? Take comfort in the fact that very few managers or organizations come out with a 100 percent positive rating. What this test tells you is how much work needs to be done to bring you and your business up to the standards that will be acceptable in the twenty-first century global economy. Managers and their organizations are gearing up throughout the world to get their share of the global gold. Some take wild swings; some learn through the school of hard knocks, and some just dabble at it and retire at the first rebuff. Others build global expansion into their strategic plans together with the need to move their corporate or organization culture from ethnocentricity to a global perspective.

Moving from Ethnocentric to Global

The transition from an ethnocentric to a global perspective is a journey, a commitment of time, learning, and money. That's why it needs to be planned and strategized and put into perspective. Most global companies like Nestle, GE, and Philips started as domestic companies; many of them opened as purely local, like Wal-Mart, Hilton and McDonald's. Their domestic growth took them from local to regional, then to national–a process that must have seemed gigantic when it was first considered by their founders. It wasn't easy. Transports, communication, delivery systems, and training were all a lot more difficult and less available than they are today. Some of these well-known companies had to struggle through the depression of the 1930s. Firms like Ford, GE, and 3M have had to contend with management reshuffles, major strategic rethinking, and internal cultural revolutions in their process of becoming the global giants they are today. Most of them have made the transition from domestic to global in less than fifty years. Many in the technology sector have made it in less than five. Some came out of the womb kicking and screaming to be global.

Driven both by the facilities available and by market pressures, our customers and competitors are moving us out of our domestic comfort and taking us global. They often do it so rapidly that we barely have time to pack our bags. Many of our suppliers will follow as we go global. It's a chain reaction.

Companies with no strategic plans to go international will find the conversion an upheaval when it comes. This often occurs during a time of domestic market growth when minds are set on handling expansion at home. This should be the very time when global development plans and strategies are made to place the business increasingly into international markets.

In the event of a market downturn, hopefully global productivity is already making a positive contribution. Sometimes the decision not to proceed with global plans is based on simple fear: fear of the unknown; fear of the size of the challenge; fear of capability. It's not a bad idea at this point to recruit a specialist consultant or business coach to work you through this process toward a satisfactory solution for the future of the business–whether it is to go global or stay domestic.

Once the decision is taken to push your business overseas and the plans are drawn up, the revolution begins, and you and your associates will take a leap that will change you and your company forever.

Global Explorers and Prospectors

A new type of leader will emerge to run the global organizations of the future. Leadership models that were once popular in the past no longer work today. These models were largely based on hierarchical control and command structures built for an expanding domestic market in the USA. Leaders developed under this system-hired people *just like them.* This no longer works for the United States, nor for the rest of the world. Human resource executives are finding that leadership development programs that have worked well in a domestic environment soon fail as they try to export them. Many other countries are having the same problem. German, French, Japanese, Korean, and British leadership styles are all different, based on long culture traditions. The importance and relevance of relationships, ethics, short-term profit, hierarchies, and risk aversion varies from culture to culture.

American Influence

In the 1960s as American firms were moving into Europe, they brought with them the American leadership and management models. These were even communicated into European chapters of service clubs such as Rotary, Lions, and Jaycees. The patient Europeans were, on the one hand, willing to learn new tricks but, on the other hand, they regarded it all as a joke. However, in the face of no other alternative and the sheer power of the American influence, many of the models were installed in European firms. Not until some years later did the Europeans build up their own management schools and develop their own corporate leadership models, reflecting the cultural backgrounds of the French, the British, and the German ways.

The new global leader/manager will grow away from his or her provincial model into one with a global mindset. Jack Welch said many times to GE managers that the future leaders of the company would not be like him. He spent his entire career in the United States; the managers would spend their careers almost entirely overseas where they would develop global perspectives.

Companies throughout the world face a serious global leadership gap. World expansion into global business has fast outpaced the management talent available to support it. Progressive companies can't train their people fast enough, and the college education source is not delivering enough qualified material.

* * *

On November 10, 2001, at a meeting of ministers held at Doha, Qatar, China was officially admitted to the World Trade Organization (WTO), opening up business to 1.3 billion new customers. The Organization of American States is rapidly developing its free trade zone; Russia is now a member of the G8; and the European Union will admit ten more countries in 2003. All this action demonstrates that global-savvy leaders will be a most valuable resource. Training and development of managers in global management skills should be put on fast track. If not, many billions of dollars could be lost and/or wasted as international deals collapse or fail to meet expectations due to cross-culture incompetence.

Corporations from Europe, the United States, and Asia are setting the pace for the future. By sheer day-to-day experience in the new world of global business, they are writing the leadership/management manuals of the future. The first criterion is the recognition that good global leaders are not necessarily born–but they *can* be made.

Recognize Global Mindset

In the early 1970s, I traveled extensively in France with a reinsurance expert named Peter Blauth. Peter was born in Poland and educated in Switzerland. At the beginning of WWII, he had been called up by his exclusive cavalry regiment. One morning they rode out from Warsaw toward the east. In magnificent formation they cantered over the Polish countryside–only to come face to face with Russian tanks. "Unfair!" said Peter, who was held captive in Katyn forest where the genocide of the Polish officer class took place.

Miraculously, Peter escaped and made his way to Egypt where he discovered that the British were signing up Polish officers for duty in the Special Air Service in return for British citizenship. The SAS assisted resistance groups in occupied Europe. Peter's fluent French positioned him in the job he did for the rest of the war: parachuting into France and blowing up bridges. In due course, Peter was captured, tortured and thrown into Auschwitz, but he never complained or held any recriminations against his captors. He told me constantly that his life had been interesting. He was a *Renaissance* man.

When I worked with him, he never stopped asking questions. We used to drive through the beautiful midi French countryside, calling on small mutual insurance companies. For Peter, everything was an interesting adventure. His copious knowledge of history led us into countless chapels, churches, and chateaux. Peter Blauth could talk to anyone about anything–his life was built around curiosity and questions. "Isn't this interesting" was his constant comment. I could imagine his saying this as he stood pondering his fate in Auschwitz. Peter's boundless curiosity mirrors the inquisitiveness of exemplar manager/leaders with a global mindset: abundant curiosity about the world and its people and the extraordinary issues and events happening every day that we call *life on earth*.

One of America's greatest authors, James Michener, was once asked how he managed to put so much detail into his stories. "I'm like a sponge," he said, "I can go somewhere or talk to someone, and I catch every word, every inflection, and every situation. I absorb it, then I write it down."

Global leaders have to be like sponges: looking, listening, asking questions, absorbing, and taking nothing for granted. The metamorphism from an ethnocentric mindset into a global mindset leader is in the capable hands of the individual.

Training Managers in Global Mindset

Unfortunately, most businesses are not focusing on training their managers or future managers to develop global mindsets. A survey conducted by Black, Morrison, and

Gregerson, published in *Global Explorers* (Routledge), found that only 7.6 percent of the firms indicated they had a comprehensive global leadership development system.

The authors go on to explain how to map out a personal plan: "It should rely heavily on the four Ts, Travel, Teams, Training, and Transfers." They divide the four Ts into stages of career development: early career, mid career, and late career. Sadly, few companies pay much attention to the early career phase for the development of global leadership skills. This is the time for the formation of perceptions, of big-picture career planning, and of considerable corporate culture influence. How you persuade your employer to widen the perimeters of your training is up to you, but it can have a positive role: it will bring you to the attention of the management.

* * *

Back in my early career stage, I recall asking the director of my Victorian employer for sales training. He looked at me with shock as if I had caught him in a private act. The company had over twenty people on the road, all totally untrained in sales skills. Since that was what we did most often, it seemed to me that we needed to become accomplished at the task and learn from experts. "What's wrong with learning from the senior managers?" I persisted. I got the support of my colleagues, and finally I found a senior ally who asked me to organize a training program. My Victorian employer crept in halfway through the seminar–and stayed to the bitter end. "Hick, good meeting that .... I am sure you learned a lot of new ideas–like I did."

Leave Home

Living in England means that one can easily travel into continental Europe. As a child, I was taken on family vacations to the south of France, Spain, Holland, Germany, Italy, and other locations on a regular basis. I played and related to children of my own age in these countries and picked up a few phrases in their language. That was a fortunate start in my global understanding.

Taking every opportunity to travel in early life makes a real difference to our view of the world as we grow up. It makes it easier to develop a global mindset. Parents should expose their children to foreign countries and cultures as soon as possible. It can be cheaper to take a family on a budget trip to Europe then a few days at Disney World, and the investment is probably longer lasting.

As you move into your career, take every opportunity to meet visiting overseas nationals, making it known that you are a candidate for overseas posting. Read everything you can to expand your perceptions of the world. Some, who cannot travel with their business at this stage, can take inexpensive personal trips: overseas church missions, study tours, and low budget tours. Even getting a job as an escort for a tour group can take you to places in the world you may never otherwise visit. Joining the international Peace Corps is a splendid way to develop a global mindset and to see how most of the world lives.

Global Explorers says that there is no end to the values gained by travel. In mid career, there is learning and sharing with colleagues and overseas contacts. In a late career stage, travel builds international connections and relationships and presents the opportunity to build the experience of early and mid career candidates.

Team Work

Black, Morrison, and Gregerson make the point that joining multicultural teams at work allows the global mindset candidate to learn the principles of cross-communication. The candidate will discover the underlying assumptions between people of differing backgrounds. He or she should look for opportunities to be a member of a multicultural and cross-functional team. In this type of team, not only do members learn how to bridge national or regional culture gaps, they learn how to bridge functional culture gaps as well. As one manager reported, "Sometimes the gap in perspective and values between finance and marketing can be as great as that between Taiwan and England."

Training Modules

Only a few business schools in the United States have a global business specialty. Thunderbird, the American Graduate School of International Management, is perhaps the best known (thunderbird.com). It offers international management degrees and was the first school to provide such a program in the country. If you can get your company to send you there, or if you can get yourself there, it would leapfrog your progress toward understanding the functions of global business. Many universities and colleges run international business curricula as part of their MBA degree programs.

Programs teaching global mindset and leadership skills are, however, rare as are courses in cross-culture competence. Global Business Initiatives (michaelhick.com) is one of the few to offer these courses as in-house training to corporations and through special arrangements with select colleges and business schools in the United States and certain other countries.

One of the best cross-culture schools in Europe is in England, directed by Richard D. Lewis, the well-known linguist. Located in an historic house tucked away in the Hampshire downs known as Riversdown, Lewis and his experienced team teach cross-culture and language skills in full immersion courses and have most of the major companies in Europe as clients. The staff at Riversdown produced *Gulliver, Performing Successfully across Cultures*, an EPS system which, as a CD, you can slide into your laptop and check on the cross-culture pointers of the people with whom you are likely to interact in the average overseas meeting. As you sit in the anteroom in Tokyo, pop in the CD and examine the cultural protocol. Lewis is one of the reasons why European managers are fast becoming more equipped with global mindset than their American, Australian, or Asian counterparts.

The best training for us all comes in the personal commitment to improve our knowledge, whether this is through experience, training programs, or both. Keeping company with people from other cultures by reading widely on world news, studying maps, joining societies which focus on foreign affairs, and visiting the countless overseas websites are all highly beneficial in your stretch for a global mindset.

Transfers

Few companies provide any formal transfer training for executives. Some progressive firms, however, do have programs for transferring high-potential young managers to overseas locations where the cross-culture exposure is practical immersion. Those managers who do not work with an organization that has any sort of organized program should look for any opportunity to get transferred. The short answer is "volunteer for everything that is going to expand your experience, your vision, and your perspectives."

Early in my career with Lloyd's of London, I realized that practical knowledge of the United States was a crucial part of the knowledge base of an aspiring executive: over 60 percent of Lloyd's business at that time originated in the United States. But how was I to obtain this experience? Since childhood, when my parents subscribed to *National Geographic*, I had read everything I could about the country. I knew its history and its geography and would seek out American servicemen in England to talk about the United States. I collected American army badges, buttons, and bits and pieces; I had maps of America on my bedroom wall; and I would go and see every American movie I could. But when it came to visiting the country as an ambitious young executive, I could never afford to do that on my own. Then opportunity came in the form of a debate contest sponsored by the Junior Chamber of Commerce. My team won the British championship. "What next?" we asked at our celebration dinner.

"America," I said. "We'll find sponsors and go on an American tour as a team." We did it and debated against university, college, and society teams from Boston to Washington D.C. to Chicago. It was nothing less than a mind-changing event for an impressionable young man. I was able to meet senators, news anchors, and major clients of our business–all on sponsors' money. A year later, I was appointed the youngest director my company had ever elected, enabling me to be transferred to the Paris office for two years. My global career had begun.

Watch for your chance to get some overseas exposure in a variety of unusual and unexpected ways. If your mind is receptive to it and your goal is clear, then it will come into your life.

Building the Global Mindset Organization

The organization that is populated with global mindsets will develop a global mindset of its own. It will have a character, a culture, and a personality that will see the world as a whole and understand how it plays its part. It can then build a global brand and hire people worldwide with impunity. But what are the ingredients for building a global mindset business?

We have determined three things from our chapter so far. In order to demonstrate global mindset, a company's management team has to:

a) Be familiar and comfortable with the world's diversity.
b) Be able to integrate diverse worldviews into its strategic thinking.
c) Assemble and manage cross-cultural teams.

A corporation's ability to interpret the world it works in, understand its market on a global basis, know every detail about its global main competitors, and hire the best people available anywhere in the world is the goal of the global mindset business. What are the practical steps it can take to get to this level?

• Be sure that the CEO and those of influence have positive global mindsets.

• Staff the human resource function with global mindsets.

• Globalize the human resource operations.

• Hold management meetings in a variety of diverse global locations.

• Reward executive promotions to those with global mindset.

• Create promotion ladders that recognize international experience.

• Reward performance which accents global focus.

It's all about leadership. Unless the influential leadership of an organization has the right mindset to move into or stay active in the global playing field, it will remain limited to its ethnocentric perimeters. Bringing the huge advantages of global cross-culture diversity to a business and managing it with ability is the supreme challenge at the opening of the twenty-first century. Those companies who meet it will reap rewards almost too hard to imagine.

Essence of Diversity

America, the *melting pot*, has always been proud of its concepts of diversity, but the practical history has been different from the vision. Minorities and women have been segregated and excluded; discrimination has been a feature of the dark side of American life; and inclusion has not been a feature of corporate personnel infrastructure. No doubt some of this still persists. Undoubtedly, there is a lot of work to be done. But in the last few decades, the mood has changed and organizations have recognized that diversity and equal opportunity are features of success and not of protection. If organizations have learned the advantages of diversification at home, then they can apply those advantages equally as well in the global arena.

Stephen F. Ambrose, the historian, believes that the greatest social tragedy in America was segregation and the exclusion of the African-American from taking part in the life of the nation for so long. Similarly women, with all their creativity, intuition, and ability, are excluded from any worthwhile activity in the majority of the world. Ambrose calls such exclusions a waste of human potential, a "loss for the benefit of all mankind."

The essence of diversity is inclusion, the principle whereby all people, regardless of gender, color, culture, or creed, stand together with equal opportunity and reward. Carrying this banner forward into the global jousting ground is a high ideal. It will be tested, teased, and challenged. It may be defeated from time to time, but it is a battle that has to be won if cross-culture competence is to survive.

Advantages of Cultural Diversity

America has a global brand known as *land of opportunity*; it's where you go to be free and make your fortune. The evidence is overwhelming. Twenty-five of the Fortune 400's richest Americans are first generation immigrants who include George Soros from Hungary, worth $7 billion; John Kluge from Germany, worth $12 billion; and Jerry Yang, founder of Yahoo who arrived here from Taiwan, worth $1.5 billion. There are hundreds of other recent arrivals, moving at lightening speed up the wealth ladder, who will be added to the list. The headlines are full of success stories of immigrant entrepreneurs–just imagine how many of the same material are waiting to join you in your global success.

World Savvy

Getting a global mindset includes getting global savvy. Understanding the way the world works and operates takes serious study and application. This is not the subject of this book, but it deserves a reference because differing cultures interpret this information and use it in negotiation, selling, and management in different ways.

World savvy managers understand the fundamental systems that are the cogwheels of the global economy. These include:

- Understanding international financial systems and markets, foreign exchange management, and venture capital markets, the World Bank, and the International Monetary Fund

- A working knowledge or global accounting methods and the capability of reading and understanding financial statements from the major industrial countries

- Knowledge of global marketing strategies, country advertising standards and culture, global market distribution, competition, and branding

- The principles of human resource management, an appreciation of the law of various countries, the movement of expatriate people, and the culture of employment

The world savvy manager will also have a day-to-day appreciation of world politics and the interaction of country leaders and governments on the global stage.

A Constantly Changing Scene

The democratization of newly liberated countries, the move to global free trade, and the development of global financial systems is a constantly changing scene. World political leaders have never seen anything like this–there are no historic comparisons to refer to. The global mindset manager is also working in this tempest. Only the nimble and the savvy will survive.

The impact of political action against a global business can be extremely serious. Exposures, such as product recall, nationalization, expropriation, and even kidnap and ransom, are real risks for some managers working in politically charged environments. Political risk insurance is a sensible protection sought by many international organizations, but by far the best precaution is a world savvy manager who is capable of global risk management.

Belgian Coke

Many times corporations simply misread cultures, thus making decisions without proper research, without consulting the local law, or without bringing in the local political powers that be into the issue. Consider the consequences of Coca-Cola's product recall in Belgium. The giant soft drinks company was the subject of a major product recall when on June 9, 1999, 42 school children in the northern Belgian town of Bornem complained of nausea, headaches, and cramps after drinking Coke. In a few days, 115 people complained of the same problems. Coke recalled over 2.5 million bottles and made the statement that the product had "a quality issue where you have an off odor or taste." Immediately, authorities in France, Belgium, and Luxembourg ordered the removal of more than 65 million cans from market shelves. Local media attacked Coke from every direction, and the Belgian minister of health made the statement that the company had not provided a "satisfactory and conclusive explanation" for the mysterious spate of colic. While the product defect was unfortunate, the real problem for Coke was its lack of sensitivity with the local conditions and misreading the culture. A simple production accident became a major culture collision.

The renaissance of the global mindset managers and the inheritance they will endow are awesome. Global business is growing and will grow faster once it has the global mindset managers it needs to direct and develop it.

If the world is to benefit from globalization, then we must put our minds into the right consciousness, develop the right skills, and do the right deals for the good of all the world's people.

3

The Culture Conundrum

F rom an early age, we realize that numerous people on planet Earth are not like us. They look different; they often speak an unfamiliar language, and they sometimes do unusual things. We sense that we are more comfortable with people who are *like us*, so our exposure to people *not like us* is limited, and opportunities for interacting with them is minimal. When we do get to interact, we tend to look for the differences rather than the similarities.

Melting Pot?

Organizations in the United States have long since ended segregation. Discrimination is illegal and laws have officially made the country *colorless*. The watchdog agencies that keep an eye on civil rights and equal opportunity are forever vigilant in prosecuting violators, and political pressure is constant on Congress to tighten up the laws that control the offenses committed in the name of culture dislike and misunderstanding. But still there are appalling examples of culture animosity and even hate. Emotional flare-ups in inner cities, accusations of police brutality toward minorities, and examples of imbalanced justice against African-Americans, Cubans, Hispanics, Arabs, and Asians fill the inside pages of our newspapers.

The economic gulfs between cultures are obvious, even to children who perceive that their educational opportunities are also different between culture types. It has often been said that you will never understand another culture unless you *walk in their shoes*. Minorities in America complain that discrimination still continuously rears its ugly head, even if it's just a casual look of distaste, a rude remark or worse still, a job turndown. All this sad litany of the state of race relations (and I am sure that there are many worse examples) goes to show that it doesn't matter how many laws governments can enact or how good a job they do at enforcing them, it is still up to the determination and high consciousness of man to make a nation a country worth living in for everyone.

If cross-culture cohabitation is so difficult, then what are the chances of cross-culture competence in the global village? We acknowledge that the United States made enormous strides in a few short years. The American social scene was very different when I first visited the country in the early 1960s. It can hardly be recognized today when compared to some attitudes and behavior of those days.

It is my belief that America's experience and her ability to work to improve race relations will be the example for the rest of the world and will help other nations and regions of the world to structure and enforce laws governing culture cohabitation without discrimination.

With all this influence going on in our lives from a young age, what is the chance of our being able to work cross culturally in transacting our global business? Well, it's going to take hard work, a determination to deal with cross-culture incompetence, and good managers making certain that all those within their responsibility are properly trained.

The key to cross-culture competence is knowing the facts about culture types, understanding our own culture, and knowing how to react, relate, and work with others.

World Culture Types

Stavos was a Greek tanker captain. He had worked with Onassis for a number of years, and then he bought a ship of his own. By the time I began handling his insurance, he owned four tankers, mainly operating charters between the Gulf and western Europe. He was a real sea dog: weather-beaten, cheerful under duress, and full of sea stories. I used to sit with him in his office as he told me tales of storms and shipmates over the seven seas. He would wave at people as they walked past his office and get up and talk to them about cargoes and contracts, crews, and charters. His *office* was a table in the bar of the Flying Dutchman, a café located on the docks in Piraeus, near Athens. To get an appointment with Stavos, you would first check with his wife to ascertain that he would be in town. Then you would tell her that you would meet him *at the usual place at the usual time* on such and such a day. The usual time would be between 11 a.m. and 4 p.m.; the usual place was the Dutchman.

I would keep my appointment, bringing all my data for the meeting: facts of cargo insurance, claims issues, and renewal information, all of which needed my client's review and approval. Stavos would give a cursory glance at my material.

"I trust you, Michael," he would say in his gravel-voice, broken English, "If there is a problem, I just kill you." A grin and a wave at a passerby told me all I needed to know.

Culture collision was in the making to the uninitiated. To Stavos, our relationship was more important than my data. To me, my data–or getting my business done–was more important than my relationship with him. We came from two distinctly different culture types.

Learning Curve

My Japanese client Ozo, whom you met in the introduction, taught me many things about culture collision. If I had understood how to deal with culture types who work in group orientation, then I might well have done a better job for my company. As it happened, I did not have the negotiating skills to deal with an ever-changing team. It seemed to me that they were always moving the goal posts, that they couldn't be trusted, and that I never heard the straight scoop. As it turned out, they saw me as the problem: unprepared to give them time for reflection, not providing consistent information to each group, and not being aware of the Japanese concepts of time and how it unfolds and how each step of the negotiation process is practically a ritual.

Three Culture Types

The world's cultures have been studied in great depth by academics and experts, and there are a variety of definitions. Most of the work on cultural dimension is based on Geert Hofstede's research. His definition of culture was "the collective programming of the mind which distinguishes the members of one category of people from another." He called culture "the software of the mind." His studies were followed by Fons Trompenaars and Charles Hampden-Turner; then came Richard D. Lewis, who made a more detailed categorization of culture into negotiation and reaction styles.

For the purpose of this book, we will look at the world's cultures strictly from the aspect of business interaction. During our meetings and in the course of our management, we want to be aware of the reaction we can expect from our interaction. We want to be prepared for the responses we are likely to get from the participants. In a general sense, the world's culture types can be divided into three groups: data-based, relationship-based, and group-based.

Data-Based Type

Data-based types are dominated by schedules, time-tables and projects and by a strong sense of individualism and personal responsibility. Members of this group like to be punctual, factual, and get on with business. Data-based people like to do one thing at a time and like to work with pre-agreed agendas, follow-up memos, and confirmations. They love information and live by statistics, back-up material, and reference books. They follow correct procedures, work according to fixed hours, and respect officialdom. For them, social and business life is separate; they are unemotional and use limited body language.

Relationship-Based Type

Relationship-based types are generally extroverts, talkative, gregarious, and believe that relationships are more important than anything. They often do several tasks at the same time and do not easily keep to timetables. Relationship cultures rarely write memos, follow up with correspondence, or prepare agendas, but they are often highly creative, artistic, poetic, and cultured. They relish excitement and colorful experiences. Plans are changed, strings are pulled, and facts are flexible to them. Business, pleasure, and social life are intermixed, and relations are often involved. They have people-oriented interactions where emotions, unrestricted body language, and interruptions are part of the behavior.

Group-Based Type

Group-based culture types tend to be introvert, patient, and silent. Their style is to be respectful listeners, exercising tolerant impartiality. Everything relates to the team, group, family and ancestors, corporate identity, or to others with whom they are temporarily in contact. Issues are seen in the context of the group picture and how to work with, assist, and conform to the group philosophy. Group-based people are thoughtful of others, avoid confrontation, and save face on behalf of themselves and others. They delegate to reliable people and base their business relationships on trust and honesty. Group-based cultures like to mix business with social life and appreciate modesty, wisdom, and respect for the elderly.

It is always dangerous to classify or pigeonhole human types because there are millions of exceptions to the rule. Yes, all these culture types overlap. Many of us see the characteristics of more than one group in others and in ourselves. However, for the benefit of managing our business, working with cross-culture teams, and negotiating deals across frontiers, it is only important to understand the outline principles.

Keep It Simple

It is not important for most international business people to get into culture behavior detail. Few deals will be lost if you shake hands rather than bow or kiss. Most overseas executives are aware of the general behavior of different nationalities and are highly forgiving of goof-ups, gaffs, and faux pas. I have watched many Americans in operation overseas, and many spoil themselves by being too condescending. Hey, just relax and be yourself. People will prefer you that way. The key to remember when interacting with anybody–which hardly needs mentioning–is to just be respectful of that person's background and culture.

In this book, however, we are concerned about understanding the cultures that sit opposite us at the negotiating table on our multi-million dollar deal, the cultures who work on the teams we manage, or those representing the important overseas customer we wish to sign up. Understanding why they think and act the way they do will not only help us to transact the deal successfully, but it will help to give it a decent shelf life.

The Time Divide

The *time divide* is one of the most important issues that lead to culture collision.

The differing attitudes toward time can frustrate, misinterpret, and often destroy perfectly good deals. We have all seen situations where lack of punctuality was interpreted as rudeness and where insistence on punctuality has been seen as destroying a perfectly good business relationship. But the time divide is not just keeping your appointment on time–it is the appreciation of how each culture type sees and values time. In your international deals, you will make many schedules, time charts, and deadlines only to have them fall short, causing frustration. We had better get into the right frame of mind about time before we end up with major stress problems.

* * *

I was speaking at a major corporate meeting in Barcelona, Spain. I had assisted in the planning and had organized a series of guest speakers. It was a tight schedule, so everything needed to run like clockwork. The mayor of Barcelona and a number of local dignitaries were invited. The meeting was held in one of the most beautiful buildings in the city–part of it was seventeenth century– and one could walk outside on the spacious balcony and look out over the Mediterranean Sea. I was on tenterhooks. Would my careful plans work out? Would all the speakers turn up? Would the caterers be on time? Would the mayor be pleased with it all?

Guests started to arrive–the rich and famous of Catalonia– with magnificent gowns and stunning jewelry worn by beautiful women on the arms of rich and handsome men. It was a magical evening: beautiful weather, city lights, and an ancient room with portraits of Columbus on the walls. Everybody seemed to know each other. The talking was incredible. Wine flowed, canapés were sampled, and conversation grew more animated. Time flew by. I looked at my watch, horrified. We should have started dinner forty minutes ago. Does anyone care?

I found my Spanish organizer. "Have you any idea what time it is?" I asked.

"What does it matter?" he said. "Everyone is having such a good time."

Four hours later, the speeches were made–two hours late–but nobody seemed to care. I, in my data-based mindset, was a nervous wreck. The important thing was that the relationship-based people had a great time.

Data-Based Time

Data-based cultures run their lives by clocks and calendars. They enter appointments, tasks, and activities into their schedules, believing that time has to be *used* and not *wasted*. If an appointment is a no-show, then the time has been wasted unless the individual can find something useful to do to replace the lost meeting. "Don't waste your time, Jimmy. Find something useful to do," said our mothers to us years ago. Data-based people see life in finite time. They have to fill it with goals, activities, and useful pursuits. Business is based on time schedules, so anything that upsets the schedule is going to be most unpopular. The Swiss have made an industry out of keeping time. For them, it is an intellectual science rather than a tool for living. Americans, on the other hand, often say, "Time's money," so time is given greater importance, particularly in a culture where people are largely judged by the money they have. The British have a similar attitude to time, but waste to the British is time not spent in social (the pub and holidays) activities rather than work related. So even among the same culture groups, there are differing attitudes to the ways time is spent.

Relationship-Based Time

Relationship-based cultures have a totally different attitude to time. They consider the data-based sequential or monochromic time system to be imposing and completely illogical. "It's not the punctuality that counts: it's the meeting, our relationship," they explain. They are not interested in appointment times or schedules–they would rather make sure that the rapport works, that the people get to know each other, and that there is a good outcome. That it finishes on time is insignificant.

"Punctuality messes up schedules," Richard Lewis says about this culture group. "They see time as event or personality related, a subjective commodity which can be manipulated, molded, stretched, or dispensed with, irrespective of what the clock says."

American business people have a hard time working in this dimension. They feel somewhat helpless without the disciplines that their schedules impose. The Arabs and the Italians are disdainful of this dependence on tools and equipment at the cost of human relationships.

For the data-based member, it is vital, therefore, to just relax when in the company of the relationship-based acquaintances. Take a deep breath and accept the basic psychology of the culture group so far as time is concerned and realize that when (not *if*) we do business with members of this group, we have to have a different set of priorities.

Group-Based Time

Group-based cultures see time as an unfolding phenomenon with a past, a present, and a future, all in place and all active. Asians see time in this cyclic form where the past "formulates the contextual background to the present decision about which they must think long term," says Lewis. History, ancestor worship, and a profound sense of destiny all add up to an attitude toward time that is at diametric odds to the data-based group. In the contemplation of group decisions, the entire *big picture*, which is also a time picture, has to be considered. The Chinese respect the value of time and, in their extreme desire not to offend, they will regularly apologize for wasting time in a meeting. Not that this is necessarily true: they just want to make the point. To understand the relevance of time in the group-based sector, it is important to study something of their religions and associated rituals, most of which demonstrate the oriental time philosophy. In Japan, the Tea ceremony, the ritual cleaning of the house, the gift-giving protocols–all have aspects of time segmentation about them. Any visit to a Shinto shrine or a Buddhist temple will demonstrate the almost placid nature of time and the sense that everything in reality takes place in eternity.

It is not hard to appreciate that foreign visitors have not been popular with group-based cultures in the historic past. As the Chinese market opens up to western trade and as we attempt to do our deals with them, we have to spend time understanding this fascinating old culture with beliefs, traditions, and attitudes literally on the other side of the planet.

Culture, Time, and the Economy

In their book, *Culture Matters*, Samuel P. Huntington and Lawrence E. Harrison make the point that the primary cultures of a nation can have the effect of promoting or withholding a country's economic growth. They break down culture groups by economic levels and determine that the difference between progressive and static economies can be identified by time orientation. Progressive economies, they say, believe in looking at the near future and static economic groups look at the distant past.

This may be true of the extreme cultures, but most fall somewhere in the middle, and some are in a state of rapid change. If we were to compare the United States with, say, India, then we are comparing a culture no more than 300 years old with one that is at least 3,500 years old. The pioneering American immigrant, escaping from the serfdom of his old country as he beheld the wide-open spaces before him, carved out the rock-hard principles of the American way. In reading the short, action-packed, progressive history of the American people, it's not hard to understand their culture, or indeed, understand their future.

On the other hand, the impact of the ancient history of India on the lifestyle of the Indian people is undeniable. Descended from the Aryan people of central Asia, who settled the Indus valley around 1,500 B.C., they developed a religion that became their lifestyle. So profound is their belief that only Islam, which ruled much of India under the Moguls for almost 400 years, gained any sizable number of converts. India would definitely be regarded as a static economy, according to Huntington and Harrison's theory. But today we are seeing a remarkable advance in the economy of India, based on technology products and development.

Most European countries have had lengthy and colorful histories, much of which has impacted the culture of the United States. Some Europeans have a problem with moving from static to a progressive mindset. It is hard growing up in an historic culture among ancient buildings and traditions and not live in a time warp.

Frozen in Time

Raised in the cathedral city of York, England, I was educated at St. Peter's School, which has an unbroken history of education since A.D. 627. Surrounded by Norman (A.D. 1066) walls, dominated by a fifteenth-century cathedral, and peppered with Roman ruins, the city is a living museum, frozen in time, which attracts hundreds of thousands of tourists every year. Everything in the administration and governance of York is concerned with the preservation and consideration of its ancient buildings and heritage. Many of its citizens live, work, socialize, and worship in ancient buildings. Their environment becomes part of their belief system.

There are millions of Europeans who live in cities just like York. Europeans love to live in this mix of static and progressive. If anything, most of them live more in the static zone than the progressive and are concerned at the onrush of progressive change. Hence, European politicians are determined to articulate the so-called *third way*, which suggests that the European lifestyle model is an alternative choice to the American model, which many claim is the model of globalization.

In their analysis of other issues in their book, Huntington and Harrison say that work is valued by progressive cultures and seen as a burden by static groups and that education is offered to all in progressive cultures but is an exclusive privilege in static. They also claim that advancement is based on merit in progressive cultures and on connections in static cultures, that justice has universal ideals in the progressive but is dependant on wealth and influence in the static, and that authority is *wide* in a progressive culture and *narrow* in a static.

Religion and Culture

Religion is culture and culture is religion. The two are inextricably intertwined so we need to look briefly at the main religions of the world and the culture types that walk with them. Religion is so much at the heart of some major cultures that it behooves managers to at least have a passing understanding of them. This book is not intended to be a definitive guide to world religions–there are many more learned publications–but it intends to demonstrate some of the features we must take into account when putting our international deals together.

A frustrated international vice president once said, "Why can't the Jews and the Arabs just get on together and behave like Christians?" Interesting!

The same can be said for that unmitigated disaster Northern Ireland, where Catholics and Protestants with deep-rooted problems going back 500 years, perplex successive U.K. governments. "Why can't they live together and get on with each other like the rest of us?" we ask. What about the Serbs and the Bosnians, the Hindus and the Moslems, the Moslems and the Christians, the Orthodox and Western Christians, and the Jews and Arabs? In the twenty-first century, these irrational conflicts and hate between people will be the dominant issues for successive governments and the cause of wars and terrorism for decades. But global business will continue despite diabolical events committed by a handful of madmen because people of goodwill will seek to trade with each other across religious and cultural frontiers: that is what the majority of us want to do.

Data-Based Religion

The principal religion of the data-based group is Protestant Christianity. There is an individualistic work ethic attitude that comes with this philosophy that started in the Calvin/Luther teaching and was continued into the Puritan philosophy. It continues today throughout the Protestant church communities in North America, Australia, New Zealand, United Kingdom, from northern continental Europe into northeastern Europe, and in parts of Russia. Most people in the Protestant Christian faith keep their religious life and beliefs to themselves. North Europeans, in particular, are private about their religion. They do not discuss it, particularly with strangers or in a business setting.

Western Christianity is the single most important factor in the development of western civilization. As it spread throughout the western hemisphere during the Reformation and Counter-Reformation, political and intellectual consequences occurred, and the modern western culture was molded. No other world culture developed the system of the separation of spiritual and temporal authority. "In Islam, God is Caesar; in Japan and China, Caesar is God; in Orthodoxy, God is Caesar's junior partner," according to Samuel P. Huntington. "This division of authority contributed immeasurably to the development of freedom in the west."

Relationship-Based Religion

Religion is important to this huge culture group that includes the largest religions in the world: Roman Catholicism and Islam. The Roman Catholic religion includes a large population in the United States, but their principal locations are in southern Europe, Poland, Central and South America, and parts of Africa. As leader of the oldest Christian religion, the pope commands respect from world leaders, and the order is well-known for its strict views on certain lifestyle issues. The position of the church vis-a´-vis its political standing varies from country to country, and its fundamental views about some controversial issues are well reported by the press. In general, people living in a Roman Catholic country enjoy an established religious environment where the stability of the church, in some cases, compares favorably to the instability of their government. The long history of the Roman Catholic Church, the ancient cathedrals built with fine architecture, and the social position of the senior church patriarchs give the church prestige and respect so that it has become embedded into the culture of the country. It's hard to go to Spain, Italy, France, or any South American country and not immediately get the *feel* of Catholicism.

Islam is one of the major religions of the world and probably the one most misunderstood by westerners. Like other religions, the Muslims have their fundamentalists, some having demonstrated their vicious behavior in the atrocious terrorist attacks on the World Trade Center and the Pentagon. People in the west probably learned more about Islam during the heavy period after these attacks than at any other time in their education.

Founded by Muhammad at the beginning of the seventh century, Islam spread throughout the Arab and Persian world, into northwest India, Malaysia, Indonesia, and

North Africa. It is now very active in all western countries to some degree. In 2002 it is likely to have more followers than Christianity, and it is expanding rapidly. Islam is in agreement with Judaism and Christianity in that it is mono-theistic. They believe in one God.

For the businessperson working with Moslems, it is important to know the five principles of their faith and their duties:

1. To profess faith in the statement that "there is only one God and Muhammad is his prophet"

2. To pray five times each day, facing Mecca

3. To give alms for the support of the faith and to the poor

4. To observe a solemn fast during Ramadan

5. To make, at least once in a lifetime, a pilgrimage to Mecca

Devout Moslems maintain strict rules of conduct. Women are expected to dress modestly, even to cover their faces in public. Sale and consumption of alcohol is forbid-den as is eating pork. Islam has always been a militant faith, like Christianity was 500 years ago, and it makes the ap-pearance of being at odds with the west. Preservation of their culture is at the heart of this attitude. Saudi Arabia's Prince Bandar bin Sultan's explanation was, "Intangible social and political institutions imported from elsewhere can be deadly. Ask the Shah of Iran . . . Islam for us is not just a religion but also a way of life. We want to modernize but not necessarily westernize."

Other religions in the relationship-based sector are Jew-ish and Eastern Orthodox Christian.

Group-Based Religion

The principal group-based religions are Hinduism, Buddhism, and Confucianism, although there are several others practiced by this culture base such as Shintoism, Sikhism, and Jainism.

Hinduism is mainly restricted to the Indian subcontinent. It has approximately 700,000 adherents. It is one of the oldest religions of the world, dating back to almost 3000 B.C. and was imported into the Indus valley in about 1500 B.C. It is a polytheistic philosophy; in other words, it relates to many gods–probably hundreds. Its teaching is based on a set of manuscripts known as the Vedas: two epic poetic works and various other writings and ancient prayers. Hindus do not assemble in a church for services. For them, religion is a highly personal and family thing. They have shrines to various gods in or around their homes and will visit temples dedicated to certain gods in order to pay homage to their favorite deity.

Hindus have a deep respect for all living things–even insects. Their holiest creature is the cow, and cattle are allowed to roam freely throughout the streets of India, constantly reminding Hindus of the divinity of life. The cycle of reincarnation is an integral part of the philosophy. Although the caste system is a part of the Hindu religion, its practice has been made illegal by the Indian government.

Buddhism was an offshoot of Hinduism and was first practiced in the fifth century B.C. Unlike Hinduism, it spread rapidly throughout Asia into Sri Lanka, Nepal, China, Southeast Asia, Korea, and Japan. The belief, like Hinduism, is based on the reincarnation of the soul, on living *right*, and seeking detachment from the material world. Meditation is an essential part of the Buddhist life, and the orders of monks, which proliferate the Buddhist world, is evidence of this. Some businessmen in this region have spent some years as monks and are now following their Buddhist responsibilities as laymen. Buddhism is a religion of stories, mysticism, and meditation, and of charity and helping others. The Dahli Lama is the proclaimed head of the Buddhist religion, and there are many groups, orders, and approximately 400,000 followers throughout the western world.

Confucianism is the religion of China. It is based on the teachings of Confucius who lived in the 500s B.C. Confucianism has had a powerful effect on the history and politics of China over the centuries and continues to influence today. An estimated 5 million people in East Asia profess to be Confucians.

Other religions in the group-based sector are Taoism, Shintoism, and Zoroastrianism.

Huntington and Harrison make the point that religion in *progressive* cultures (Protestant and Confucianism) has a *poverty-fighting* philosophy whereas in *static* cultures (Catholicism, Hinduism, Buddhism), religion has a *poverty-valued* philosophy.

As we work with our international relationships to do our international deals, we will gather experience and savvy about the philosophies and beliefs of others. The vital key is to recognize that all cultures have their beliefs, and we have ours. More damage has been done to the peace of the world through trying to force-feed religious beliefs into those who do not welcome them or to convert others to our ways of thinking. The arrogant theory that we know how to save the world is at the heart of culture collision. Not only have deals been wrecked on this road but also lives have been lost on the journey.

Language and Culture

The historic development of language–along with its ever-changing style, nuance, and expression–is deeply embedded in culture. Its purpose is to enable people to express their ideas, needs, and emotions to each other through audible speech and through the written word.

There are about 8,000 languages worldwide plus about 50,000 dialects. In the United Kingdom alone, there are about twenty-five major dialects. It was said that in cockney London you could tell which streets persons lived on as soon as they spoke. In Yorkshire, to my knowledge, there are at least seven different dialects.

The United States has approximately 300 dialects and scores of sub-dialects–from the numerous spoken by African-Americans to the hundreds heard in New York and from the Cuban-American varieties to the San Franciscans. Language and dialect are woven into culture and as cultures change, so does language.

It is a constantly changing phenomenon. Some cultures feel that the preservation of the language is the most important thing to do in the face of globalization. This is like trying to stop the clock. Language has always changed with the times. The French or English language cannot be suspended or frozen as an art form because as ideas, needs, and emotions change, so does our language. Shakespeare would not recognize the language in London streets today, let alone the streets of New Orleans, and neither would Voltaire understand the French spoken in the salons of Paris today.

For our purpose, we have to realize that in transacting our international deals, we are at a disadvantage if we do not speak the native language of the other side.

Multilingual

Chris Geenson was born in Scheveningen, Holland. His father was Danish and his mother, Walloon. He attended university in Brussels and got his first job in Mannheim, Germany. Later Chris went to work for a reinsurance company based in The Hague, so he took many trips to London. He was sent to Milan to open a territorial branch that included the entire north Mediterranean countries. By the time I met Chris, he could speak Dutch, Danish, English, German, French, Italian, and Spanish fluently and could get by in Greek and Portuguese. He used to say that after a few *Amstels*, he could order a round of drinks in Serbo-Croatian.

In multiple-language meetings, he would slip effortlessly back and forth through various languages, addressing persons around the table in their own language. My pitiful efforts to speak schoolboy French were embarrassing in meetings when Chris would chitchat and backslap with the mono-linguistic French client. At that point, I realized that being born and raised in the English language could have serious drawbacks when doing global business. We may do all the study of culture behavior; we may know when to shake hands and when not to; we may understand the ways time is valued, but unless we can communicate in the language, it is not easy to read the culture fluently.

Monolingual

Less than 2 percent of English-speaking Americans can fluently speak another language. The Brits themselves are not much better despite their proximity to the European continent. It is fortunate, therefore, that most of the business world we will relate to will be able to speak English as a second language or that, at the very least, we will be able to use the services of a translator. But translation often loses something in the process. Interpreters at the United Nations run into these problems every day as they try to convey meanings behind statements, particularly in emotionally-charged debates. Richard Lewis reports a case where the English speaker said, "I assume," the French had it translated as "I deduce," and the Russians heard it as

"I consider"–by which time the idea of assumption had been lost.

Brit Speak

Between the British and the Americans, there are well-known gaps in communication, or " . . . divided by a common language," said George Bernard Shaw.

We all hear of the difference in vocabulary, such as windscreen, boot, and others–what we have to be aware of are the nuances behind the statements.

American tough talk like "it's in the bag," "have we gotta deal," "you've gotta be kiddin'," "no way," " down the tube," and "up the spout" are all part of the American cliché vocabulary developed by a free-rolling, entrepreneurial society. To the conservative European, some of these come over as brash or perhaps may even be taken literally by the Germans.

The British understatement is regularly misunderstood by Americans when they use their vague, fuzzy clichés like "good show," " bad news," " good shot," " a bit thick," and "sticky wicket" many of them related to sporting activity. The British use of cutting invective is part of the *inter-Brit* banter but is much misunderstood as being personal and rude by the more sensitive American ear.

If there is so much division in a common language, then what can we expect in a different language and a totally different culture? The answer is: a great deal of difference. But don't worry; people are not lying in wait to ambush you whenever you miss a point or fail to understand a nuance, misunderstand a cliché or fail to appreciate their jokes. If they are, then perhaps we shouldn't be doing business with them in the first place. The key is to recognize that these idiosyncrasies of language are all part of the culture mix and deserve to be appreciated as we move forward into our deal-making activities.

Globalization and Culture

There is much chatter today about the breakdown of culture divisions and types due to the tsunami of globalization. It is a cause that has been embraced by the street-protesting class, by leftist newspapers, and by some fundamental religious groups, but it is also a concern to us all, particularly when we witness the speed by which all this is happening. The fact is that culture breakdown, change, and rebuilding in another form have always happened throughout history. Successive invasions and settlement by Romans, Vikings, Angles, Saxons, and Normans destroyed the old Celtic cultures of ancient Britain. What emerged was a distinctive cultural soup that included, we hope, some of the best attributes of the ingredients. Man has always traveled and traded, taking with him his lifestyle, his attitudes, his religion, and his values, as well as his goods and services. Traders spread Islam throughout the Middle East. As the camel trains plodded along the silk-road, so came the practice of Islam and the consequent change of culture in its wake.

In some cases, it was war that invaded and attempted to destroy a culture, but very rarely did the aggressors destroy an established culture entirely. Holocausts, genocides, and ethnic cleansings in our time do not wipe out a deep cultural core built over generations. Today we are witnessing the rebirth of old traditional cultures long suppressed by communist regimes. They are claiming their place in the list of world nations as they dig out their traditions, rituals, and religions. As they do so, the swing of the pendulum takes some of them to the extremes we have seen from time to time in the past.

4

Cross-Culture Incompetence

The history of man is essentially a story of cross-culture rows, disagreements, quarrels, fights, settlements, and patched-up agreements. The earliest records tell us of misunderstandings and wars between people of different tribes based on land possession, hunting territory, and crop production, but the enmities between them became fueled by cultural differences. People searched for the variances rather than the similarities, the inequalities rather than the equalities. Disagreement turned to dislike; aversion turned to hate; prejudice became second nature. The Bible is a continual story of cross-culture prejudice with numerous accounts of tribes, mini-tribes, and nations disliking each other. In some cases, the aversion goes on for centuries. More recently, the horrific accounts of culture persecution, murder, and genocide from Londonderry to the Gaza Strip, from Sarajevo to Phnom Penh, and the attacks of September 11, 2001, demonstrate in graphic detail that the problem is alive and active.

If this is the story of man's second nature, then there is a lot of work to do if we are going to avoid wrecking our international deals because of cross-culture incompetence. Let's look at some of them.

Prejudice

Hopefully, despite the daily news of atrocities, we are living in different times when the values of diversity are appreciated, and smart countries and companies abolish the walls that create the perception of differences based on race, gender, nationality, ethnicity, age, and social orientation. Evidence demonstrates that this might be happening. In the last fifty years, the United States has legally moved from segregation to integration and law has been enacted which gives clear rights to women, children, the disabled, and minorities. Thousands of activists tell us there is a lot more to do. Probably so—it's not easy to clean up thousands of years of prejudice in a lifetime. However, globalization waits for no man, and we have to recognize that cross-culture prejudice lies dormant in the human psyche, ready to spring out and wreck an otherwise good deal at any time.

Prejudice is defined as a preconceived judgment or opinion, leaning toward one side of a question from other considerations than those belonging to it. It has no grounds for existence based on logic or even experience. It has no place in the corporate environment, particularly among international teams and managers with overseas responsibilities. Cultural prejudice cannot find a place where there is global mindset; the two are incompatible with each other. If leadership and training cannot remove it, then it has to be discarded. It is like having a germ of bad attitude in a hyper-motivated sales team; its influence can rot the core if it is not cut out.

Stereotyping

Supreme Court Judge Clarence Thomas made the point during his memorable Senate hearing that turned a sexual harassment hearing into a legal milestone. He referred to the stereotyping of the African-American male and complained that he was being subjected to this prejudice.

Our inclination to lump a culture group, nationality, or race into a general category or overall opinion is stereotyping. "The French are rude." "All Americans think about is making money." "English food is dull and boring." We have heard them all. We may have given vent to a number ourselves. I tell my English friends not to judge America on the taxi ride from JFK to Manhattan, and I tell American visitors to England not to go home with the idea that the whole population spends its time in the pubs.

It makes good conversation to talk about other nationalities as if they don't measure up to us. Newspaper tabloids love that sort of thing, and it makes good media material, but they are deepening the stereotyping rut by doing so.

Stereotyping is a product of gossip, ignorance, superficial knowledge or perhaps an unfortunate experience in a country. Perhaps it just makes comfortable conversation– the *not like us* scenario. The international manager, when confronted with stereotype conversation, should dampen the fire by contradicting the stereotype with stories showing how the experience was the total opposite. Nothing confounds gossip like truth.

Chauvinism

Gender discrimination in the business world is still widespread, even if illegal in the United States. It is often hard to detect, but its effect is frequently evident in promotions, job selection, and opportunity. Women have made great strides in overcoming, working around, and even fighting male dominance in the workplace, but there is considerable work to be done in education and example. Progress can be made when it is realized throughout the business world that women bring a vast creative, intuitive, customer-caring intelligence to the enterprise, along with a natural work ethic, instinctive loyalty, team spirit, and commitment.

Likewise, female chauvinism is a form of cultural incompetence. Excluding men for the sake of gender discrimination is just as stupid. If it is done as a sort of backlash against male dominance or to teach them all a lesson, then it is a wasteful exercise that culture competent managers should recognize.

Fear

When, at the age of twenty-three, I was instructed to negotiate the renewal of an insurance contract in France, my first reaction was outright fear. *I don't know how to deal with the French. What happens if they don't understand me? What about the money? Do I have to drive? I could get lost. I could be robbed. I could be murdered and nobody would know.* All these fears and hundreds of others filled my mind and cluttered my excitement at having been given this new and interesting opportunity.

Fear of the unknown is well-known to us all. Traveling abroad and experiencing fear of the unknown is fairly common, certainly to those going for the first time to a distant land and a remote culture. Even experienced and seasoned travelers feel a measure of apprehension when they prepare to leave for a faraway destination, particularly now that we are involved in a war against international terrorism.

John Simpson is an independent geologist with Halliburton and works out of Houston. I met him on an

Aeroflot flight out of Tomsk, Siberia, heading for Moscow. Halliburton has been active developing oil and gas prospects in Siberia for many years. Simpson, age 43, works six months at the wellhead sites then returns home to Texas for two. He has been through five Siberian winters. "But the summers are worse," he says, "with mosquitoes as big as birds and every type of bug known to God." He gets an attack of nerves every time he travels, he told me. "I've survived plane crashes, cholera, and earthquakes. I've worked everywhere from the Indonesian jungle to the Saudi Empty Quarter, and I'm always glad to get back to Texas. I'm getting too old for this crap!" But John Simpson likes adventure and new experiences, and he will keep going back over there as long as there is a job to do. "Maybe it isn't really nerves," he then said. "Its my adrenaline. That's why I smoke too much."

Fear of interacting with other cultures may not be a problem unless it paralyzes. Bob Atkinson, an oil and gas pipeline engineer with a division of Chevron, was traveling with a colleague to Mongolia. After a long flight from Beijing, they arrived at Ulan Bator. As Bob reached up for his carry-on, he realized that he was getting off alone as he looked at his colleague. His friend couldn't move. He was stone cold, white with fear. Bob checked his colleague onto the return flight to Beijing to be met there by his wife.

Some people find it difficult to travel to new and distant places. Managers should appreciate that it is not for everybody but much can be accomplished by training and on-site acclimatization. Pre-travel briefing on culture issues, money, accommodation, travel, and food should be mandatory before sending off valuable personnel. Finding that they could not operate up to their potential or, at best, that they needed two days to get used to their environment could have been minimized with a two-hour briefing.

Language

Fear of interaction with remote cultures usually stems from a feeling of incompetence with the local language. "How will I be understood?" is a valid question. English-speaking business people are fortunate in one sense, but mightily unfortunate in another. The fact that the majority of business is transacted in the English language is helpful, but the inability to relate to the culture through their language is an outright disadvantage.

AVERAGE number of LANGUAGES spoken

Dutch	4	Belgians	3
Germans	3	Singaporeans	2
French	3	Japanese	2
Swedes	3	Canadians	2
Americans	1	British	1

Clearly touching the frontiers of other languages has its advantages as does a native tongue not spoken by the mainstream business world.

Any English-speaking manager who is required to spend a minimum of three months interacting with another language must develop a working knowledge of that language. Any business that creates an alliance with another should employ people who are fluent in each other's languages. Any sales representative should have a social knowledge of the language of his or her customers.

Lifestyles

The differing lifestyles we experience around the world are the triggers for our comment, "They're not like us!"

While walking with our female guide through central Mumbai, I asked, "Why don't they clean the street and get rid of this garbage?"

Her reply was, "What garbage?" Approaching the streets of India with squeaky clean western eyes is an exercise in futility. Traveling with a criticizing eye-comparing everything from sanitation to table manners to the conditions at home–is cross-culture incompetence.

American absorption with bathroom conditions can ruin an otherwise good opinion of a country. Until immigrating to the United States, I had no idea that the loo was such an important piece of household fixture. Frankly, I had never even thought about the ridiculous thing. I had used hundreds of varieties, including my grandmother's *two-holer* down the garden path when I was a child in Yorkshire.

In most countries overseas, the bathroom, toilet, lavatory, or loo is an irrelevant, unimportant sparse facility that rarely gets maintenance or modernization. As any woman from the United States knows, you have to plan way ahead if you are on the road in any European country. Further east or south, forget it!

Most cultures outside the west have a different standard when it comes to hygiene. It seems the older the culture, the worse it is. Some tribes in central Africa are still scooping up rainwater puddles and drinking stagnant lake water with all the associated killer bacteria. Egypt is facing total salinization (the process whereby salts accumulate in the soil due to slow moving or stagnant water) in areas below the Aswan High Dam. Those who travel into such areas, of course, need to take proper health precautions for which there is plenty of good advice, not only from your doctor but also from the State Department. However, we have to accept that this is the way it is. The issue for global managers is "Can we live with it?"–if not, then it becomes a roadblock in our effort to become cross-culture competent.

Interaction

Becoming globally savvy is a practical hands-on type of learning process. It demands travel to foreign countries and cross-culture interaction.

Recently an international friendship organization in Houston asked my wife and me to entertain a group of Japanese businessmen visiting the United States. We hosted a dinner party for six of them at our home and planned to give them a formal evening. They duly arrived on the dot with their translator, and we exchanged gifts. Having studied our culture guidebooks, we were careful about our protocol and all seemed to go well until the translator said, "The group wants to know if you are always this formal."

"Well, no. It depends on our guests. If its family and old friends, then we are informal," he translated to the group.

Then translating in English, he told us, "The group would like you to be informal tonight and demonstrate an American family evening!"

Its not easy to act informal in front of a group of Japanese salarymen, but we did our best. Frankly, I was relieved to do so in the middle of a Houston July evening.

Our guests loved it as they explained that they all worked for Mitsubishi Bank, and they were traveling America at company expense to study the culture and get to understand its people. Their days were filled with lectures, political briefings, and factory visits. Evenings were spent just like they were with us: visiting American homes and experiencing the family environment.

Its easy to believe that these managers will become cross-culture competent. Mitsubishi is one of a number of large international corporations that take this competency seriously and are raising a globally savvy group of executives who have experienced the real world outside their own. Most of us don't get this type of opportunity; rather we have got to find the main chance and afford it on our own. It is often cheaper to fly to Brussels and stay there three nights than to spend five days at Disney World.

Ethnocentricity is a major drawback when it comes to doing global business; it is one of the main reasons for cross-culture incompetence.

Poverty

The first abject poverty I remember seeing was when, as a youth, I visited the slums of Naples, Italy. It left a scar on my memory. *How was it that a country with obviously wealthy people could also have so many poor people?* I asked myself. For years I blamed the systems that allowed such atrocities. Its not easy for the western mind to understand this issue.

The same thoughts went through my mind when my wife and I, on the first morning of our recent visit to India, stepped onto the sidewalk in front of the Royal Taj Hotel in Mumbai with its exotic rooms, white marble halls and lobbies, and mosaics of gold and precious stones. The Taj looks out over the famous India Gate where the Viceroys came ashore as they arrived to govern the country during the British Raj. We hadn't walked twenty yards before the world's poor, mainly children, besieged us. In India, everything is multiplied tenfold: poverty, population, and persistence. We couldn't shake them off. My wife gave them every rupee and paisa she possessed until we were rescued by the hotel doorman. "Shoo; go away; be gone," he shouted at the dirt poor followers and then turned to us and said, "Tell them to go; don't give them anything; otherwise, they will never leave you."

"You have to realize," explained Homi Davier, a Parsi friend living in Houston, "most of them are actually content to be living in poverty. It is necessary for them to go through this experience in this lifetime. If not, then they will not be able to obtain improvement in the next." Right or wrong, I don't know. What I do know is that it was information I could store in my culture understanding file.

Countries with huge populations perplex us. The problems seem so gigantic and insoluble. It is probably because the data-based western culture likes to be able to solve its problems and control its environment. That doesn't seem to matter in India where time is an ever-unfolding tapestry of the law of karma. China believes that its population size is its advantage. Whatever the reasoning offered by the culture or country, it is inevitably foreign to the western way of thinking. Critical remarks demonstrate cross-culture incompetence and are unhelpful in our relationships. Even if we get answers to our questions, the chances are that they will not be in our framework of thinking, so let's just move on.

Non-Christian

The Indian Mutiny of 1857, sometimes referred to as the first war of Indian independence, was one of the bloodiest disputes in the gory annals of human conflict–brought on because of cross-culture incompetence—big time! One of the main reasons was because the sepoys (the Hindu and Muslim Indian troops employed by the British) believed that they would shortly be forced to adopt Christianity as their religion. This had been attempted before. Missionaries had been murdered; converts had been slain, and church buildings burned. Proselytizing civilians were roaming the barracks, claiming that their role was to regenerate India and make it a land of Christians. A leader of the people at that time, Dwarakanath Tagore, is accredited with the remark, "If the British represent Christianity, then I think I will remain Hindu."

The English were more successful in Africa with their conversions. Tribes who converted were spared death. Very simple, really!

Christianity Versus Islam

History is packed with examples of cross-culture incompetence when it comes to religion. The old antagonism between Christianity and Islam has been going on for fourteen hundred years. As the message of Mohammed was carried along trade routes–through the Middle East, into Persia and northern India, and by ships to north Africa and into Spain–it constantly clashed with Christianity. In 1095, the Crusades were launched. For almost two hundred years, Christians attempted to take the Holy Land with ghastly cruelty and diminishing success. Meantime the Islamic Ottoman Turks ruined Byzantium and occupied the Balkans, pushing up through Eastern Europe to the walls of Vienna. Early Christians saw Islam as a constant threat.

Samuel P. Huntington in *The Clash of Civilizations* says the following:

> The causes of this ongoing pattern of conflict lie not in transitory phenomena as twelfth-century Christian passion or twentieth-century Muslim fundamentalism. They flow from the nature of the two religions and the civilizations based on them. Both are monotheistic religions, which, unlike polytheistic ones, cannot easily assimilate additional deities and which see the world in dualistic, us and them terms. Both are universalistic, claiming to be the one true faith to which all humans can adhere. Both are missionary religions believing that their adherents have an obligation to convert nonbelievers to that one true faith.

Managers intending to do global business are advised to have a basic understanding of the religion of the culture, particularly in the case of Islam and Christianity. As we have learned the worst way, these two religions are the source of potential collision between and within working teams, alliances, customer service providers, and joint ventures. The best defense is knowledge and understanding.

Back to History

Culture and history are woven eternally in concert. Together they make the tapestry through which the people tell their story. Their trials, triumphs, and tribulations are embroidered into the fabric of their society. They are what they have experienced. This is where we start if we really want to understand our market and its people.

Most of the world is not only fascinated by their history, but they *know* their history. They talk about it, read about it, and are proud of it. For today's managers who are starting to do business with new countries and employing people from different nations, there is an urgent need to learn something of international history. To do otherwise is cross-cultural incompetence. The deeper we study the history of nations, the more proficient we become in understanding the people and realizing why they think and act the way they do.

* * *

"Would you like to go to Texas?" asked my boss, Derek Bryant, on a winter's day in London.

"For how long? Three days? Three weeks?" I inquired.

"No, three years. We would like you to go and develop some big-ticket oil rig insurance for Lloyd's." Back in the early eighties the North Sea was booming, and Houston was the offshore energy capital of the world.

"When do I start?" I responded, thinking about wide-open spaces, cowboys herding cattle, rolling tumbleweed, and swingin' saloon doors.

My arrival in downtown Houston was delayed due to airport construction, freeway expansion work on I-45, and the huge number of new arrivals checking into the Hyatt. "Where are the wide-open spaces and the rolling tumbleweed?" I asked myself. A few people look like cowboys, perhaps, but no cattle and no hitching posts. I had better start to learn about my new home before I jump to any more stupid conclusions.

I found that the only way to start learning about Texas was to head west about 175 miles to San Antonio. There I learned why Travis, Crocket, and Bowie are regarded as heroes. Next I drove to Goliad and discovered why Fannin is thought of as a *scumbag*, then on to the San Jacinto battleground to understand why Texans can forgive Sam Houston anything, then to Spindletop, where in 1901 the first gusher rushed in the Texas black gold rush. Texas history is about larger than life characters making a mark on the events of their time, not too different from the guys I was starting to meet.

Some guidebooks do a moderately good job at providing the history of the subject country. Fodor has consistently done this well for its tourist guides, but this should only be a start, a taste of what's required if we are to be culturally competent.

Even on short trips to a country I have never before visited, I read as much as I can find on its history. I try to arrive two or three days early, visit the cultural capital, and spend a few hours in the museums, the parliament buildings (if open to visitors), the major art galleries, libraries, and street cafés. By the time I meet the client, I am pretty well briefed on the things he's most proud of–his country and its glorious history–or at least, I better understand why the country's leaders behave in the way they do.

Geography Again

We have all heard the stories about college kids not being able to place the state capitals. Presumably, education in geography took a back seat to math and science after Sputnik. Today the lack of geography knowledge is cross-culture incompetence and can lead to some embarrassing moments for the global manager.

"It's Tuesday; it must be Brussels," was the breakfast comment we passed to each other on the road in Europe. One capital city after the other, in a mad round of reinsurance renewals in the weeks before year-end, led us to get confused about where we were.

Many travelers are confused about where they are. Many people cannot put countries into positional order; some cannot relate location with compass directions or, particularly, with time zones. If we are to be globally competent, then we have to have a working grasp of these things.

The English sometimes refer to Australia and New Zealand as the *antipodes* (pronounced an-tip-odeez). If you drill through the planet from London, through the center of the earth, you would come out somewhere in Australia. So it is the opposite of London in time and season.

When I traveled out there, I could never figure out the time in London, so I started to carry two watches, one on local time, one on London. After getting confused about whether it was day or night in the United Kingdom, I switched to a twenty-four hour timepiece.

Practical knowledge of where we are in relation to other countries (i.e., time zones, the climate zone, topography, demography, and economic base) is all basic to the understanding we need to do business there. It's the minimum preparation our customers expect; it demonstrates that we pay attention to detail and that we care.

Most of all, it gives us the information to make decisions, hopefully as good as any local; and, if the *local* is making the decisions, then we have the knowledge to understand what he or she is talking about.

Geography has always influenced culture and the way people think and act. Consider the Russians. We often think of them as being the product of successive autocratic rule over many centuries–first the Tsars, then the Communists–when, in fact, it is geography that has had more influence on their collective personality than anything else.

Russian Enigma

Russia is massive with eleven time zones–that's almost halfway round the globe. It is the biggest country on earth. The enormity of it has made the people feel highly vulnerable and suspicious of foreigners. It has encouraged them to be inward looking and defensive, inclined to warfare, and protective of their long borders. Collectivization was an agricultural system used by the Communists. In fact, it is an old method of banding together for survival, long practiced in Russia. Most Russians, of course, have never traveled their country, but at school, they have been taught about its size, its diversity, its rich resources, and its climate.

Russia's harsh climate, unremitting, unrepentant, and unsympathetic, has had a large hand in molding the Russian character. Alexandrovo is a village of approximately 1,500 people located one hundred miles southwest of Tomsk, Siberia. Most of the people live in four-room log houses with corrugated iron roofs. They lost 414 men and women in World War II. The Alexandrovo district was a dairy collective in Soviet times. Now each farmer has his own two or three cows and grows a few vegetable crops and winter fodder for the cattle that graze the common land, mostly around the village street. The winter of 2000/2001 was not good; temperatures were in the -40°C range, and there was up to eight feet of snow. The first snow fell in mid-August and continued through late May.

Routinely, for two and a half months, there is frantic activity: nature bursts forth, flowers bloom, and bugs fill the air and reproduce. The farmer must grow winter food for his family and his cattle, and his wife preserves it. Wood fuel has to be collected and cut for the long winter. Then, there is virtual hibernation. Nothing can be done–it's survival time until the snow melts and the sun comes back and the whole cycle starts again. This unending, severe climate has made Russians cautious and pessimistic, a tendency to accentuate the negative and take a bleak outlook on life. It has ingrained obstinacy in the Russian character, but it has also built a nation of people who have substantial strength and endurance.

The culture competent manager will take time to become familiar with the country and its people through traveling the byways and remote areas. Here one finds living evidence, the grass roots of the culture makeup. Here one learns by immersion.

Political Naivety

Understanding the political game is understanding the culture, and that can be a powerful and highly expensive problem if it is not competently handled. Jack Welch, recently retired chief executive of General Electric, found this out, to his cost, when the gnomes of Brussels quashed his proposal to merge Honeywell into GE.

Reported in the *Financial Times* on June 29, 2001, GE and Honeywell endeavored to get the approval of the $41 billion merger from the European Union Competition Commissioner Mario Monti after getting the go-ahead of U.S. regulators. Welch was keen to make this his swan song and predicted that the combined operation would secure the future of GE for years to come. Little did he and his team think that the politically motivated bureaucrats in Brussels would scotch the deal. Mario Monti argued that the bundling of GE/Honeywell products could cause damage to the much smaller European aero engine industry. "In the United States, bundling is a reason to approve a deal," says Kevin Arquit, a competition lawyer who was short-listed for the head of the Department of Justice antitrust division. U.S. experts, brought into the negotiation by GE, were amazed at the arguments put forward by the EU commission, which issued the statement, "If a company becomes very efficient after a merger, the Europeans are not going to allow it."

The Europeans listened to competitors' arguments rather than to consumers, something that U.S. regulators have long since stopped doing in antitrust cases. Local industry protection comes naturally to European politicians brought up left of center in the political spectrum.

The political culture of a country or a trade bloc can be a subtle thing, but we ignore it at our peril as I found out when I rushed into a promising deal and its promise of rich business without doing any political homework.

Uruguay Sugar

For months, we had been trying to put insurance together for a new government-backed sugar mill being built on the outskirts of Montevideo, Uruguay. Our agent, Donald Cameron, was an expatriate Scot who had been the manager of a British insurance company with a branch in Uruguay. Donald asked one of our people to go and help him put the deal together. It needed to be done in a hurry–before the government fell to the military junta that everybody believed would take over. A good technician who spoke Spanish, Tim Griffiths, went as our company's representative.

Five days later, I was in the room at Lloyd's where the underwriters sit and do business with the brokers. Mr. Taylor, a marine underwriter, called me over and showed me a copy of the *Herald Tribune*, not a newspaper I normally read. "Hope you don't have any premium due in Uruguay–look at this," he said. To my horror, there was a report of a military coup that had successfully taken over the government and had arrested numerous foreigners, had put an embargo on currency transfers outside the country, and had curtailed all the government-sponsored building activity.

Back at the office, phone calls met brick walls; telexes and cables flew into the ether. Uruguay was off the map–and our man with it. Tim's wife called in a panic. "We know nothing, but we're trying" was all we could tell her. Next we called the British Foreign Office where we met bureaucratic put-offs, "no-news-is-good-news"–all the usual hyperbole that civil servants seem to learn at some inhuman diplomacy school. Finally, we heard that Donald and Tim were in jail. Well, that was a relief; at least they were not dead or in some concentration camp. But then we heard that they were accused of "economic crimes against the state of Uruguay." Now that sounded bad.

Slowly the diplomatic system got into gear. Tim was to be released, but Donald was going to trial, along with scores of other businessmen from the world over, all of whom were accused of "currency evacuation and law evasion." Three years in jail ruined Donald's health, and he died a premature death.

Tim arrived home, a thinner and pastier version of his old self, accompanied by a foreign office official who berated us for spending taxpayers' money unnecessarily.

"Hey, hang on, old boy; isn't old Tim worth it?" someone cheerily said to the official.

"That's not the point," he replied crisply. "We issued warnings that this coup could happen any day, and you merrily went ahead, putting your people in harm's way. Why don't you read our warnings?"

"We don't ever get them," I admitted sheepishly.

Here we were–a multi-million pound business with operations and customers around the world–not doing our homework, wasting thousands of pounds of company (as well as government) money because of cross-culture incompetence. We had failed to read the information and to do our research in understanding the way the country was moving.

Geopolitics

The study of geopolitics is to understand the ways of culture. Briefly, geopolitics is the study of the geography, demographics, and economy of a country. Its conclusions give pointers to the future actions of the nation. The geopolitics of the United States, simply put, is determined by the two large oceans on either side: *folks like us* to the north and friendly amigos to the south. It means that the United States of America has frequently taken an isolationist attitude to foreign policy. When it does get involved with the rest of the world, its spheres of influence are a long reach across the oceans to Taiwan and the western Pacific and to western Europe. This remoteness has given the American people a buoyant independence and a temptation not to get involved with the *problems* of other nations–something that we have referred to previously as a difficulty for those who wish to give their business a global mindset. Take Poland, for example. Two traditionally aggressive nations to the right and the left, Germany and Russia, and the Pripet Marshes, to the south, determine its geopolitics.

Germany is influenced by Russia to the left, France and allies to the right, sea to the north, and mountains to the south. Britain's geopolitics is that of an island race, independence, trade, and sea power. Those who visit India are impressed by the uniqueness of its culture. Again, geopolitics has played its part. India's heart lies in the densely populated plains of the Ganges. To the north is the awe-some Himalayan range; to the south, east, and west are the peninsula and the Indian Ocean.

Remote Locations

We are going to have to get used to working with cultures in remote locations where there is no Hilton, no decent phone service, and little, if any, acceptable medical attention. If we are only prepared to work in places where American standard hotels are available, then that limits our scope. Those pioneers who spread through Europe after WWII, planting the young trees of American businesses such as IBM, Xerox, GMC, and Dupont, knew what it was like to heave a suitcase up three steep flights of narrow stairs in a small Dutch private hotel, then come down for a hard-boiled egg breakfast with ersatz coffee. Then came the Holiday Inns springing up like mushrooms overnight. I was in Gibraltar when they opened there. It was turnkey luxury compared to the usual offering. "Do you know how many towels you get?" asked my local friend, Mike Garcia. "A whole rack of five."

"They are short changing you, Mike," I replied. "They normally provide ten."

Holiday Inn set a standard that made the local lodgings wake up, and European travel was never the same, even off the beaten track. It's going to take a long time for some lesser-traveled areas in China, India, Africa, Russia, and South America to catch up, but that doesn't mean that we must wait that length of time to do business.

The thing I appreciate about the energy business is the fact that companies will go anywhere to find oil. And oil always seems to be in the most remote and arduous places in the world, where the living conditions are dirt primitive and there is anarchy in the air. In Baku, the capital of Azerbaijan, on the western shore of the Caspian Sea, the now defunct soviet system has left an ancient fine city in ruins: decaying infrastructure, choking pollution, corrupt government, and a penniless economy. However, Baku could have a bright future as it is located near the vast oil field of the Kashagan. It is said this could be the biggest find in the last two decades. It is the proposed head of the huge pipeline that will carry the oil to the Mediterranean near Tarsus, but there are problems. Here, at the fulcrum of the Middle East between the Caspian Sea and the Black Sea, is a checkerboard of cultures, all in an unnatural game of *who's on first*. Islamic Azeri Turks rub shoulders with Christian Armenians who cohort with Orthodox Russians. The problem is that many Armenian children are raised to bring death to the Turk; the Turk has had a history of genocide toward the Armenian, and they both hate the Russian. Iran is to the south and Russia to the north. They feel hemmed in like rats in a trap. But it was not always like that. Oil was first discovered here in the 1870s, and the Rothschild's bank backed the development. A cosmopolitan metropolis was built: a Hotel de Ville, an opera house, and hundreds of fine apartments, most of which are now in a state of collapse.

Now western entrepreneurs have moved into town and are helping to build Baku back to its previous glory. If only all the factions and potential culture collisions can be contained; if the concerned recognize that a growing economic base can bring prosperity, health, and education to the people, and that cross-culture incompetence is no way for a society to live, Baku will rise again.

Nationalism

In 1990 I was climbing into my tourist bus in Red Square when I felt a tug on my sleeve. A middle-aged Russian wanted to talk to me. He was a teacher, he told me, and had a message "for America." My interest, doubt, suspense, and excitement rose as I pictured myself enacting some John Le Carré part. In perfect English he said, "The flag may have changed, but the people in there have not," as he pointed to the Kremlin behind him. At an international conference in Moscow later that year, delegates from all over the world gathered to hear what ideas the new Russia would use to build its economy along democratic and free market lines. A delegate from Sweden tagged an official and discreetly pointed out that the flag at the back of the stage was upside down. The official changed it during the intermission, but on entering the room again, the chairman of the meeting said that the flag had been hung upside down. An argument ensued. Finally, only a call to the office of the president of the Russian Federation could solve the problem that had almost taken over the conference, and the flag was hung back the way the Swedish delegate had suggested.

Flags Up

Nations can get hung up by flags and patriotic symbols and, if not careful, can develop a kind of national arrogance around the symbol. If not handled with common sense, it can be put into the category of cross-culture incompetence.

The final night of the Proms at the Albert Hall in London is a traditional grand night of national pride and flag-waving. Patriotic songs, such as "Land of Hope and Glory" and "Rule Britannia," are sung to the accompaniment of the London Symphony Orchestra in an auditorium of waving flags. It's enough to stir an Englishman's heart and to recall the days of the empire. Fortunately, it's just playtime.

The problem with blatant patriotism is that it can drive a gulf between nations and cultures. Most people understand national pride: the honor due to the collective group for their achievements. It is when we step over the thin red line—start believing that we are a master race, that no other country has anything as good as ours, that everybody else is inferior—that we demonstrate cross-culture incompetence. This act has led to some of the most awful wars in history.

Flags, national emblems, and patriotic songs are all right at home, at veterans' parades, at ball games, and Fourth of July celebrations, and certainly in support of national unity when the country stands shoulder to shoulder in the face of a cruel enemy. Under normal circumstances, however, we should all experience restraint when in mixed cultural company.

Getting cross-culture competent is a fascinating journey of education and experience which every global manager will enjoy. The diversities of the world go deeper and deeper as we delve into them and travel down strange and unfamiliar alleys to satisfy our curiosity. Not far into the mysteries, we realize that we know more about our customer's culture than he or she does. That's cross-culture competency.

5

Cross-Culture Competence

Taking your business global is likely to be the most important action you can take to ensure its survival in the first half of the twenty-first century. Being able to stay in business makes all the effort worthwhile, and cross-culture competence is the most vital skill to practice to remain existent. Few companies with an established international presence manage to keep the initial momentum in place, either because of inflated expectations or because of unexpected circumstances that overwhelm the project. Clearly lack of planning, research, and preparation are major contributing factors, but the most significant reason which impacts both inflated expectation and unforeseen circumstances is the lack of cross-culture competence–the inability to read the cultural tea leaves which will poison the deal.

Like a diagnostic warning, there is a list of the key competencies we need to work on to give us the skills we need to accomplish successful and lasting international deals. Each competency is a personal attribute that can be worked on individually.

Change Again

Western business has been embroiled in change since the seventies. Managers have been given the message of change or die at an increasing volume for twenty years, and they have valiantly handled everything from civil rights to gender equality, from reengineering to no reengineering, from quality excellence as an advantage to a given, customer service to customer empowerment, from fax to email, from computerization to B2B, and from regionalization to globalization. No wonder we're confused. John Naisbitt told us what to expect; Tom Peters told us how to deal with it; John Drucker was our mentor; and people like Jack Welch, Bill Gates, John Chambers, Ned Gove, and Michael Dell were our examples. We stood by with a mixture of amazement, punch drunkenness, acceptance, and resistance.

Some people are born to change, and some have change thrust upon them. Most people fit into the last bracket and cope as best they can with the change that whirls about them while carrying off all their traditional beliefs, comfort blankets, and preconceived ideas.

Of all the change that managers have had to face in these wild decades, nothing will be like the change that confronts us in the maelstrom of globalization. We will never be the same again. So if we haven't gotten used to change by now, we had better get ready because we are about to step into the tornado.

Rapid Culture Change

Speaker Carl Hammerschlag, M.D., publishes an e-zine called "Schlagbytes." In August 2001, he wrote:

> Just released records from Japan reveal that in the first six months of 2001 the Japanese crime rate has risen to record highs (most of it juvenile related). This small island nation, with a thousand year code of honor and mutual respect has seen a huge increase in juvenile delinquency. There has been an uproar in Japan with parents saying these problems are due to the breakdown in values and traditions. Commentators cite a rapidly changing culture has transformed the structure of families and the entire educational system.
>
> No one denies the Japanese have experienced a radical change in their culture. An emperor once considered divine was declared ordinary. A nation defeated, arose from the ashes of annihilation to become a world power of free-market capitalism.

Clearly, what it takes to survive economically is different than what it takes to survive emotionally and spiritually. Survival in the physical world of a rapidly changing culture is predicated on its ability to adapt quickly and for its constituents to be able to apply unencumbered, logical thinking to make them change. Those not bound by preconceptions can think more expensively. J. Paul Getty once said that in times of rapid change, experience can be your worst enemy. He is alluding to the fact that old judgments can inhibit creativity. On the other hand, disconnecting from old traditions also separates us from credible values of our soul. Tradition provides the structure that lifts our spirit during the hard times. Survival in the emotional world requires more than our analytic minds; it requires connections to something other than ourselves, something we trust and believe in.

It is not just the Japanese who are in the process of rapid cultural change. We are all sitting in the frying pan amidst the fires of a rapidly changing technology. That technology has provided us with some enormous benefits, but it has not yet provided us with better answers for dealing with the catastrophes we face or just the ordinary ups and downs in our lives.

Juvenile crime is a worldwide problem, and I believe it is a reflection of our disconnections. Survival in rapidly changing cultures is ensured by allowing the mind to think nontraditionally but the heart has to stay connected to a traditional ethic of morality. Strong families build character and teach values that help us survive emotionally.

The ratio between good and evil has remained constant throughout the ages. If we lose touch with these values that once sustained us, we will lose our balance.

Life Change

Going global, if it's done properly and is not treated as an adventure or a *trial run*, will change forever the way you see your life, your customers, your products, and the human resources you work with. It is, in fact, a *way of life*. Getting a global mindset is, in effect, becoming a *global citizen*, and your view of the world and its people is totally different from anything you have experienced before. You and your business can never retreat from this condition since such is the philosophical and attitudinal change it demands.

My first visit to Russia was in 1974. Apart from the fact that it was during the winter, it was soviet gloomy: gray sky over Leningrad, gray people in gray suits talking about gray things, giving gray answers over gray food. The historic royal way Nevsky Prospect was empty; maybe one car passed every five minutes.

My next visit was in 1990. Perestroika was in full swing. Nevsky was being dug up and repaired by hundreds of brawny women as the tour buses wound their way around the barricades. The next time I was there was in the summer of 2001. It now is called St. Petersburg. The Nevsky is vying with the Ave. des Champs Elysées as one of the fashionable streets of Europe. Tall elegant Russian women walk the sidewalks, calling in at Cartier and Louis Vuitton. Mercedes and Lexus SUVs cannot find a place to park. There are dozens of superb international quality restaurants up and down the famous Prospect. If we think change has upset our apple cart in the west, then we ought to spare a thought for Russia. Their change has been nothing short of revolution, which is, after all, part of their rich culture. Chaotic change is part of the global business condition. The whole world, almost without exception, is in the whirlwind, and we have to ride it if we want to be cross-culturally competent. Social, political, and lifestyle changes are rattling the doors of traditional institutions, governments, and religious orders. There's no let-up in this dynamic condition, and there is little, if anything, that politicians can do about it. Politicians, you may have noticed, are probably the most perplexed about it. They look at the march of globalization and see the potential of a tax revenue flight and the movement of corporate governance into less regulated and more tax-advantaged locations. Without any doubt, however, the democratic surge is on, and the system that Winston Churchill referred to as "bad, but it's the best we've got" is standing up and making the dictators look a lot worse.

Religion is yet again getting the bombardment of change it has been used to through the ages. In the wake of political freedoms, religious enthusiasm has been rekindled in the Russian Federation and the new republics. Fundamentalists of all complexions are active to the point where it almost dominates Islam which is daily claiming new converts, and there is a revival of Buddhism in Thailand, Vietnam, and through the killing fields of Cambodia.

This ever-changing backdrop to the play in which global managers must act their parts sets the stage for the way in which the characters are never the same; the main plot is invented as it goes along; the players are from everywhere; and the whole theatre could close for any reason. In other words, they must be cool under any circumstance and be flexible, adaptable, and functional.

Teacher, Coach, Mentor

Cross-culture competent managers are teachers, coaches, and mentors to everybody within their inspiration. They are world-class trainers, encouragers, and motivators who leave behind them a real tangible improvement in people. Of all the competencies, this is likely the most rewarding as we see individuals in their turn grow, develop, and help others in their sphere of influence. A strong personal desire to assist others to mature and succeed is at the root of this skill, and it can have a dramatic effect for good on the morale, output, creativity, and spirit of the organization.

George Bagshaw was nothing less than all this. He was a paid-up member of Tom Brokaw's *Greatest Generation*. George, at the head of his platoon, had landed in Normandy on D-Day in the first wave on "Sword" Beach. They had been together at El Alamein, Anzio and the assault on Casino. He had won every medal for bravery offered by the king except the Victoria Cross. His men would follow him anywhere. He taught them all to win and survive.

I first met George when he gave me my first job. What an incredible start to any career. George believed that everybody had a talent and a quality that made him or her exceptional; it was just a question, he said, of finding it and bringing it to the top. As managing director of one of the largest insurance organizations in the United Kingdom, his life was spent selecting, training, motivating, and mentoring the next succession of managers. I once calculated that he had influenced at least four layers of managers who would supply the business for fifty years. In a recent meeting I had with some people at my old company, there were four active senior managers who were directly influenced by the example of George Bagshaw in the mid-1960s. Not only that, the George's spirit still runs strong in the business. All the managers who were trained and mentored by him continue the traditions he established all those years ago, and the George Bagshaw Management Development Award remains the most coveted trophy in the business. George Bagshaw was way before his time and, as guardian of his company's future, he knew nurturing his protégés was his most important role in securing that future.

Jack Welch would tour the world of General Electric, attending staff meetings and seminars. He was an education junkie. But there was a more significant reason for doing this. He was looking out for talent that he could divert to fast-track management development.

Global managers are no different, but they are likely to have a group of protégés who are a good deal more anxious to be educated than the average. They feel honored to be part of the protégé process: they can't absorb their education fast enough. Have you noticed the commitment to education of Asian students, how their parents encourage them to succeed, and how they crowd the graduation honors list?

Most western managers have been immersed in corporate training, mentoring programs, example exposure, and experience education since their college graduation. This is not likely to be the background of the cross-culture people in their charge. This massive talent pool is ready and waiting for our intense education like new fresh clay ready to be molded by the master potter's touch.

Coking the Chinese

A research study conducted by professors from the University of South Carolina and two Chinese universities showed that more than 400,000 Chinese jobs were linked to Coca-Cola's operations as of 1998.

Although only about 14,000 Chinese worked directly for Coca-Cola in 1998, roughly thirty times that number were employed by Coke's independent suppliers, distributors, wholesalers, and retailers in China, the study said.

Coca-Cola's bottling system directly contributed 8.16 billion yuan ($985,590,500) into the Chinese economy in 1998 and paid 387 million yuan ($47,743,082) in taxes to the Chinese government.

"Coca-Cola's direct employees, tax payments, and output, while significant, are only the tip of the iceberg in China," said Douglas Woodward, an economics professor at the University of South Carolina, who co-authored the study. "Coca-Cola's greatest impact on the Chinese economy–through its enormous network of independent suppliers and distributors–is much more massive," Woodward added. It is their ability to help China to modernize inefficient state-owned companies, teach managerial and marketing expertise, and upgrade production technology in over thirty manufacturing facilities belonging to them in China.

The innate desire to help others succeed, to become a superb trainer, a respected and indulgent mentor, and an esteemed coach to our multicultural coterie is possibly our best competency as a global manager. It will certainly be the most rewarding.

Respect for Others' Beliefs

This cross-culture competency is at the heart of good global management. It is the ability to take the trouble to

learn about the individual beliefs, religions, and philosophies of the people under our responsibility. More importantly, it is to know enough about them and not just to tol-
erate them but also to respect them.

Ruth Colbert was a well-regarded marine underwriter
who had developed a strong following in a business dominated for two centuries by men. Shipowners, ship brokers,
insurance brokers, underwriters, and associated cohorts
were a small group who knew each other well. They were
a close-knit bunch who worked together, exchanged business, went on business trips, and drank with each other.
When Ruth cracked into this *clubby* set, she did so on sheer
ability. She got deals done that no one else could–not by
female charms but by knowing her business. Her personal
fame spread throughout the business world as she wrote
articles for large circulation publications in the shipping
and insurance industry and frequently spoke at seminars
and conferences. It was only a question of time before the
largest shipowner in Indonesia asked his broker to introduce them with a view to making her the lead insurer of his
fleet. Ruth had been preparing for that potentiality. During
the previous two or three years of mid east travel, she had
learned everything she could about the Islamic culture and
religion. She had even taken a side trip to Riyadh to understand the pilgrimage. Ruth took some vacation time and
arrived in Jakarta five days prior to the meeting: it was not
relaxation–it was education.

The sights, smells, and sounds of this extraordinary city
are serious culture shock if you are from the west. One of
the first things you notice is the *big durian*, the foul smell-
ing, rotten odor that comes from durian, the favorite fruit
of the locals. Here is a bustling community of multiple
cultures–Bataks, Bugis, Timorese, Moluccans, Sudanese,
and Javanese, as well as the smiling indigenous Batawis.
Ruth walked the cluttered quays in the Sunda Kelapa, the
Old Colonial Kota District, and the flamboyant buildings

of the Kiningan. She spent most of her time in the national museum with its incredible ethnographic section with Chinese ceramics and models of traditional houses. Later, to immerse herself in the appreciation of her potential client's faith, she spent some quiet time in one of the most elegant mosques in the Muslim world–the ten-thousand capacity Istiqlal Mosque, designed by a Christian architect.

Some western women understandably find the precepts of the Moslem religion to be unacceptable–due to the perceived treatment of women in that society–but this English-born and educated woman found some major aspects of the Islamic religion that she immensely respected. She found that, in fact, the Muslim people have great respect for family, for the elderly, and for charity. If anything in the Muslim faith upset her, it was the treatment of women; however, she found that a great deal of progress had been made in Jakarta and that the veil and purdah had been discarded and replaced with the business suit and the business office.

Needless to say, the Indonesian shipowner had never met a woman like Ruth. There developed a close and lasting business relationship and friendship, based on mutual respect.

Global managers seek out the values and beliefs of people in their charge by getting to know and appreciate them and by learning to respect the unique aspects of their cultural and religious beliefs. It is much the same in all inter-human relationships. We have to look for the similarities that bind us rather than the differences that separate us.

Interest in Other Cultures

We are all fascinated by other cultures: why they think and act the way they do. Thousands of books, movies, and stories tell of large and small, humorous and serious examples of cross-culture differences. It's part of the fascination of life on earth. Vacation travelers back from overseas tell their friends less about the history, museums, cathedrals, and palaces but more about mad drivers, good food, customs officials, and bottom-pinchers. In other words, it's the current raw culture we are interested in because they are not like us.

Managers engaged in cross-culture competence have to be genuinely interested in other cultures to the point that it is a real fascination. They cannot read or experience enough; they keep a journal of incidents, quotes and anecdotes that demonstrate cultural nuances, differences and similarities; they ask questions, communicate with foreigners, read foreign newspapers, and watch foreign movies.

Some kids have the advantage of being raised in homes with a multicultural attitude. Bill Jones works for an oil company. He has traveled into every *rat hole*, as he puts it, in every country, looking for oil deals. Every time he comes home, he brings something very special for his twelve-year-old daughter, Angela. She currently has sixty-eight dolls dressed in different national costumes, about twenty stuffed native animals, children's toys, books, and money from all over the world. The collection is her pride and joy, and she takes family friends up to her room to see an Aladdin's cave of exotic treasures from around the world. The best thing is that she can tell you where every item came from and a little story about it. When Bill comes home, he relives the fascination of the culture he has visited and conveys his excitement to Angela who can't wait to tell her friends. What's the betting that Angela will grow up with a global mindset and be associated with a successful global enterprise? As for Bill, he gets his cross-culture kicks from the major personal project of his trip: looking for that extra special doll which will make Angela's eyes light up and challenge her curiosity to know all about it.

Empathetic Leadership

Empathy is a rare quality. It's not easy either. Cultures with a tradition of dominance, such as those of western Europe, find empathy an unnatural act. Those whose history has colonized others find it difficult to get into an attitude of understanding and sharing. Likewise, the American way has often been *if you don't like it my way – then tough shit!* Most dominating cultures find empathy difficult, but it is a substantial cross-culture competence, so we have to master it.

Empathy in this context is the ability to accept differences and build on these differences in a positive manner, to understand and share with others, despite culture, creed, color, nationality, or gender. It represents a profound leadership quality and requires careful training and development for it to become embedded in the corporate mindset. The qualities of empathy are flexibility, tact, humor, sensitivity, politeness, compromise, patience, warmth, trust, willingness to listen, and the ability to see issues from the other cultural side. Empathy is a formidable list of qualities, but it puts management into a new level–the level of the world-class leader.

The world will not belong to *managers* but to passionate, driven leaders: people who not only have enormous amounts of energy but who can energize those whom they lead. Empathy is all about great leadership in the global enterprise.

We know enough about good management to know that it is inseparable from good leadership. This is more appropriate in the global business context than perhaps any other because here our decisions, our example, and our abilities have a more profound impact on results than in the domestic environment. Global consequences are like domestic results on steroids. Everything we do in the international context is magnified. Our leadership style as global managers takes on an importance unknown to most domestic companies.

Global Leadership Styles

Leadership styles are vastly different around the world and are almost entirely constructed on the history, climate, and the mentality of the people within a particular society. In a deeper sense, the language of that society also influences leadership style in that certain languages have restricted liberties of thought, vagueness, and lack of descriptive vocabulary. This tends to restrict communication between people.

Over millennia of time, cultural groups have organized themselves in remarkably different ways to deal with power, authority, and leadership. Many influences play their part. Geographic features like size and topography, extremes of climate, such as long cold winters and hot dry summers, natural catastrophes of disease, famine, drought, earthquake, and flood, war, invasion, genocide, ethnic cleansing, religious concepts, and language structure all participate in the way a culture perceives leadership.

Empathetic Leadership

Empathetic leaders have to understand these principles and have to take them into account in their management style. How is this done?

Culture groups usually organize their commercial organizations in the same way they organize themselves, their institutions, and their government. Things change, however, and the influence of today's events will permeate into the cultural mindset over time. Nevertheless, we are dealing with business today, and we need to know what cross-culture issues will affect our leadership style, recognizing that it's *me* who has to change, if need be, not the culture.

The variety of leadership styles is considerable and can be complicated and obtuse. Even countries almost next door to each other may have diametrically opposite leadership styles, such as Swedish and German, or French and Italian. Even cultures in the same culture group, such as British and American–both data-based cultures–have very different styles due to a combination of history, topography, and country size.

The global manager will be able to adjust his or her leadership style to the culture group concerned. There will be an immediate recognition of the basic structure of authority, and the manager will drop into the rhythm: no criticism, no comparisons with how it's done at home, and no instructions to change. Any effort to change would be met with disgruntled disagreement followed by sulking disapproval. Often the leadership style, obtained outside the basics of that culture, returns to its original way. It's a waste of time, money, and talent to try to change deeply embedded ways–and it's not the way of the cross-culture competent manager. It is, however, the way of the empathetic leader.

Humility, Modesty and Respectful Behavior

Humility and modesty don't come easily to western managers or, indeed, to western people as a whole. The concept of *cow-towing*, as the British say, is totally foreign to the culture personality, and the *macho* male image encouraged in the American personae is not easily shed. However, for more than 50 percent of the world's population, humility is a virtue, and others see the strutting westerner

as a cross-culture incompetent. Competent managers understand why humility, modesty, and respectful behavior
are virtues, and they know how to empathize with them.
All the major management models during the last few years
have tended toward the Japanese systems. Corporations
have accepted teamwork over individualism, collaboration
in place of competition, and alliances instead of exploita-
tion. As managers incorporate more Asian management
techniques into their global companies, we are seeing a
shift from western to eastern culture in business.

Asian Adaptation

Humility and modesty are largely group-based features,
part of the Asiatic and Indian culture types. They are in
noticeable contrast with data-based and relationship-based
people. Those who have traveled in these areas know how
all economic levels–both to foreign visitors and to each
other–demonstrate these characteristics, particularly when
relating to people in a superior class, caste, or position.

The Chinese consider modesty, courtesy, tolerance, and
respect for the elderly as their principal values. The Japanese are well-known for being ultra-polite, for their respect
for the feelings of others, and for their obligation to the
group. Indians appreciate humility, patience, and being
treated with respect. They also like to be *proper*; therefore,
gentlemanly behavior is important at meetings and social
functions.

* * *

I was invited to Mr. Depong's home for dinner. He
owned one of the largest insurance companies in Taiwan.
Before leaving home, my wife had packed some small gifts
to give to my clients. They were all neatly wrapped in shiny
white wrapping paper with red bows attached. I picked one

out of my suitcase and caught a taxi to the address Mr. Depong's secretary had sent me. A servant met me at the door of the spacious, elegant house, and I was led into a reception room. Mr. Depong could speak very little English, and I spoke no Mandarin; however, he had a colleague at the table who could translate. The three of us sat down to dinner in the tastefully decorated dining room. I knew he had a wife, but *where was she*? The servant brought in the main course–a huge whole baked fish–and placed it in front of Mr. Depong. Taking a porcelain spoon, Mr. Depong deftly divided the fish into three pieces, serving the tail to the translator, the middle to me, and the head to himself. When in doubt, watch the host. Depong cut out a spoonful of fish and put it in his mouth; I followed suit. To my horror, the fish was packed with tiny sharp bones. The deliciousness of the taste was overcome by the discomfort of the eating. When in *serious* doubt, stare at the host. Mr. Depong masticated one final time and spat the remnant bones onto the polished wooden floor beside his chair! The translator followed, so I thought, *here goes*. Splat! What a mess. Hey, this was fun! I was starting to enjoy myself as the floor became littered with bones, scales, and fish eyes, and nobody seemed to care. When it was all over and we were licking our lips, a beautifully dressed, attractive young lady came in with a small broom and dustpan and promptly started to clean up the mess. After doing so, she bowed to us and retreated to the kitchen. As the dessert was brought in, a lady stood at the kitchen door and inspected the food.

At the close of this interesting evening, I was introduced to the ladies at the kitchen door: Mrs. Depong, her attractive daughter, and the servant. I rounded off the evening with some embarrassment by giving Mrs. Depong my white-wrapped gift signifying, in my ignorance, that a funeral was to take place in the household! But the underlying impression I had of this calm, devoted, and kind family was their humility, politeness, and respect for each other and for their guests.

Rugged individualism is out of place in these cultures, and the management style often associated with American business does not fit the culture style. Old cultures of high-density population and group support, as in Japan, have become homogeneous where the group is more important than the individual; therefore, individual needs, ambitions, and outlook are subservient to the group.

Understanding Ourselves

In all the information the global manager needs about cultures, it is the manager's own culture that needs particular attention and understanding. If we are to work successfully with others across the globe, we need to be conversant with the perceptions and realities of our own culture. In negotiating, marketing, hiring people, and managing overseas assets, we need to understand how others perceive *us*; that is, why we think and act the way we do.

Understanding our culture is about as difficult as understanding ourselves, with one exception. We can read about our culture in this book or in some others, but there probably isn't a book written about *you* unless you have a biography about yourself and even multiple biographies sometimes disagree about their subject.

The same rules apply to understanding our own culture as understanding anyone else's culture. You have to have a good grasp of the history, geography, language, and religious background of the people. As culture changes (and you only have to ask grandparents about the lifestyle of their grandchildren to understand that it does), most people vaguely keep abreast of the modern world or the way the world about us reacts. We should have a pretty good grasp of our culture, you may say. Oddly, the opposite is true.

Most of us have little idea of how the rest of the world really perceives us because we spend most of the time listening to and reading biased material. Newspapers are full of stories showing how much better we are than everybody else. Beating the patriotic drum sells papers.

Self Stereotypes

We tend to develop stereotype attitudes about ourselves. The phrase *ugly American* seems to stick in the psyche: some believe that's what they are and start to live up to the statement. Some have the belief that they are somehow socially inferior to foreigners, particularly Europeans and, more particularly, the French.

Charles Handy, the English management guru, had a French student in his seminar. "In America," said the student, "they know how to make things work, but they don't know how to live. In France, we know how to live but can't make things that work."

What do Americans really think about themselves? Do we see ourselves as kind, generous, giving, smart, hardworking, God-fearing, good people? It is often when we experience the onslaught of hate against us that we finally realize that we really *are* made of good stuff.

The British are also severely stereotyped by others. I have heard them all–arrogant, amateurs, vague, pompous, sarcastic, and untrustworthy. Sounds pretty bad. It's a wonder anybody would ever do business with them. The truth is located somewhere in the middle and far less emotive. Most Brits believe themselves to be world savvy, culturally and socially sophisticated, reliable, inventive, and well-educated– a highly *top-heavy* opinion but with an element of truth.

Before we move into the understanding of others, let us get to know ourselves better. That applies to our own lives as well as to our culture. Sometimes we can only move forward in life by splashing cold water in our face before looking into the mirror.

Big Picture Perspective

Moving from an ethnocentric to a global mindset does things for our outlook on life. Inevitably we get a different perspective of the world in which we live. We hear all these contradictory clichés like *Think Global, Act Local* and *Act Global, Think Local* and get really confused. So what do we need to know to maintain our global cross-culture competency, and how are we going to keep it together?

Management schools and reputable universities throughout the world teach business studies to management students that only take them to the rim of the canyon. They then say "There's your world; go for it." Where are maps to help them across the canyon and the tools to climb the peaks and rappel the slopes? For example, where are the mind-broadening courses that give the big picture perspectives, the understanding of international politics, Asian history, scientific developments, social change, world health issues, feminism, ethics, and new religions?

Management books do not give the answers either. Peter Drucker pointed out that the best book on management of strategic alliances is Winston Churchill's biography, *The Duke of Marlborough.*

The cross-culture competent manager in his role as mentor, teacher, and coach is also student, pupil, and apprentice. The learning never stops. So how do we develop the *big picture* perspective?

- Think in broad concepts. When you are presented with a problem, for example, see it in the context of other problems you have on the table and rate it (one to ten) on its seriousness and attention need. Also give it a time context. Can it be solved immediately, or will it take time? Dealing with problems scientifically rather than emotionally is 50 percent of the solution.

- Have wide interests. Most people's interests are in a fairly narrow band: sports, youth work, fishing etc. Widen your interests; go to events on different subjects, and try some new hobbies. You have heard of people known as *Renaissance* men or women. These unusual people always seem able to turn their hand to anything. They are often musicians, artists, carpenters, and speakers, for example. When sitting around the table with your colleagues, ask them to tell you something about themselves that others may not know. You may be very surprised how many Renaissance people you know.

- Network. Join associations. Don't just join for membership–get involved with committees, conferences, and local chapters. Get onto the presenters list so that you can develop recognition in the industry you are part of. Get to be well known in your industry. Be a volunteer. Join breakfast clubs, business networking societies, and downtown clubs. I joined the National Speakers Association in 1995, and it has been one of the most useful things I've done because it has given me a wide perspective on my opportunities as a speaker, presenter, and author, as well as giving me invaluable contacts which have helped my business.

- Fill out your résumé. Seek employment that will widen your career, not just pay more money; that will come later. A career needs strategic planning just like a business, and we need to plan our moves so that we add more to our big picture. Of course, overseas postings will be invaluable, providing you can see around the corner to the job after that. If your existing employer can't give you the career experience or breadth you re looking for, then move quickly. The global business world waits for no one. Your résumé plan for the future should map the road that you wish to pursue, including the names of companies you would like to work for, your salary, and your job description.

- Be an extensive reader, writer, speaker, teacher, and traveler. All this is interactive–at least it should be. There is nothing quite like teaching to learn something. Everyone you interact with will widen your picture of the world. Writing is a remarkable way to clarify your thoughts and widen your horizons. Articles for trade magazines, industrial papers, association newsletters, and Internet publications are all hungry to fill column space with useful information for their readers. Finally, travel wherever you can and whenever you can to unusual places to do unusual things. Go and help a charity in a third world country or volunteer on a *mercy* ship to a distant port to provide medical attention to indigent people.

- Keep you curiosity alight. Do research on a specific subject you know little about but which interests you. Attend classes on a wide variety of subjects such as art subjects, culture issues, public speaking, current affairs, international politics, or history subjects. Most universities have excellent adult education classes that cover a vast variety of subjects at very reasonable enrollment prices.

- Last but not least, read kids' books. Seriously. Reading kids' books gives you a perspective you will never get reading the *Economist, Forbes, or The Wall Street Journal*. Why? Because one of the first things you need in order to get a big picture concept is creativity – and lots of it.

Cross-Culture Creativity

Lisa Sybert knows how cross-culture competency can give rise to creative, innovative, idea-packed corporate culture. She was hired when the Connecticut based software giant was a half-billion dollar company. An MBA graduate of University of Illinois and a post-graduate of Thunderbird, she was appointed with the grand title of vice-president of international operations and global development. At this time all the company had was a small manufacturing unit in Malaysia which was always giving trouble with delivery and communication. Her colleagues thought she had taken a graveyard job. "This is the end of a beautiful career, before it's begun," said her railroad engineer dad. Certainly nobody at the software company had volunteered to do it.

"I wonder if I have done the right thing," said Lisa on the first day as she looked at the map of the world she had hung in her office. She went to evening school to learn some basic Malay and booked her flights in coach to Kuala Lumpur to check out the Malaysian problem.

"I'm setting up a think tank unit here with the most enthusiastic people in the plant," she said to the manager. "I don't want the most senior–I just want good attitude people. I also want cultural variety. I understand we have Singaporeans, Chinese, and Indians here; I want a real cross section."

Starting with improvements to the productivity of the plant, then with the communication with the U.S. divisions, the think tank team couldn't stop the outpouring of their ideas. They called themselves Sybert's Cyclones. They put out an e-zine letter on the company Intranet and became the talk of the corporation. From the Cyclones came the start of the Bangalore program development unit and the Singapore manufacturing unit that will outpace the Malay plant in productivity. The Cyclones are currently brain-storming the problems of pirated products in China. Wherever she went, Lisa formed creativity teams based on the successful formulae of the Cyclones. In Bangalore, Singapore, Sydney, and Manchester, she sought out the extreme contrasts of culture and encouraged them to play with their creative spirit. At headquarters, she gathered a multinational, multicultural team to help her with ideas for international development and got them to empty their natural resources, their innate beliefs, and dreams in front of the open-minded group.

From being the whelp in the litter, Lisa became the favorite child. Refusing to take credit personally for the achievements, she always said that it was her Cyclones that blew down the barriers and flooded the place with ideas.

The Creative Team

Here is an exercise you can do to get you and your team more creative. It's called *vive la difference!*

Encourage members on your team to recognize their differences and talk about them to others. In the corporate atmosphere, there is often a desire to submerge into sameness and conformity. Creativity is not born in this incubator. It flourishes in a spirit of diversity and difference.

Sometimes we forget the fact that we are all different from each other and that our uniqueness is our greatest asset. The imprint for each lifetime is like no other since life on earth began. Just by that appreciation you can change the way you feel about a thousand things and about one's own self esteem.

Ask these questions of yourself and your team:

• What unusual thing will you do today?

- What adventure will you experience this year?

    - Take some trips to unusual places

    - Read magazines that are outside your normal interest areas

    - Volunteer some time to organizations outside your experience

    - Make friends with widely diverse culture groups

    - Employ new immigrants and refugees

    - Take up a brand new hobby

    - Commit to the regular experience of adventure

Cross-culture competence is a lifetime journey: a vertical learning experience filled with constant blind corners and surprises. It is a journey only for the open-minded, the willing to learn human types, and those who, in the process, are prepared to take a nonjudgmental view of our fellow man and stick to it. It could probably be the final challenge of the human race.

6

Global Cross-Culture Business Skills

Now that we are on the way to becoming cross-culture competent, we have to put these abilities to work in the real world. We have to test them in the key areas of building, leading, and managing an international business and negotiating, marketing, and selling products and services in the multicultural world we all inhabit. You may be, like I was, one of those who was thrown into the deep end with the minimum of briefing, training, and *know-how*, or you may have gone through all the preparation possible to get to this point. Whatever the situation, now is the time to take a vertical climb in your learning experience. Nothing in this or any other book will substitute for the hands-on experience you will acquire when you start traveling and meet your foreign customer, colleague, and prospect. It's like standing up to make your first big speech or asking for that first big order or firing someone for the first time. It's as if all your experiences, education, character, personality, and upbringing are focused laser-like on this one event at this moment of time.

Panic in Manhattan

I was thirty-five floors over Manhattan. Even at that height I could hear the city noises, the taxi horns, and the sirens of emergency vehicles coming up through the canyon. To a twenty-six-year-old Englishman on his first visit to New York, the size of everything, the pace, the frantic energy was almost overwhelming. I felt stranded, alone, up in the sky without friends and utterly naive among these heavyweight tycoons who seemed so much larger than life, so sophisticated, so rich. My self-confidence had drained down the plug hole. These Americans were ultra confident– the complete reverse to me. My emotions were running wild as my thoughts went from negative to positive and back to negative again. *I wish I had never come here. But this is what I've always wanted to do–this is it. I have dreamed of this moment for years, and here I am acting out my dream–but I'm dreading it. I'm scared. What am I scared of?* All my education, upbringing, and training were focused on my ability to handle this moment. Yes, I was scared to death of looking foolish in front of these people and failing in front of them–letting my side down–failing England!

Just when I was ready to collapse like a pile of shivering jelly, Art Baker came into the room. He had the biggest smile I've ever seen on anybody, and on that day it was the best smile I had ever seen in my life. Art must have been to charm school; he put me at ease in no time.

"Mike, if you want to call your bride, just pick up that phone, give my secretary Nancy your home number, and she'll dial it through for you," he said. "My wife's driving into the city, and we're all going to take in a show and dinner before we do anything else."

If first impressions mean anything–which I think they do–then my first impression of New York changed from hate to love in two minutes. What a personable start to some tough but friendly negotiations. There I was, over-influenced by the bricks and mortar of New York and forgetting that at the end of the road, it's all about people getting on with people and knowing how to deal with them–it's all about cross-culture competence.

Creating the Cross-Cultural Organization

Outsourcing has been a feature of global expansion for more than thirty years. This method gathered momentum during the nineties and is likely to be the most active form of building an overseas presence. Traditional reasons for outsourcing include:

- cheaper labor rates
- lower taxes and duties
- customer pressure for local representation
- better access to local market
- less pressure from labor unions
- economies of increased scale

There are a number of additional reasons to outsource the dynamics of a business into other areas of the world such as:

- accessing information about other cultures
- gathering intelligence about competition

- developing wider creativity and innovation
- obtaining local country information
- developing a global mindset

Finding Global Talent

Companies are also scanning the world to locate the best talent available. Finding the right people to run the global companies of the future will be the biggest challenge facing managers. Only by knowing where this talent resides and where in the world it is being educated can business find its succession management. The level of education varies considerably throughout the world, but some countries have better educated young people than others; many countries, due to their location, history, and the popularity of their native language, have a large multilingual population. Literacy percentages are an important guideline, and high rates usually demonstrate a high quality of basic education up to college level. The Soviet Union had a tradition of literacy that has carried over to the post-communist era, and children with little or no personal advantages are capable of reading and writing. In 2001, a tenth grade reading and writing test was given to forty children living in a Siberian orphanage whose average age was thirteen. They passed it 100 percent. The same standards will be found in Eastern Europe. India has over 300 million people with good quality degrees, and we can only guess at the educated competency of millions of people in Asia. In other words, we haven't yet tapped into the massive human intelligence resources available to the global enterprise. First, we have to recognize and accept the fact that some countries have far superior basic educational standards to those in the United States and Europe. Quality human resources are like gold. They are often difficult to discover, usually in remote places, and are invaluable after refining. Every organization, no matter what it does, is only as good as its people, so when creating the global cross-culture organization, we recruit the best, regardless of culture, creed, or gender.

Cross-Culture Mix

Worldwide business should also be a cross-culture representation because this is the surest way for an organization to learn about working with, selling to, and producing product for a culture-varied customer base. How better to understand their nuances, differences, and similarities than getting close and personal in the confidentiality of the corporate campus.

One of the reasons why the United States has had such an ongoing problem with Japanese competition is because American companies in the past have not taken the time nor trouble to understand them. For decades, U.S. auto and consumer goods companies beat their heads against the wall of Japanese competition. This feeling culminated in a remarkable display of anger during a well-publicized TV event when four U.S. congressmen took sledgehammers and burst a perfectly good Japanese-manufactured radio to demonstrate their anger at the loss of American jobs. How much better it would have been to admit that the Japanese were doing something right, to find out what it was, and try to adapt it to our own ways.

Include the competitor's culture representatives in your group, and you will understand your competition that much better. We have to be able to read and interpret their minds. In the North African desert while he was fighting German General Erwin Rommel in WWII, British General Bernard Montgomery had a life-sized picture of the German hanging in his mobile headquarters. When asked why, Monty replied, "Every morning I stand in front of his photograph and ask him, 'What are you going to do today?'" That's what we should ask our competition–every day. Foreign competition, however, is nothing like domestic competition. You simply can't read it anything like the same, so you have to have some serious help from the culture. Hire someone to interpret it for you.

Variety Triggers Creativity

Building a cross-culture organization will bring creativity and innovation to the enterprise. One of the triggers of creativity is variety. The act of taking your mind into different and unusual territory will stimulate the *idea juices* and get innovation into action. Relating with people from entirely different backgrounds will certainly divert your traditional thinking. Besides, people from these different backgrounds will look at your problems in a new and different way. Diversity of culture is one of the most potent ways of attracting creativity. The great strength of America and the success of its future is vested in its tradition of cultural mix and its willingness to attract immigrants from diverse cultural backgrounds, despite tough immigration checks and safeguards to avoid potential terrorist infiltration.

When you want to know something, ask the question and start the research. When you want inside information, ask someone who's been inside. When you want to know about a country, ask a native. Country know-how is a subtle thing, a matter of personal opinion mixed with experience and knowledge. Personal opinion, particularly opinions of immigrants, can sometimes be biased regarding specific issues in their native country, but a well educated, knowledgeable, and communicative individual can provide invaluable information about his or her country, its lifestyle, work style, and philosophical beliefs.

In Chapter 3, we have outlined the essential need for managers to get a global mindset and spread that attitude throughout the length and breadth of their business. Staffing an organization with people of differing cultures and national origin is a sure way to build a global mindset in the workplace environment. Brown and Root, Houston, the international civil engineering company, holds team meetings that include overseas members talking about and briefing colleagues on their home countries. In this global mindset company whose open atrium lobby is filled with the flags of every nation they work with, managers constantly seek ways for international personnel to interact with others to improve cross-culture understanding. Every foreign member of an organization is a potential trainer and can assist in giving it a global mindset.

Leading the Cross-Cultural Organization

One of the most obvious advantages of a cross-culture work force is that it presents a local face to the local customer. It can communicate in the same language, understand the behavior, interact with government officials, and talk to local bankers and investors. It can also be a scout group to attract and retain local talent by installing training systems. In many emerging markets, the competition to hire local talent is intense. By providing quality training, locally potential hires will be attracted to join the organization where skill development is available rather than taking a position based solely on salary and benefits.

Managers who lead cross-culture teams know that one of the first things they must do is to lay down multiple consistencies. Diversity indicates multiple differences, but teams can only work together if they understand certain commonalities. These consistencies or commonalities include such things as establishing the following:

- a basic value level of ethics, trust, and integrity
- common verbal and written language for all communication
- shared decision-making procedures
- standards of professionalism
- procedures for handling individual creative innovation
- reporting and recruiting procedures

It is important that leadership should encourage cross-cultural groups to discuss and debate their diversity issues and legitimize open discussion of differences. Cross-culture incompetence is all about frustration, anxiety, misunder-standing, and ignorance. Open communication is one very valid way to overcome this.

Blending the Best

While recognizing that management methods can differ from culture to culture, it is important for managers to understand that information sharing and the blending of leadership styles are important. The successful Mercedes plant operation based in Vance, Alabama, demonstrates how a hierarchical German management style, with emphasis on quality and workmanship, was applied to an American workforce accustomed to an atmosphere of openness, democracy, and informality. The key was the blend. The German managers relaxed on their hierarchy, and the Americans accepted the hyper-efficiency. Bull, the French computer company, acquired a U.S. division of Honeywell in the late 1980s. The acquisition became a dramatic example of misunderstanding and miscommunication leading to frustration and attempted abandonment. After that experience, Bull decided to have inter-company *open* discussions on their differences, allowing the workforce and managers every opportunity to frankly discuss their cultural, emotional, and practical differences.

The methods applied for recruitment, promotion, pay, and redundancy of people within the organization should be explained clearly to each cross-culture group. Any suspicion that there is selectivity or favorites would affect employee confidence as well as morale. Cultures have differing expectations regarding these issues, which, of course, go to the heart of personal well-being, job and financial security, and career progression. We regularly hear of cross-border expansion being selective as to national location due to labor laws, wage levels, union power, and/or welfare. Obvious differences in work conditions and benefits between countries–for example, France and the United States or Germany and Great Britain–can create serious problems. Exercising high value flexibility, understanding, tolerance, and communication is essential when dealing with these issues.

Human Resource Priorities Are Different

According to much research, very few people know their own cultural values until those values are threatened by another culture. That is why so many cross-culture integration programs commence with high expectations only to end in failure and resentment. In the leadership of cross-culture teams and organizations, it is imperative to examine the human resource policy applied to the local culture. All the cultures working there will have differing basic assumptions and expectations about what employees and employers can demand from each other. A British chemical manufacturer, for example, had trained a group of up-and-coming managers for overseas responsibilities. The time came to send them off to their respective locations–France, Spain, Canada, and the United States. They all presumed that local remuneration and benefits would apply wherever they went. Their headquarters' human resource department had never thought to make any change to their existing arrangements. Months later, after argument, frustration, and some resignations, the HR department finally relented, costing the company over $250,000 in wasted effort and compensation.

In a survey conducted by Vista Communications and reported in the *Financial Times* May 29, 1997, executives employed by 248 U.K. companies managing over 1.3 million people admitted that staff received too little information to properly understand the expectations of their tasks or their job. For the global company, the responsibility of leaders/managers to communicate effectively with their people is daunting. As companies work across frontiers, outsource, and employ multicultural personnel, identifying the most efficient ways to relate to staff is of major importance.

There are two main messages every organization must convey to its people:

1. They must communicate the values, goals, mission, and vision of the business. The objective is to unite each employee's attitude and to foster commitment and loyalty to the organization or the project.

2. They must communicate specific work related issues, tasks, and project objectives. This not only communicates how a job should be done but also conveys the employee's views and opinions.

The HR Factor

Global human resource departments know better than most that there is no such thing as a *common culture*. Even a company with different sites throughout the same country has to take into consideration the differing mores, customs, and languages that lie entrenched–sometimes dormant and deep within, like a sleeping volcano. On a worldwide basis, these differences can be immense.

In working one-on-one in relocating personnel to different countries, HR professionals have done a good job in the legal and physical sense. Normally there is someone inside the HR unit, or available through outsourcing, to provide housing and necessary integration of the transferring family's everyday living needs such as visas, work permits, bank checking accounts, government identification cards, and driver's licenses. All this is fine; however, understanding the similarities and differences in the work and everyday life cultures is still largely ignored. Many times the transferring employee and family is just expected to *catch on*.

Numerous surveys and published interviews with top executives confirm that having the *right people* in the *right jobs* and having *people work effectively with each other* are the number one to number three critical issues for meeting business goals. And we all know this is tough to achieve, even in a one-site-only business, regardless of the country.

Knowing the business's mission to meet the customer's needs by providing the best product or service in a faster, competitive market has led HR to contribute in a critical way to the success of global business expansion. Out of the desire to have employees work well together have come many trainings and assessments around the different behavior and learning styles of individuals. These individual differences seem to be the greatest threat to working well together. When cultural differences are considered more important than individual style differences, the results can be anywhere from disappointing to disastrous.

What the Global HR Professional Can Do

- Think global, not territorial. Because company locations in the past housed only employees that worked in the same division, it's easy to think of an individual *site* as a territory, rather than thinking of the location as a meeting ground for several different facets of the business. A division may be housed in two or three facilities around the globe. For example, many different groups of the business can be housed in one site so it is not the *Newark, New Jersey site*; it is the place where different sectors of the business come together working for different divisions but housed in this same site. The tendency is to think site, rather than company or division. This thinking excludes other employees of the same group in different sites and helps create the silo culture.

- Learn the differences between the country cultures and share them with everyone. For example, HR could make a list of the major holidays within each country to help in the scheduling of global meetings. Recently one executive of a global company grumbled that his corporate office, located in Europe, had never learned that Thanksgiving was a major U.S. holiday and generally scheduled meetings for that time. In the last seven years, he has been out of the country almost every year and has missed Thanksgiving with his family. No one has taken the time to understand his needs, helping to perpetuate silo or *us versus them* thinking. It weakens productivity and any chance of first-rate achievement. Yet, these differences are subtle, rarely noticed or observed as a cause of a slowdown.

• Publish information on the do's and don'ts of the firm's different culture representatives. For example, how do your various cultures handle the importance or lack of importance of being on time? As we have seen in certain cultures, an eight o'clock meeting means precisely that: the meeting begins at eight o'clock. In others, an eight o'clock meeting means the meeting will begin when all participants have come in and are ready. These differences are neither right nor wrong, yet they drive wedges in the group. Ask employees what differences they see in working with people from differing attitudes then, with everyone's agreement, decide the rules.

By implementing new ideas and awareness, the HR function becomes a contributor to the strategy and success of any global business and, in so doing, develops a company culture in which all employees are working effectively and productively.

Interest in Issues That Affect Them or Their Teams

Research at Templeton College, Oxford University suggests that employees are much more interested in issues that directly affect them or their teams than in general corporate information and developments. A *Financial Times* survey of staff in one multinational company revealed that 86 percent of employees felt that information on changes affecting their team was very important while only 21 percent felt information on the financial performance of the company fell into this category. In summary, therefore, they attached much greater importance to mechanisms for communicating information more immediate and applicable to them. Around 40 percent found one-on-one meetings with their manager very useful while less than 5 percent gave computer video interaction the same rating.

Cross-culture communication depends on the leadership qualities of the manager and his ability to interact with his group. Without doubt, the most tested success is derived from the success in getting an upward flow: a fluid flow back that is fair, freely given, and honest. This compares with the German corporate communication system that is based, for example, on works councils. Here management must consult these groups on issues such as new working procedures and organizational changes. They are also entitled by law to be given the economic and financial information on the company. They can also ask for the company's investment policy and its attitude toward political parties and viewpoints.

The most interesting fact to come out of the *Financial Times* survey on this subject is that there is little feedback from these councils back to management. Perhaps the legal requirement to flow information down did not build in the plumbing to flow it back!

Working in Cross-Culture Teams

Managers have a particular interest and need to develop the best from cross-culture teams. We have already made reference to the creative energy that develops from these collectives and, when effectively managed, how they can be of substantial benefit to the corporate information and education base. The leadership qualities of the managers will have to hone and build these contributions.

As long as team projects and endeavors are running well and the exercise is on target, the groups will work well together. If, however, they get off track, local cultures usually tend to retreat into their own deep-rooted beliefs and take sides when the going gets tough.

Leading teams from different cultures deserve some research before they get into difficulties. Let us imagine that our team consists of Japanese, German, American, and French members. The Japanese will seek to garner group support, will work for compromise, and will be hesitant to make decisions. German members will be more comfortable with a strict hierarchy, exact timetable, and precise instructions. Americans will be all for active participation, quick decisions, and relaxed cooperation; and the French members will wish to debate the important issues, will be keen to know the qualifications and education of the individuals, and will not be inclined to make intermediate decisions. Team members may not voice their attitudes openly, but these cultural ways of thinking will always be at the back of their minds. A Swedish mobile phone company lost over $15 million when it moved into Mexico with a group of European managers. Their urgency to catch the mobile market led them into precipitous action without training and briefing of personnel. They did not relate to the work style, objectives, and leadership traditions of their Mexican counterparts, and they had to retreat, rethink their strategies, and train their people in cross-culture friction within work teams. Interaction between team members can easily break down if frustration and aggravation start to dominate the proceedings, so we need a way to divert the problem. How do we do this?

The Ground Zero *Lesson*

Teams weld forever in the face of tragedy, a life threat, or serious challenge. We saw this hour after hour from the heroic New York Fire Department and the team of tireless volunteers at *ground zero*, the World Trade Center ruins of twisted steel, rubble, and death. We don't want to have to go to this extreme to test our teamwork ability, but it does prove that people band together in the face of crisis. Individuals assist each other based on their individual capabilities and the available resources. In a cross-culture team, we find that members put aside their cultural preferences and strive to place their individual qualities and skills at the disposal of the group. Leaders emerge naturally; innovators come out of the woodwork; practical thinkers come forward, and hard workers keep up the pressure. Caring, thoughtful ones bring humanity to the mission.

Some companies take teams on work missions for charitable causes to give them a sense of purpose, endeavor, and mutual aid. One team, working for ten days in extreme discomfort in the appalling conditions of an orphanage in Siberia, felt that they should never be split up again, so profound was the relationship, trust, and confidence that evolved among them as they shared frustration, sickness, exhaustion, and high emotion on a worthwhile job done well.

A similar group worked in the Costa Rican rain forest, building a community center for the indigenous Indian people. The team welded on the third day when they had to face mudslides and foundation collapse from the heaviest rain anyone on the team had ever experienced. International companies may face challenges different from rain forest mudslides and Siberian orphanages, but when teams are faced with the wild, risky, experience-busting challenges of the global business environment, their mudslide foundation rescue experience will be invaluable.

Facing a training experience of physical challenge early in an international team's history may not be possible, but interface in the seminar room is essential so that the cross-culture representatives can get their attitudes on the table.

At the beginning of the session, depending on the size of the group, leaders explain to the group how they like to work and what they expect of their colleagues. I recommend that these meetings be facilitated by an outside seminar organization so that an atmosphere of impartiality, openness, and free interaction can be maintained. With outside facilitation, there is a greater possibility that personal information, emotions, and strongly held beliefs will emerge all of which could be withheld by the individual if he or she felt that the session was a corporate inquisition. Successful companies that take time to go through these preliminaries will be rewarded in the long run.

Team Quiz

There is no *quick fix* when it comes to cross-culture understanding. Before seminar interaction begins, team members complete questionnaires about themselves for their own use. This helps them focus on their own work style and leadership preferences. Certain national culture questions are asked to help the individual move mentally into his or her personal dimension. These questionnaires will be the property of each team member and should never be asked for by management.

After the questionnaires are completed and questions answered, team members are asked to speak briefly about themselves, their attitudes, and their expectations regarding the way the team will operate. The better the spirit of openness, the more adept the members are communicating; the better the skills of the professional facilitator, the greater the outcome of this session which will be reflected throughout the life of the project. The seminar program will be devoted to respecting individual differences and identifying the strengths, similarities, and synergy of its team members. We already know that our differences are what make us lively, creative, and energetic, but it is our similarities that will build our strengths and synergy to produce a dynamic productive team. Daimler Benz and Chrysler had to go through hell and high water in their merger before they really understood how to harness the wild horses of American creative enthusiasm to the strong plough of German planning and supervision. Appreciation of the cultural skills, talents, and innate abilities of team members developed during the seminar phase will settle in the mindset of the individuals involved.

Before getting down to everyday work with an overseas acquisition, alliance, or branch development, I recommend the same type of interaction seminar if local people are involved. Translators can provide continuous translation facilities, if necessary. If the seminar members are all adept English-speaking people, the seminar facilitator needs to be an expert at understanding and translating *Britspeak*, *Amerispeak*, *Aussiespeak*, and second language English.

Language

The issue of language is ever present in the international team building, negotiating, and marketing exercise. It has to be addressed and taken seriously as it is at the heart of cross-culture relationships. Knowing the language of our foreign colleagues does not necessarily teach us the culture, but it helps considerably and should not be ignored. According to Richard D. Lewis, chairman of Richard Lewis Communications that teaches languages to over 5,000 executives every year from its centers in England, France, Finland, and the United States, achieving just modest fluency in a European language requires 250-500 hours of direct teaching, preferably over a three-month period. Languages such as Japanese, Chinese, Arabic, and Russian, for example, will require double that time and, in order to be fluent in any language, a period of *immersion*–either with a personal tutor or time in the country involved–is essential. If formal language education is not a possibility for us, we should all learn some key words and phrases for the country we are visiting. It is distressing and embarrassing to witness an English-speaking visitor in France getting angry with a Frenchman who can't interpret the visitor's needs. Wouldn't it be better, at a minimum, to learn some basic French? That at least would be respectful.

Mike Wallace on *60 Minutes* interviewed several ex-CIA top brass. Some of them had run Arab desks for years and included one Wallace had met in Beirut. Surprisingly, none of them could speak Arabic. American education has been tardy about language training, and business is taking the hit. Expecting your foreign counterpart to speak English, just because it is your language and you can't speak his, seems to be the wrong way to start a happy and productive business marriage or get a good deal off the ground.

Managers who pay scant attention to the use of local language do so at their peril. Americans abroad are open to criticism of arrogance and insensitivity if they do not pay attention to language skills. Teams operating on specific country projects should have highly qualified local language support and the services of professional translators.

Working with translators and interpreters is a perfect example that thrift does not pay. In short, get the best you can; it's worth it. Mistakes, misunderstandings, and misinterpretations are nightmares to undo after the wrong idea, the wrong emphasis, or the wrong notion has been planted in your counterpart's brain.

Translator or Interpreter

There are thousands of people who say they are interpreters. College students are only too pleased to volunteer their services, even just for food. Language professors, retired people, and expatriate housewives wanting to make a little money will work as interpreters; however, most of them are really just translators with varying degrees of ability in making literal translation of language. Interpretation of nuance, emphasis of point, and deliberate asides are all heard, understood, and conveyed by the experienced interpreter. Care should be taken to interview interpreters who should either have, at minimum, a business background or be able to understand business terms, phrases, and procedure. Information should be provided about the companies who have used their services (and references should be checked), the professional organizations they belong to, and the professional degrees and qualifications they have attained. The interview is crucial. Here the interpreter should be involved in detailed conversation with questions and technical words and phrases and use of the English that he or she will hear around the table. The interpreter's written abilities in language translation should also be checked in case that service is required for any business transaction.

Managers build teams with the resources, both financial and human, at their disposal. They are the delta force troopers who move into projects and opportunities with speed, tenacity, and determination. Some are in place for weeks; some for years.

Effective Management Across Cultures

Good management across the frontiers of culture and politics, distance and communication, and education and experience is a practice that is dependant on having what we call a global mindset. Without this vital ingredient, the international manager (or his or her superior) will probably find the challenges too onerous and the failure rate of his deals too high. Everyday, normal management in a domestic environment is difficult enough; in fact, running a business in this complex world of endemic change and constant stress is as much as most people wish to handle in a working lifetime. As if this isn't enough, the way of the world is forcing managers to expand their territory, and many have even asked for it through reading the mega-popular *Prayer of Jabez*. We get what we ask for!

Lifestyle choices are presented to us every day, and that's good because moving into global management responsibility needs to be considered seriously, carefully, and with the input of family. The main thing is to take a deep breath, think about the consequences, and make a considered judgment before going headlong into the maelstrom.

* * *

It was the early '70s. The flight for Hong Kong left London via Rome, Bombay and Bangkok. I was in the hotel in Hong Kong by Sunday afternoon. In those days you could order a lightweight suit, have the tailor come round to your room, measure you and deliver the finished suit to the hotel before breakfast Monday. Total cost $25.

On Monday I had a meetings with three agents in Hong Kong. Tuesday I caught a flight to Taiwan, saw an agent in the afternoon, and had dinner with an insurance company in the evening. The following day I flew back to Hong Kong for another meeting and calls on prospective customers. The day after I flew to Singapore.

After a day and half in Singapore, I travelled south to see clients in Sydney and Melbourne, Australia. After a quick side trip to Auckland, New Zealand to deal with a debt problem telexed to me by London, I was back to the original itinerary to sign up a new agent in Perth. I then flew the longest non-stop section then in operation by any airline by flying the Quantas Perth-Johannesburg run in a stretched Boeing 707 with long-distance tanks. The engines coughed as we put into Mauritius for fuel.

In Johannesburg, I took a side trip to Cape Town. My Hong Kong suit had started to split and my suitcase looked like a wreck. A telex awaited me at my hotel asking me to divert to Beirut on the way back to London. Didn't my ethnocentric boss understand that I was tired? In Beirut my taxi picked its way through bomb blast rubble, and I wondered why I did this job.

Crazy, you may say, and you are right. Before we assume the lifestyle of a global worker, we must look at the consequences and understand the effect of what we are undertaking.

Pressures on Global Managers

Clearly, the everyday pressures on global managers put leadership qualities high on the list of best practices. Leading from the top by demonstration and by example is universally accepted in any culture. When tough decisions have to be made, when the going gets rough, and when people in the field are losing their direction and faith, then it is the individual leadership, attitude, and understanding of the global manager that will keep the ball rolling. And global managers should never give operatives any task they would not willingly do themselves.

Commitment to building a culturally diverse ensemble, conducting an innovative cross-culture, friendly orchestra, and playing fine-tuned music for your customers is a work of art. Every leader understands this. Jack Welch said, "The world will not belong to the so-called managers or to those who can make the numbers dance but to passionate, driven leaders—people who have not only enormous amounts of energy but who can energize those whom they lead."

Research has shown that management decisions concerning recruitment, promotion, compensation, and workforce reductions are among the most sensitive issues any global manager must address. These criteria directly touch the cultural norms of people and their sense of well-being and order. Decisions about finance, accounting, or production rarely produce emotive reactions, but any tampering with human resource issues, benefits, and working conditions will excite visceral comeback across the human race.

Multinational mergers get column inches in the *Business News*, but the *human* story comes later on another page. Human resource management is all about cross-culture competence.

Global Citizenship

As business crosses political and cultural borders and brings a whirlwind of change in its path, the ensuing altered state to human lifestyle is in some cases overwhelming: culture traditions are challenged; local politics are influenced; economies are set on new direction; rural people drift to the cities; cities become unlivable, and religions are tested. Population growth skyrockets in areas already devastated by privation, and those already in the poverty ditch are emaciated by AIDS brought in by men who work in the towns. The anti-globalization movement sees the specific horrors which economic change has wrought and rises up expecting governments to stop their onward rush to prosperity in the face of human misery.

As business people working in the global arena, we know a different story. We are aware of the massive advantages that have been brought to huge areas of the world: how the globalized financial system brought down communism in Russia and set free the aspirations of millions of people in Eastern Europe, how China comes under the spotlight and her human rights record is available for inspection before she can enter the international community, how democracy is preferred over dictatorship in the economic support of nations, and how the infrastructure of roads, airports, communications, education, and hospitals can only be installed with money made from trade.

The choices are not easy for any culture that has been in the gutter of ignorance and poverty for centuries. In countries where power is vested in one family or a group of religious fanatics, the idea of change is anathema. Yet many of those countries are only too anxious to open up their natural resources to development in return for money and other forms of wealth. They walk a precarious balancing act. Neither is the choice easy for any country presently emerging from those conditions. The tumult, the lawlessness, the confusion, and the lack of know-how alone demonstrates uncontrolled change, as we see in Russia, where well educated, intelligent people wake up every day to a new system, a new law, and a new way of thinking, totally different from the ones in which they were brought up. In the west we say we're overwhelmed by change. If you *really* want to witness change, go to Russia.

The free market looks set to be the dominant form of economic activity in the twenty-first century, yet more people are questioning its ability to deliver real progress rather that just economic growth. The global manager must be aware of the wider horizon and the broader responsibilities in addition to stockholder returns. Likewise, stockholders need to be educated into the long-term values of good global citizenship that may not produce the returns they have been used to in the short term.

The Making of the Good Global Citizen

World public opinion has determined that, at the moment, a free economy system is preferable to the state controlled, but the state, as we saw in Russia, provided security from cradle to grave. It may not have been considered high quality security, but it was better than nothing. Today the Russians have next to nothing. So there are arguments and challenges to the free market theory. Many see unbridled free enterprise and the power of huge global companies as worse than dictatorial government. The pendulum never ceases to swing.

As managers, we sometimes find ourselves stepping into the shoes of government where employees, local public, and our customers look to us for leadership. As we increasingly distinguish the roles and responsibilities of *leadership* from those of *management* for achieving more visionary, more dynamic, and more engaging business goals, we must make the same distinction with respect to achieving broader social progress. Management alone cannot get us there; true leadership combined with world market forces might.

The definition of *progress* is hard to interpret in the global economy sense, not only because of the divergent opinions and pressures put forward by market forces but also, and probably more importantly, by a wide variety of culture groups which we call *good global citizenship*. Global progress cannot move forward if we ignore either.

Some of the issues that determine good global citizenship are as follows:

1) Environmental sustainment. The old way of thinking, which is still evident, is that companies should only react to environmental issues when there are economic reasons, but bad environmental sustainability is poor business in the long run. Traditional cultures such as Hindi, Buddhist, Moslem, and Shinto are close to nature, and pollution or destruction of nature's gifts are an affront to their be-

liefs. Managers need to be clear, both in word and action, that they support environmental sustainment.

2) Career and job creation. The role of business is to create value for customers. In so doing, it creates opportunities for employment. Government's traditional role has been to protect workers from undue upheaval due to market changes, as when western Europe which went from smokestack to high tech. Such protections can often have the opposite effect and prevent people from moving freely into new industries that have a longer life span. Managers need to explain their job creation, work, and education beliefs and practices to governments and to the local public.

3) Ethics and standards. Good citizenship anywhere is law-abiding and is the setting of high standards of ethics and behavior. It also means keeping promises but, more particularly, it is understanding, respecting, and obeying the laws and principles of the local religious teaching. The laws of the west are based on precedent, but the laws of many cultures are based on rules and prescriptions. Good managers set high ethical standards. They also provide quality training and interaction on these subjects for the people on their teams, recognizing and respecting the diversity of opinion and behavior.

4) Public good. Corporations have infrastructure. Some are the size of a small country. In the United States, companies organize blood drives, marathons for the disabled, build houses for Habitat, and lend executives to United Way. The idea is catching on in Europe. It will catch on throughout the world–not just because it is good citizenship but also be-

cause good global managers cannot ignore local needs if they have the means to satisfy them. The Coca-Cola Company has a long and impressive record of public good in India. The company's twenty-six operating bottling plants are located in rural areas. These plants are involved in providing medical services from serving as local ambulance facilities to weekly visits of medical doctors at remote villages. Often vaccines are supplied free of any charge and, in times of major disaster such as the earthquake in Gajurat, medical supplies, pure drinking water, disinfectants, and baby food are delivered by company vehicles. Coke also provided resources and expertise in publicity, community mobilization, and volunteers in the recent national polio immunization project in India.

5) Education and training. Few can doubt the value of well-constructed and maintained global training programs providing career and personal advancement. Most major companies long ago recognized this huge contribution to good citizenship as well as its huge practical contribution to the success of the business.

The success of any enterprise is due to the quality and performance of its people–a simple truism that bears constant repetition. In our globalized world with its cross-culture frictions, misunderstandings, and antagonisms, we are again forced to focus on the burning issue of human relationships. How on earth do we live and work with each other for the common good?

7

Negotiating, Selling, and Serving the Global Customer

B russels is an attractive old city with its famous Grand Place and Cloth Hall. It has some of the finest restaurants in Europe and the people are friendly, educated, and cultured. I was sitting around the negotiating table with a Flemish-speaking director of the Belgian branch of an insurance company we wished to buy. He was flanked on both sides by Walloon (French-speaking) lawyers and accountants. I was accompanied by a Cockney-speaking accountant who had rarely been anywhere east of Dover. I knew absolutely no Flemish; my schoolboy French was restricted to reading menus; and my knowledge of the Belgian negotiating style was less than zero. These conditions did not bode well for a successful deal. As we proceeded haltingly through the negotiation, I started to realize that the advisers were really in charge. Authoritative, formal, and distant, these notaries and financiers were blocking, nit-picking and arrogant. The friendly, relaxed director was not getting a word in edgeways, and my colleague was just staring at his paperwork. Three hours into the meeting and still nothing accomplished, we adjourned for lunch. At the restaurant, the director and I were in the restroom at the same time–a place for honest conversation.

"If we leave it to these Walloons, we will never get anywhere," said the director in broken English. "I agree to going ahead with the deal if you do–let's just move on with business."

We returned to the table, ordered a bottle of Dom Perignon and, to the horrified surprise of the Walloon brigade, he toasted the completion and success of the deal.

The solution-oriented Flemings looked for compromise, and the official, autocratic Walloons looked for exactitude–both important in their way–but for many years I was thankful that the culture patterns fell the way they did.

So, culture does matter when we are around the negotiating table.

Getting the Messages

Often when we're sitting at the table in the global workplace, we may believe, on first impressions, that the people we're facing think and act just like us. Certainly, they have the same emotions and feelings as we have: they want to love and be loved; they have a basic need for security; they feel anger at injustice; and they want to be respected. But then, national culture takes over. At a certain point, we all come under the influence of our learned background beliefs and behavior that we move into automatically. Sometimes, if we have spent many years as an expatriate, we can slip effortlessly into a familiar, local culture whenever we move into its environment–like an actor moving into a variety of roles. Now deviations of attitude and view come into play, subtle codes emerge, and we have to be watchful to avoid irritants and offenses. We must look for similarities between us and find common ground. Most of all, we should know when to agree to disagree and recognize that the other culture may not be able to see our point of view but that's OK! Cross-culture collision at the negotiating table can wreck your deal before it ever gets started.

Mexican Stand-Off

A Texas hotel supply company wanted to do business in Mexico. Their *deal-doing* vice-president of sales went to meet the Mexican agent in Cuernavaca. He had allowed one day for business; he then planned to drive to Acapulco for some marlin fishing. Dressed in *resort casual* attire, he arrived at the rendezvous hotel at 9:30 a.m. as arranged by e-mail. The vice-president could speak no Spanish, so he was relieved that the agent would have a basic knowledge of English. Nearly two hours later the agent, dressed in a business suit and tie, arrived, apologizing profusely for being late, explaining that his brother had had a family problem. After almost an hour of chatting about generalities, the agent suggested that they have lunch at the beautiful restaurant overlooking a lawn of strutting peacocks. By this time, the vice-president was getting frustrated. He wanted to be finished by 5 o'clock so that he could drive down to the coast before dark.

"Let's get down to business," he said, businesslike.

"Tell me about your family," the agent replied. "Where in the United States were you born? What did your father do? Have you been to Mexico before? Have you been to our Anthropological Museum in Mexico City?"

At 4:30 p.m., they were still in the restaurant looking over the peacocks, and the vice-president was beside himself. Three days later, he returned to his office in Texas, convinced that doing anything in Mexico was a waste of time and money, that the people were unreliable, and that they have no motivation to do business. Little did he know that the agent had formed a *good* opinion of *him* and *his company*–perhaps a little rough at the edges–but the Mexican contact felt they could have a business relationship. Weeks later, he still couldn't understand why the vice-president had not been back in touch with him.

If the vice-president had realized that small talk, the development of confidence, the demonstration of national pride, and the importance of meaningful social time together are all vital to the negotiating Mexican businessman–if he had made less premature judgment about the way the meeting should go, then the meeting might have turned up trumps for him, but he had left himself with no options.

Look for Options

In their groundbreaking book on negotiation, *Getting to Yes, Negotiating Agreement without Giving In*, Roger Fisher and William Ury point out four reasons why people do not search out options when they negotiate:

1)   Negotiators tend to make premature judgments that hinder the imagination and lock a certain set of possibilities in place.

2)   People tend to search for a single answer that leads them to progressively constrict the range of options rather than expanding it.

3)   The assumption of a fixed pie locks people into a win-lose mind-set.

4)   Negotiators concentrate on the home side's problems and needs instead of considering both sides' problems and needs together.

The negotiating phase of most deals is at the beginning–right there where reputations and first impressions mean so much. Overseas business representatives are often meeting each other for the first time; sometimes it is the first meeting they have had with foreigners. Our negotiating style procedure and conclusion, therefore, will be the standard that we will have to live with, perhaps for many years. Tough, smart tactic, win-lose negotiators may leave an unsatisfactory attitude behind which will haunt them when they try to garnish support from the group at a later stage.

Trouble in Tangier

I visited Tangier for the first time when it was an *open* city, an international port that had enjoyed its strategic position at the gates of the ancient world serving as the southern portal of the Straits of Gibraltar for centuries. The major world powers had *quarters* located in various parts of the city: the French quarter, the American quarter, and the British quarter. Barbara Hutton lived in the American quarter as did Malcolm Forbes and one or two other interesting types. A few shady British characters were there avoiding English justice. The really interesting quarter in Tangier, however, is the Kasbah, that frantic, mysterious warren of narrow alleys and heavy doors, of bazaars and veiled women, of brass and copper vessels, of carpets and silk caftans. *Bazaar* is a Persian word meaning *market*. This is where the *bazaari* class is raised and spends its lifetime trading with each other and bargaining with travelers. Open almost all night, the stores are filled with watches, cameras, perfume, jewelry, brass camels, incense burners, and copper candleholders. In such a frenetic school of practical negotiation are these entrepreneurs raised and trained. Here I tried to do my first deal with an Arab bazaari–not in the Kasbah, but in an exotic office at the port. Ali Achmed owned dry docks and ship service facilities. He looked just like I imagined a pirate would look on the Barbary Coast. I was out of my class, but he needed our insurance (it helps to work with a brand like Lloyd's of London on those occasions). From the outset of our discussions, Ali wanted some quid pro quos (literally, something for something) every time I ticked off a coverage extension he should buy.

"Will Lloyd's give me a contract to repair ships in the western Mediterranean?"

I replied, "I don't know. It's not in my power to determine that."

"Can you put in a good word for me to be a Lloyd's agent?"

As he sat close to me, his garlic breath wafted over me like a heavy cloud. He went on and on about reducing the premium rates and kept going over the issues, making them personal as he asked, "How will I survive this year with business down and a family to feed?"

It all became highly personal–very Arabic, very bazaari–to the point that I had to end my inexperienced misery and retreat to my hotel, deal unfinished.

"Let's get him to London," said my ethnocentric boss on the phone. "Give him some night life, and he'll renew all right."

We didn't renew all right. We didn't renew at all. I heard later that Ali had gone to a competitor who had made some introductions and helped get him a nice dry dock contract.

Arabic cultures have been traders for centuries. We should treat that experience with the respect it deserves–

they live and think and have their being in a totally different world from the westerner. For the Arab, personal relationships are everything; remember, they are in the relationship-based culture group.

Take the Long View

Americans, on the other hand, are linear thinkers. American prosperity was not made by negotiating in the bazaar but was built on quickly seized opportunities and immediate profit. Most of the rest of the world do not see deals that way. Most cultures, including those in western Europe, see deals more as long-term arrangements that are built on confidence, trust, and personal relationships. Reinsurance companies, for example, in Germany and Switzerland will show you their one hundred year loss results that include two world wars, revolutions, insurrections, recessions, and depressions plus earthquakes, hurricanes, sinkings, and sabotage, and they are still in business, some very successfully. Their fifty and twenty-five year results are a regular feature for discussion. American reinsurance companies are under constant pressure to produce good quarterly results with the probable result that the Europeans dominate the international reinsurance industry.

The expectations of U.S. stockholders and the system of rolling forecasts put massive pressure on U.S. negotiators to come up with something quickly, which often means that overseas deals are flanged together with built-in obsolescence. If, for example, we are negotiating with the Japanese, then the current negotiation is trivial compared to the gigantic problem they have–deciding whether to do lasting business with this foreigner. To them, this encounter is to merely *inform us of their intentions*, not to make decisions: their group outside our meeting makes these. The French are not obstinate when they will not compromise.

They just believe that their logic is correct. The Mexican agent spends time in developing personal information and close contact with the Texan vice-president in order to reflect his position of power to his colleagues and family. He never loses when he negotiates: his social position is on the line; his dignity must be intact, and it all must be done in an eloquent manner.

Differing Views of Outcome

The negotiating journey, therefore, is a process viewed in differing ways by different cultures. Others see its participation, purpose, conduct, and outcome in vastly dissimilar ways to the point that a deal can be wrecked quite easily on the launch pad long before the trip starts.

As the talks commence, the values, phobias, and role-plays of the culture groups involved start to become evident. For the Americans, Dutch, Scandinavians, Swiss, and Germans, time is money. It is extremely important to compress as much action as possible into the time available. The Germans will also insist on meeting deadlines, full information, punctuality, and having clear chains of command. The French, on the other hand, are committed to logic and rational argument. They pay attention to form and verbal presentation skills. The British insist on fair play and debate issues in quite reasonableness and diplomatic form. Latins are concerned with building trust, personal relationships, and honor. The Japanese are devoted to a complex set of obligations, the welfare of the group, and the maintenance of *face*. Russians are sensitive to status: they negotiate like they play chess–several moves ahead– and they are very patient in getting their way. The Chinese like meetings to be formal and structured in a hierarchical fashion: it will be a slow and repetitious process often regarded as too slow for western taste.

It must be obvious that probably 90 percent of the world's population negotiate at a slower rate than managers in the United States are used to. If we are going to avoid cross-culture collisions, we had better understand the pace of business in the rest of the world and obviously amend our pace and style accordingly.

The Decision Making Process

Another aspect of culture difference is the decision making process during negotiations. Second to the *time factor*, it is this process that causes American managers such frustration. For many cultures, the decision does not belong in the negotiating process, and it can often be taken remotely from the operation. For example, the French never like being rushed into making a decision that may finally be made by someone of seniority not involved in the process. The British like to be vague and leave the issue hanging out there so that nobody can actually point the finger–somehow the issue gets into action in the *fullness of time*. Latins and Mediterraneans defer to their leader to make the final decision that is then cast in stone. This is rather like the Japanese who go through a long process of agreement, consensus, and digestion before it ends up with the company president: he will not take his responsibility lightly as he will likely be forced to resign if it goes wrong – and that would reflect badly on the whole team.

Honorability

Another aspect of frustration for the American manager in the negotiation process is one of *honorability*: "How binding is this agreement?" "Will they keep their word?" The British, Germans and Scandinavians feel that they can *take their agreements to the bank*. The Japanese, on the other hand, believe that the agreement, written or otherwise, is subject to being altered in view of fast-changing circumstances that could impact the success of the deal. The French like to talk about decisions but do not care to make them intermittently. For them, the process is a brainstorm and a debating exercise on situations that could change any time–so the decision can wait until the answer comes from time and logical thought. This also reflects the way Latins see agreements. There must be room to maneuver.

Misinterpretation

Cross-culture negotiations are inevitably impacted by language differences and made more difficult because English is the language of choice in business today. American English has flexibility and a colloquialism that few other English-speaking people use, so managers should be aware that they could be seriously misinterpreted without knowing it. And we are not just talking about words that are regarded as vulgar in one country and commonplace in another. Most people, particularly the Asians and the Europeans, interpret spoken English literally. So if you use the statement "Don't pull any punches," be aware that if your counterparts around the table are from these regions, they may think that a fistfight is about to start!

American English is the language of an optimistic *get up and go* society that does not have a tradition of debate or fine oratory. Political invective and the quick turn of phrase that has demolished *high horse* British politicians and entertained theatre audiences for centuries are missing from the American culture. However, the relaxed, disarming colloquialisms and repartee so well-known throughout the world from movie and TV shows is as much part of the American style as the friendliness of the people. Nevertheless, managers should be careful to avoid using this type of language at the negotiating table. It can be misinterpreted unless your counterpart has been well-informed or has spent many years in the United States.

British English is totally different. George Bernard Shaw said Britain and America are "divided by a common language." The British manager talks in circles interspersed with humor, small talk, understatement, and innuendo–finally reaching a laid-back, vague, and fuzzy conclusion. Some British managers make use of the wide and wonderful vocabulary in the language and love to make a turn of phrase. English, whether spoken by Americans or Brits, is packed with codes that most people do not notice. Your foreign counterpart will be mystified with the codes you use with other English speakers, so it is best to be aware of that. If native English speakers are in the meeting, interlocution with them should be watched carefully by the savvy counterpart contingent.

Articulation is a skill in any culture, but for managers it is essential. Across the negotiating table there is little else but the free flow of ideas–converted to words, put into phrases. Having said that, it is then our ability to listen and interpret the other side's position. That's the hard part. It does no harm for any of us to be reminded of how to listen.

Listening Skills

For the cross-culture communication expert, listening is 75 percent of the skill. In a later chapter, we will look at presentation skills, but here we are still sitting around the negotiation table: all agog to do the deal but where the slightest slip 'tween cup and lip can mess up a perfectly good opportunity.

English nineteenth century novelist, Anthony Trollope, wrote about a character named Lucy Morris who was a person of outstanding listening skills. She possessed the ability to listen empathetically and encourage people to talk. Trollope referred to it as *hanging on their lips*. This means watching the speaker intently, hanging onto every word, giving eye contact, and conveying nods of understanding and encouragement. This conveys to the speaker that you are not just listening, that you're not only concentrating and understanding what your counterpart is saying, but that you are also demonstrating respect for what he says.

Ken Hughes had a terrible stutter, but he was a phenomenal salesman. Once in front of the prospect, all he did was ask questions, and because it was so difficult for him to talk, he just kept quiet. I was with him one day. Ken said no more than fifty words the whole morning; the prospect did all the talking. "Thanks for a very interesting conversation," said the customer as we walked out with an order.

These are the keys to listening at your cross-culture negotiation meeting:

- Let your counterparts tell their stories in their own way. Encourage them to talk about their hopes, their problems, their successes, and their failures. Ask them further questions about their business, their interests, and their family (if they mention these topics first).

- Use good eye contact. Give them affirmative nods and a yes from time to time. Exercise discipline to block out the distractions, such as noise in the next room or on the street.

- Resist thinking about how you want to respond as a comeback or as a contradiction until the speaker is finished. Pause and then make your comments. If you haven't been filling your mind with your comeback, then you probably haven't missed some good information.

- Don't be judgmental. We jump to conclusions about people as they sit across from us and get into conversation. *Personal stuff* gets into our head–old prejudices, racial profiling, stereotyping–all the useless junk which takes our mind off the subject at hand–trying to understand our counterpart and, do a deal.

- Don't jump to conclusions too soon; hear them out. Many a cross-culture deal has collapsed because of trying to add up the totals before all the numbers are known or because we go to the table with preconceived opinions. Keep an open mind up to the end or until you know all the available facts and have heard all the opinions.

- Put yourself into the speaker's head and figure out where he or she is coming from. Read the body language. Find the areas of trust, similarity, and need. Understand and empathize with the speaker's problems and concerns. It is here that opportunity for business with the other side is revealed. As your counterpart unloads the issues that worry him or her most, you understand where you can provide the solutions and, thereby, make a deal.

- Finally, be patient. It's against the instincts of many American managers, but in the fertile cross-culture soil, it may take time for ideas to seed, put down strong roots, and grow into a nutritious harvest.

The Negotiating Paradox

Negotiation skills are the subject of many good publications and seminars, and this is not the place to add to the number. However, one particular book does suit the skills of the global deal maker involved in the complexities of cross-culture give and take. *The Negotiating Paradox: How*

You Can Get More by Giving More, by Bernard Hale Zick, demonstrates the paradox that "you can get more by giving more" by being a *Friendly Persuader*, that is, a person who negotiates calmly and stays in control. He says:

> By knowing your Negotiating Nemesis, by mentally climbing into that person's head for a moment, you assess your own position from your client's perspective. You mentally prioritize your strengths and present those in the order and format that your Nemesis most values. What your client most values becomes your strength. This strength is what makes you uniquely valuable.

Zick goes on to make some highly perceptive observations that apply to any negotiating condition in business wherever it may be located:

> Since most negotiations are somewhat unbalanced, you can strengthen your position by reminding yourself that you have benefits your Nemesis desires. Why else would that person be negotiating with you? The practiced Friendly Persuader knows the real wishes and needs of the Nemesis, not just what the Nemesis says they are. This rule applies to large and small labor unions, government organizations and large and small companies.
>
> A good way to let your Negotiation Nemesis know that you are listening is occasionally to ask, "Let me see if I understand you correctly" and then repeat your version of what was just spoken. Confirming in this way assures your client or customer you are both listening and that you understand the desired wants and needs. Such assurance builds trust and boosts your credibility while increasing the chances of the relationship prospering.

Listening habits can play an important part in the negotiating procedure. I stress this point because most data-based people have a hard job staying silent compared to some other cultures. The Chinese have a proverb that is loosely translated: "Those who know do not speak; those who speak do not know." The Japanese, Finns, Scots and, to some extent, the Russians are all happy with silence. To the silent races, quiet means learning, and talking means telling everyone how clever you are–a display of arrogance and even egoism. Think of the horror when, for the first time, the silent Japanese is confronted with the verbal opera of the Italian, the oratory of the Arab, the drama performance of the French, or the continuous chatter of the American. To them, talk is expensive. It is a serious commitment to be honored, unchanged and not to be contradicted in the next phrase.

The international cross-culture negotiating game is filled with pyramids and pitfalls. Talk about learning by doing–books on this skill will never stop being written. Only those managers who are prepared to risk failure, embarrassment, or possible humiliation will get the deals they desire in this wild marketplace. If we learn our lesson every time we get tossed over and fall flat on our faces, we will soon realize that this arena is not good ground for perfectionists. The bull is an unpredictable beast, and the matador demonstrating grace and civilization can only keep his skill well honed if he spends as much time as possible looking directly into the eye of his opponent.

Selling and Marketing Across the Culture Gap

As the global sales manager reaches out across the world, one thing becomes apparent early in the process: understanding cultural differences is essential in the international buying process. When multiple sales teams from different cultures enter into negotiations, the inevitable question is "What culture style should be adopted–the sales partner's, the client's, or the home country's?" The answer is none of the above. Culture styles are what they are –the style of the culture–and the manager confronting the culture opposite must be aware of that particular culture's unique features. It's part of the preparation process.

It must be a truism that expert salespeople have to be expert negotiators and that international salespeople have to be cross-culture competent. These days there is no such thing as *business is business wherever you are.*

In the push by global corporations to integrate global strategy, there is a temptation to adopt home-style methods to overseas situations. Nothing could be further from good sense. Almost everywhere outside your native country is different, and the global sales executive must understand the differences.

People, for the most part, interact differently when relating between their own culture and another. They put on a *face* to others and instinctively guard against the codes that they use when communicating with their own. Salespeople must be acutely aware of the differences that apply.

American Stereotype

American selling techniques have received *bad press* overseas. The stereotype hotshot salesman selling used cars and using tricks and ploys to get his innocent victim to buy (along with that *ugly American* stereotype) has unfortunately gone down into the *bad file* of American cultural types. In the United States, it has almost disappeared, but the memory lingers on in the rest of the world and examples to disprove the theory are not only welcomed by other cultures but are noticed.

Gordon Prentice was the first American manager who sold me his services. Living in Denver, Gordon was a skier, hiker, nature lover, and man of the world. Soft-spoken, relaxed, and full of good humor, he knew England well and understood the eccentricities of the British. My concern when I first met him in London was that he would be the quick-fire, hotshot salesman. How mistaken I was. By sheer American charm, knowledge, and quiet humor, Gordon won the hearts and minds of all he dealt with. We couldn't do enough for him. My opinion of American salesmen changed from that day forward.

Culturally Sensitive

In dealing with a particular market, the global marketing manager is, in reality, dealing with the culture. The product design and style must fit in with the aesthetics of the culture. The promotional message is acceptable only if the symbols are meaningful or recognizable to the customer. The success or failure of the product or service, therefore, is dependant on whether it is culturally accepted or resisted. For example, trying to sell a product in a Muslim country using scantily clad women in the advertisements would certainly be a cultural snafu. Managers must take care not to apply their own values ad lib to other cultures without a great deal of care and research. This is referred to as *the self-reference criterion trap* in which a person unconsciously applies his or her own culture values, knowledge, and experience in evaluating a situation. When in Moscow, drink the vodka if the host offers it; when in Teheran, say a prayer to Allah and eat the sweet cakes; and when in Rome, expect your customer to be late for the meeting.

Cultural Universals

Global marketing managers carry with them some awesome responsibilities into the cross-culture environment. Critics of the global economy and the erosion of traditional cultural norms point to business activities that act to change or amend culture. There are influences called *cultural universals*, which are activities that apply across cultures such as entertainment, courtship, marriage, children, healthcare, education, and social welfare. Importing product and services connected with cultural universals are subject to culture collision.

A company simply exporting to a foreign country may only have to take into account the implications of price, product, place, and promotion without the more permanent implications of employees and business establishment. But for the global marketing manager, these four areas of concentration are also seriously impacted by culture. Let us look at the influence of specific cultural issues on the marketing role:

Religion

- Christians, for the most part, believe in the work ethic and individual personal success. The measure of achievement is in material success and wealth. In contrast, the Hindu religion is fatalistic about the acquisition of wealth.

- Some religions prohibit the use of certain foods: Hinduism prescribes abstinence from beef, Muslims from alcohol and pork, Jews from shellfish and pork.

- Gender roles are controlled by some religions. Muslims do not allow women to work, and their dress and conformity are also controlled.

- Disputes based on fundamentalist religion will expand in the twenty-first century. The collisions taking place all around the Islamic world, in Kashmir, Northern Ireland, Cyprus, the Balkans, and other hot spots are essential information.

- Religious holidays must be understood and worked around. Trying to fix an appointment on a holy day shows lack of understanding and preparation.

Education

It is important for the manager to appreciate the education standards of the country or culture. For example:

- The literacy rate will affect the marketing promotional strategies.

- A low education standard will have an impact on the products and services and the quality of trained personnel available for support services.

- Some countries focus on science and math related subjects in their education curricula.

- Other countries, such as France, have elite schools for wealthy and scholarship pupils.

Taste

The design, color, shape, sound, and aesthetics of articles, buildings, advertisements, and the like are interwoven in the culture. The global marketing manager needs to be sensitive to these important issues. Cultures in countries such as Italy, Austria, France, and Spain, with a long history of fine art, classical music, historical architecture, and elegance, put good taste at the forefront of their national character. Product design, always important, is particularly so in these countries.

Color, which is an important part of brand identification, should be researched. The meanings of color and its connotations are important in some overseas venues. In Muslim countries, for example, green and white is associated with death. White should be avoided in Asian cultures, but red is associated with good luck.

Design of product, buildings, signs, and advertising material is noticed carefully by many cultures. Their impression of your business, your people and your acceptability into the market can be made in a moment based on the quality of design. It is vital to get local expertise involved in these subtle matters of national taste. When you travel, learn from other big brand expatriate companies like McDonald's, Coca-Cola, Nestle and General Electric and see how they do it.

Social Structure

American marketing managers who work overseas need to understand the social structures that prevail in the region or country of their focus. Social structures are highly cultural and, while subject to change over time, provide the permanent governmental, commercial, and family fabric of a nation. Most countries have a class system. Some, like India, are extreme; some, like Scandinavia, are negligible; and each structure is reflected in the business methods and product marketing in the country.

The family is the core social structure of most cultures. Western countries tend to have smaller family units, often due to decades of mobility. Here each member has buying potential to some degree or another; each is precisely identified by the marketer to the product and services the individual is likely to purchase. Other cultures, such as Latins, South Americans, Africans, and Arabs, have more extended units, including grandparents and grandchildren, aunts and uncles, and cousins. Asian countries, as we know, go much further and include ancestors.

Social structure also affects the role and status of people in society. Men and women may adopt different roles in the family and in social institutions. In the west, women now assume as much, sometimes more, financial responsibility as men. In raising children, the differences become blurred, but the marketer has the fullest information on shopping habits, selection, and brand preference. In the Middle East, it is women who do the shopping, and it would be a mistake to target men. Professional women in Asia are rapidly assuming roles of financial importance and responsibility that a decade ago would have seemed unlikely.

The social hierarchy of a nation/culture is something to be studied. The population is graded or ranked according to some criteria based on wealth, income, power, profession, religion, education, etc. In some countries, people are able to move through the ranks easily, sometimes *up*, sometimes *down*. Americans take pride in the fact that an impoverished boy from the backwoods can become president or that the child of working class parents can end up as chairman of General Electric. The *American way* is the envy of the world. Some countries still have to contend with age-old class systems that prohibit upward mobility with only a few exceptions. However, the marketing manager has to accept and appreciate these circumstances and work within the system by segmenting their markets effectively and positioning their products appropriately.

Values and Attitudes

The global marketer should also understand values and attitudes. Cultures easily slip into an opinion or a mindset that takes longer to dislodge than to install, as trainers, teachers, and consultants know. Fixed attitudes about quality control plagued the Japanese market in the two decades following WWII. Cheap and crude was the belief. The great leaders of the industrial renaissance of Japan in the 1960s and 1970s changed all that. By sheer driven determination, they changed the mindset of the world by consistently producing quality product to the point that today Japanese goods are well respected for their outstanding quality.

Land Rover, the hardy British off-road automobile, was seen as the vehicle of choice in tough territory. It starred in exploration and military movies; it went on well-publicized expeditions across deserts and jungles and became famous. The attitude was that the Land Rover could do no wrong. Attitude sold them.

The world has a good attitude about American goods, products, and services. A reputation for being technologically sophisticated, reliable, cost efficient, and customer friendly has taken root in most cultures. America has taught the world about customer service that sprang from the highly competitive, constantly creative American marketplace. The world believes that America delivers good customer service. It's an attitude that marketing managers can take to the bank.

The Whole World Customer Service Provider

In the next ten years, 65 percent of American business will have to be skilled in the techniques of international business. Managers will have to understand how to negotiate, how to purchase and sell products and services, and how to deliver world-class customer service on a global basis. Globalization is the biggest economic change dynamic of our era. It is a giant compared to the technology revolution, but technology is certainly helping to drive it. It is changing and will continue to change, to varying degrees, the lives of every man, woman, and child on the planet. Globalization is altering the way business thinks about the future. Managers have to quickly learn new skills to understand and operate in this uncertain, rapidly changing, and wildly different environment, and consumers are discovering new liberties and choices never experienced before.

The grab for global market share is on. Every day a glance at the business pages or a click to the stock market channels will announce mega-deals as juggernaut corporations–many of which never existed a few years ago–form global alliances bigger than many countries. Emerging nations with backward communication systems find that they can leapfrog over the developed countries and install a digital wireless infrastructure, providing service to their most deprived areas. Suddenly, almost overnight, their cities are filled with a working population who live on mobile phones.

Customer service providers–the people who set and keep the standards by which most companies are judged–are now faced with looking after a newly educated, wired, savvy global consumer class who will be the making, or breaking, of their company's worldwide reputation.

Is global customer care any different from domestic customer care? In many respects it is the same. The same commitments, standards, and principles that keep your company's reputation at the top of the list at home also apply overseas. The key is to have consistently high standards wherever you do business. For example, the McDonald's mantra, "An excellent fresh meal in a clean restaurant" is the same throughout the world. It's simple, totally understandable, and loaded with customer benefits. It can be translated without loss of meaning and applies equally to every race, creed, color, and nationality.

Five Principles

The practice of keeping up your current standards is not easy when working in the global marketplace. Managers in this environment have to deal with an unfamiliar set of challenges; any one can bring on long lasting problems for recovery. Old certainties are replaced by unpleasant surprises. Everything on the global stage is under the glare of the spotlight–in front of an audience which remembers your every word and movement. There are five principles of good global customer attention as follows:

1. See everything you do on a local basis and be capable of meeting local needs. To that end, the manager should become highly conversant with the local market. Local history, politics, and economic issues should be reviewed and mastered if possible. Develop an understanding of the geography, culture, and lifestyle, for only then can the customer service manager make the flexible decisions that are the difference between success and failure. It was only after years of losses that Disney, for example, realized that wine has to be offered at Euro Disney in Paris.

2. Good leadership is an essential management quality, but overseas the customer service professional is setting the standard by which everything the company does is judged. The three essentials of high quality global leadership are high ethical standards, excellent communication, and superb training. The manager is often working with people fresh to the world of international business, and the lasting impressions left by good example companies cannot be overstated.

3. Infinite patience. The western essential of time does not have the same priority in many overseas cultures. Dealing day to day with consumer issues is regarded as a labor of love, wherever it may be, but in the wide world of global business, it's more so. The international manager will recognize that cus-

tomers like to build relationships. Meetings take longer, decisions take more time, and negotiations can, to the western temperament, go round in circles. All this is part of the relationship-building process and one that we have to get used to.

4. Build long-term relationships. In the western experience, loyalty is hard to find. The influences of competitive pricing and overcrowded markets have tended to subvert old-fashioned loyalty. Recognize that your patience in the negotiation and in the decision-making process will be rewarded with the type of loyalty that is rare in the west. You have to earn loyalty in foreign markets, just as you do at home. Personal friendships are gained over a long time, but when they are won, they are lasting.

5. Exceptional flexibility and creativity. The role of the customer service professional is constantly made up of agility and innovation, but the global operator has to be more so. In this unfamiliar zone where everything is different, you sometimes have to make up your job role as you go along. You certainly have to be able to bend the rules and make sizable decisions in the field. You have to have a substantial amount of entrepreneurial spirit, ability, and the capacity to work alone in the jungle of uncharted business territory. American business wrote the book on customer service, and it has served the U.S. economy well. Professionals know that you can never let your guard down because there is always someone else who will come along and do it better. Many overseas consumers have not enjoyed the standards American consumers now take for granted, but they are ready, waiting, and looking forward to the experience. The vital issue is that when we are ready to provide our service, we should

give them the best we've got–no compromise on
standards–no half measure.

The standards you set now, at this moment in time,
will set the benchmark not only by which you and your
company will be judged overseas for decades but also by
which your national business standards are judged. It will
also serve as an example and a blueprint for your local
graduate managers who will in due course set the standards
of their own country's business future and the economic
well being of its people.

8

Making Global Alliances Work

As regional and global expansion builds in size and pace over the next two or three decades, companies will seek alliances of almost every description. These arrangements will be the relationship of choice among most firms as mergers and acquisitions are shunned in favor of more flexible and changeable deals. The traditional corporate growth, through purchase and control, has often put a company's future success in jeopardy. So often time is taken up with managers fighting for turf and territorial establishment or trying to combine and integrate systems to adapt to the new corporate culture that real business is put on a back burner. Rarely are the customers consulted or considered in mergers and acquisitions. The principal reasons for the actions taken have been to increase market share, to make attractive stock deals, or (and this certainly happens) to ingratiate the ego of the chief executive.

Alliances, on the other hand, particularly in the international arena, are significantly more suitable and provide companies with many answers that mergers do not address.

Personal Relationships

An alliance or partnership depends almost entirely on its success from the development and maintenance of personal relationships. It takes longer and can be more complex than an acquisition; it needs constant care and attention from people of responsibility; and, most importantly, it must be reviewed and tested. Mergers rarely make that grade. International mega mergers and the behemoths they produce will be the target of antitrust officials and the anti-globalization lobby as they roll over governments, consumers, and local interests. Alliances, on the other hand, if properly constructed and understood, will be seen as helpful, progressive, and contributing good citizens.

Governments Do It

Strategic alliances have been around a long time. Think of the alliances that have been built between countries. For centuries, nations have made treaties concerning trade, territorial boundaries, peace, and defense, and also such things as importation disputes, fishing, flying, and extradition. In the modern era, strategic alliances have been made between countries for mutual protection from aggressors (as in the case of NATO) and for inter-commerce, monetary union, and free trade (as in the case of the European Union). Governments have concluded that it is better to make such alliances rather than resort to aggression or imperialism as attempted in the not too distant past. Likewise, corporations are discovering that aggressive takeovers and empire building are not as popular or successful as in the past.

Alliances or partnerships are equally as effective with small companies as large ones, by units or product lines, by departments or subsidiaries, or indeed, between individuals in competitive companies. Strategic alliances have become a reality for most firms, and the concept has spread rapidly to the international sector. They are defined as "collaborative organizational arrangements that use resources and/or governance structures from more than one existing organization."

Numerous Ways

This definition includes many ranges of organizational structure including equity joint ventures, licensing arrangements, franchises, marketing development, and shared product development projects. Global strategic alliances are described as "enduring *interfirm* cooperative arrangements that utilize resources from autonomous organizations based in two or more countries" (Ardvind Parkhe, "Interfirm Diversity, Organizational Learning and Longevity of Strategic Alliances," *Journal of International Business Studies*, 1991, Vol. 22).

Joint ventures will grow in popularity as companies seek out their compatriots in other countries. Specialist and niche industries will seek out their match company in the international marketplace and commit to co-branding, cross-marketing, and research cooperation deals. Competitors will increasingly make alliances together, as did Ford Motor Company with Daimler-Benz in late 1997 when they invested $420 million in a research project to develop an electric car powered by fuel cells manufactured by Ballard Power Systems of Canada. Their current goal is to manufacture 100,000 such cars by 2004. International joint ventures enable companies to share expenses in complex bold new undertakings that the constraints of their domestic limitations may otherwise prohibit.

The Best at Alliances

International alliances depend on cross-culture competence for their success. As we have seen, successful business partnerships are the product of good relationships between people. It is, therefore, easy to determine that alliances are likely to be second nature to the relationship-based and group-based culture types but have to be worked on by members of the data-based who find the multilinear structures and interplays of alliances less than comfortable (compared to a *slam-dunk* takeover with a built in hierarchy). Creating higher value from mergers and acquisitions is no easy slam-dunk, particularly in the global ball court. Integration into corporate culture and marketing techniques, rejuvenating an entrepreneurial spirit that existed in the previous independent entities, and just getting the new model motivated is challenging enough in the domestic zone, but it is multiplied in an overseas partnership.

Alliances succeed only when the purpose of the partnership is owned emotionally and when all participants buy into the concept. Too many are organized for hopeful immediate profitable return then fail to live up to their expectations because the members are not committed in an emotional sense. The reasons for the arrangement—both its purpose and its goal—must be 100 percent understood.

Why Make an Alliance?

Alliances of any type are for the mature. They are more complex, complicated, and confusing than almost any merger. They require a measure of high maintenance that most managers of mergers do not engage, and they often have unclear outcomes that have little or no contribution to the bottom line. It has been said, "Like a marriage, alliances are made in heaven; and, like marriages, when they're bad, they're awful!"

Understand the Benefits

So establishing the reason for making your international alliance has to be the first and foremost task and the one that will take the most time and care. When you understand the benefits, the reasons become apparent. In listing the benefits of an alliance, you are only limited by the quality of your relationship (including its cross-culture competence)—and your imagination.

Ed Rigsbee, the strategic alliance guru, states that there are seven general areas where you can profit from building alliances:

1. product
2. access
3. operations
4. technology

5. strategic growth
6. organization
7. finance

Overseas alliances have been successfully built to benefit from any one or all of these areas. Often we embark on only one to find that another becomes apparent and takes precedence.

European Alliance

Shortly after Britain signed the Treaty of Rome, giving her membership of the European Economic Community (EEC), now known as the European Union (EU), I wanted to establish a presence in continental Europe. My company joined a transnational association of independent insurance brokers. Each firm was a native of each individual country in the EEC: one member per country. Membership in this alliance was by strict adherence to non-compete rules and exchange of business protocols. Members met once a year at a select place like Monte Carlo or Amalfi to discuss the year's results and future developments. The alliance was a success, principally because its members liked each other and had a clear understanding of the benefits of their co-operation. Great care had been taken in the original selection of members based on their compatibility, personal relationships, and professional competence.

When the huge international insurance organization Marsh first came to Europe in the mid-1960s, they did the same thing and selected like-minded firms to service the fast expanding American investments on the European continent. It worked well for a number of years until Marsh started to buy up their alliance partners and the old entrepreneurial spirit died on the vine. Accountants replaced salesmen and homogeneity replaced diversity.

Overseas Representation

Overseas representation is the most basic and oldest type of international alliance. Some of these relationships have lasted for generations. They are scattered around the developing world in every seaport and every national capital. Many have served their companies with distinction, based on years of solid personal relationship. Through the relationship-based culture types of Latin America, the Mediterranean, Africa, the Middle East, and the Indian subcontinent into the group-based areas of China, Southeast Asia, Japan, and Korea, the representatives of manufacturers, engineers, contractors, mining operations and agricultural companies have flourished. Some since the early nineteenth century include Jardine Matheson and Swire Group in Hong Kong and Inchcape in the Persian Gulf. Service companies have created international alliances for decades. Accounting firms, lawyers, shipbrokers, insurance carriers, publishers, and news agencies all tie up deals with other like-minded operations to obtain representation in the country or the region.

Benefit for one side may be totally different from the other. An American company, intent on developing market share, may do a successful deal with a representative in a developing country because of the training and exposure to modern management techniques. A European drug company, wanting to get more involved with research, may construct a joint venture with a Canadian company in return for credit lines from European banks. An Indian software entrepreneur may want to access Chinese university talent in return for teaching and research commitments. A global business consultant structures a deal with a local politically connected consultant in order to win a bid to work with the country government.

International deals like these are being worked on every day. The ones that succeed are the ones with clear benefits, clear goals, and exceptional relationships. All these exceptional relationships are cross-culture competent.

Types of Global Alliance

Apart from the tradition of international representation, the most active form of international alliance developed over the last fifty years is the franchise alliance, with McDonald's and Coca-Cola being the global leaders. Coke has written the textbook on global alliances through their bottling franchise arrangements. Doug Ivester, past chairman of the company, said that 100 percent of Coke's revenue comes from alliances with bottlers and distributors. McDonald's, of course, is one big alliance-maker and has found that building its partnerships in every nook and cranny of the world has given it a severe education in cross-culture skills.

These companies have become the models for large corporation alliance builders that don't just focus on franchise stores. Coke, for example, created an alliance with Swiss-based Nestlé to develop canned and bottled coffee and tea for the worldwide market: a combination of Coke's distribution/bottling/canning expertise with Nestlé's marketing/coffee/tea expertise. Both companies are well-known for their cross culture competence and the deal is working well, even in some remote and unfamiliar locations.

Global strategic alliances take many forms. The most common are as follows:

1. The International Customer Service Alliance. Built to provide *on location* service to customers in that country or region, this is perhaps the most popular type of alliance, (and structured in as many ways) from shared equity deals to agency representation and franchises.

2. The Geographic Strategic Alliance. Located in a specific part of the world for representation, information, contacts, government relationships, and the like, this relationship may be with a manufacturer's agent, a law firm, a consultancy, or simply an individual.

3. The Business Development Alliance is organized to develop new business in the area. One partner provides the product and know-how; the other provides the market. BDAs are often structured as joint ventures, franchise alliances, co-operatives, etc.

4. Competitor Alliances. As global competition surges, companies are seeking ways to cooperate with their competitors by sharing information, cooperating on research, co-branding, and product development.

5. Distribution Alliances. Some companies have outstanding distribution networks that they have built up over years–for example, Coke's distributions system in India. Alliances with organizations capable of distributing your product are invaluable.

6. Supplier Alliances. Major retailers have created these important partnerships for years to secure their supplies. Global supply chains are distant, competitive, and often erratic. Manufacturers, raw material providers, and assemblers all come under this category and are subject to alliance arrangements.

7. Global Mastermind Alliances. CEOs like to talk to other CEOs. Research scientists like to compare notes with other research scientists. In the global arena where the world is changing at breakneck speed, people who make decisions of magnitude like to talk and compare notes with each other. The G8 is a mastermind alliance of heads of state.

We are all one world now with the wish to work together for the happiness of all mankind. We cannot do this on our own. We will increasingly depend on alliances with others for a multitude of reasons.

Managing the Global Strategic Alliance

The management abilities to be brought to bear in running a successful international alliance are heavily accented toward relationship skills. They can be summarized as follows:

1. Perfectly understand the culture style of your alliance partner: how and why he or she thinks and acts a certain way.

2. Treat your alliance partner the same way you wish to be treated.

3. Discuss and review your relationship with each other regularly.

4. Recognize that it's more important to have a good relationship and achieve your goals than to be right.

5. Know what your partner's goals are in the alliance.

6. Be sure to share your goals for the alliance with your partner.

7. Commit to the venture with passion and confidence.

8. Resolve all conflicts and disputes as soon as possible.

9. Give more to the partnership than you promised or contracted.

10. Celebrate your successes together.

Making sure that the relationship is the predominant factor in the maintenance of the agreement is the key. Remember that the alliance has to be run jointly and that the responsibility must be shared. The commercial graveyard is packed with tombstones of failed international alliances, many of which were caused by cross culture incompetence and differing management styles. Take the Bell Atlantic/

Olivetti joint venture that was organized to compete with the Italian state-owned telecom giant. After twenty-four months of bickering and disagreement over cultural details and mistrust, the deal was off. Expensive and time wasting, the project joined the graveyard when, in fact, it started as a bold and brilliant vision that could have become a considerable benefit to the Italian public.

Many alliances are not successful because the relationships have not had time to mature. Thousands of joint ventures are made between strangers. Most fail. A negotiating table where strangers sit is often a war zone where strong minds battle for supremacy. Remember that you may be moving straight from the table into a deal where you have to manage a business with people you know little about. What then are the immutable laws of constructing and managing a global strategic alliance (GSA)?

Law 1.   Do business together before you make an alliance.

Nothing is so transparent as the day-to-day business experience. Business is a two way street. The longer you do business with another, the more transparent they become. This is the time to do your research and homework on the people, their business history, and their operating style. This is the time to check the chemistry and the financials. As the personal relationships develop and the opportunities become clear, the way opens up for a more permanent and lasting cooperation based on the relationship. There is no time limit or minimum to this stage. Sometimes it takes years; sometimes it takes months, but it will be the most important decision of the process, so take your time. The questions you need to address at this time will be vital for the future of the partnership.

Important issues are as follows:

1. Are my potential partners winners? Do they demonstrate attitudes and ingredients of natural winners, or do they quit when the going gets tough? Are they prepared to make an *emotional investment* in the alliance project – or is it purely business?

2. Do my prospective partners understand that the success of any alliance is up to them and that they are ultimately responsible for their own success? Do they understand the principals of synergy? How well do they understand the true nature of *partnership*?

3. Are my potential partners good listeners? Can they absorb detailed facts and discuss them? Are they prepared to listen to other people's point of view? Are they willing to learn?

4. Are my potential partners interested in my business? Have they asked any questions about it? Have they expressed any interest in visiting our facilities? Have they asked questions about the structure of our operations, its management, and my bosses? What do they really know about our product and service?

5. Do my prospective partners realize that an alliance is a relationship of interdependence, and that neither of us must depend on the other for success, rather we must be co-dependant, like overlapping circles of equal radius?

6. How do my potential partners respond to feedback? Are they willing to take advise and even criticism? Are they highly independent?

7. How communicative are they? Do they talk about deep issues or is it superficial conversation? How good are they at communicating with their own people? Is their information accurate?

8. Are the potential alliance partners flexible? Are they open to change and to making major shifts in attitude and policy?

9. How trustworthy are my potential partners? How reliable are they regarding small everyday issues? What is their history with money? What is their debt position?

10. Are my potential partners cross-culture competent? Am I going to run into trouble down the line with cross-culture collisions in this organization?

Law 2. Negotiate a win/win deal.

When negotiating mutual value from the collaboration, it is essential that both sides understand, respect, and support each other's objectives. Our partner's objectives are often dissimilar, but that should not be difficult to accept as long as both sides understand what these objectives are. Longevity is not an indication of value. Alliances are often formed for short-term reasons. A short-term cessation may be warranted, depending on the circumstances.

How do we negotiate a win/win deal? There are two ways: by giving more than is expected of us and by showing how we will help our partners achieve their goals.

The negotiation needs to build flexibility into the deal, recognizing that all joint ventures are subject to change, that corporate objectives change with time, and that priorities of people alter. Learning by one partner, for example, can lead to a movement in bargaining power and the subsequent instability of the alliance. Market appreciation through local knowledge may also be a factor to change the deal. However, if the relationship is strong and the mutual benefit is still worthwhile, many partners find other useful ways to cooperate and may even decide to make the marriage permanent and merge.

When data-based individuals negotiate with relationship-based, we perceive two opposites at work–often dedicated to different objectives. We have already determined that data-based types think in a linear manner and relationship-based types think and act multilinear. In other words, the first is a one-track thinker and doer and the second works and thinks on multiple tasks at once. Don't worry, therefore, if your deal gets sidetracked, marginalized, or otherwise confused to data-based eyes.

In the data-based western societies, status is achieved through hard work, accomplishments, and, in some cases, wealth. In relationship-based Mexico, for example, status is often obtained through nepotism, friends, contacts, and insiders: a complicated network that starts from birth. Favors are sought, usually granted, and ultimately reciprocated in a complex understanding among equals. The owner or senior manager of a business will expect and receive unquestioned obedience from subordinates and, in return, will reward them with courtesy, protection, and loyalty. Your Mexican alliance partner will see your organization in the same way as he sees his own, and he will see you in the same way as he sees any other insider. It's all part of the cultural glasses we constantly wear and of which we as global managers must be constantly aware.

Take the fine art of compromise, for example. Compromise is regarded as an essential negotiating skill in Anglo-Saxon business. However, other cultures deal with impasse in totally different ways. The French insist that their logic is right; the Japanese have been totally misunderstood; the Arabs retire for prayer and come back more conciliatory; and South Americans see compromise as a *climb down* and an affront to their dignity. Mexicans will often display resistance to such a slap in the face and will refuse to concede anything to the arrogant *gringo*. How then do we conciliate and compromise in the face of such antipathy? These principles are bound up in the various cultures and are, therefore, wrapped in emotion and passion. Meaningful solutions for impasse can only be sought if we are able to understand the other side's priorities and goals and relate these to the concepts of dignity, understanding, and reasonableness. Putting ourselves into their culture condition, wearing their glasses and seeing things from their perspective helps us to relate to the other side's point of view. Churchill used to say that once he got to know Stalin he could get into the mind of "Uncle Joe" and figure out the *enigma wrapped in a riddle*. Ask yourself, "What would he do in this position?" In the case of our Mexican partner, he might go to one of his friends to help get the compromise through. It perhaps would save face. Maybe you should give that a try.

Law 3. Get the organization right.

Even after cross-culture competence is in place and the deal is beautifully structured, there is still yet another minefield to cross–that of the organizational fit. This is when alliances struggle with systems, management incompatibility, and structural misfit.

I negotiated a joint venture in Barcelona, Spain, with a local insurance business owner. We were to write a volume of hotel and resort accounts along the burgeoning Spanish Costa del Sol and Costa Brava where all Europe seemed to be holidaying due to the attractive weather along the Mediterranean coast and the currency advantages against the peseta. My Barcelona partner had the accounts, and we had the insurance market through Lloyd's of London. I knew the owner well, and we had developed a good relationship over many years. He was a bit light on administration, but he was a great salesman. Now was the time for making serious money.

"What do you want out of this arrangement, Eduardo?" I asked.

"Money," he said.

We agreed that we both wanted the same thing and signed the deal.

It worked well for twelve months. I went to see him a couple of times and was satisfied that all we had to do was collect, so I put the accountant in charge of the alliance. Bad move. The accountant decided that the systems were wrong, and he also wanted Eduardo to send the premium on time and stick to his side of the agreement. The first awareness I had of any problem was when Eduardo called and told me he couldn't continue the deal. I had stopped calling on him and, instead, he had been forced to put up with a difficult accountant and all our bureaucracy. Our long term trusted relationship was in jeopardy.

How many deals suffer the same indignity when proprietors, CEOs, salesmen, and entrepreneurs negotiate the deals without bringing in the operatives? I turned my back on Eduardo and left it to someone who had not been around the table when the question was asked, "What do you want out of this deal?" It was a mistake I've never forgotten.

Two lessons were learned from this fiasco: a) a poor relationship/management fit will lead to poor performance; b) a bad organizational fit will lead to collapse. Both deficiencies can be corrected if caught in time, but sour relationships and unnecessary bureaucracy can shadow even good money.

Law 4. Keep the negotiators in the management.

Alliances are built on trust. In the global world, trust is a highly valued commodity that's difficult to replace or repair when it's damaged. It is essential, therefore, that the persons involved in a negotiation be involved with, or at least be a part of, the team responsible for the day-to-day management of the alliance. Operational managers from the firm's operational units should be involved with the formation process and the implementation of the start up. They are the ones who need to ask the tough questions about operational problems, system integration, and who does what. Personal relationships need to be made at the founding of the alliance and constant attention to the objectives of the venture well understood by all the people concerned, and publicized to all those likely to be involved. A successful alliance manager must be cross-culture competent and capable of working in a collaborative relationship with multiple bosses or in a high state of ambiguity with non-aligned performance objectives of the partners concerned.

International alliance managers can run into problems with job titles. Foreign managers often put great store behind titles and may be affronted by a title less prestigious than they would like. It is important to stress the job role rather than the job title. The negotiation phase is the best time to explain and demonstrate all these quirks and potential misunderstandings.

Law 5. Review your joint commitments with your partner.

Members of the relationship-and group-based types understand the integrity of a solemn commitment. Family feuds and tribal hatreds, read about in novels and in the news, are the extreme of this devotion that often goes on for generations. They often criticize the data-based for their lack of obligation and commitment to their word. They see this as major risks in doing business with data-based members who are sometimes considered opportunists and fickle minded. Remember, therefore, that our commitment to an alliance and our *solemn obligation* will be the way we are judged. If we renege against the relationship-based and the group-based, we jeopardize our chances of doing any further business with them.

It is essential, then, to go into our alliance with the intention of keeping it in place and making sure it's healthy as long as the mutual goals are sought after.

The key is communication—communication between the members or leaders of the original negotiation. If they change, then communication and revised agreement between the new parties must take place.

We live in a world of change. Goals change, priorities change, and the original intentions of our alliances will change. Review them on a regular basis. Active alliances need goal reviews every year and progress reviews at least every quarter. Slow or semi-active partnerships should also be reviewed every eighteen months and questions asked concerning the ability of the endeavor to continue fostering its goals. Deals left in limbo are an accident (or lawsuit) waiting to happen. Most disputes are caused by communication breakdown.

Law 6.   Review the alliance with your organization.

The champions of the alliance should be sure that they have the support of their organization and its upper management. They have to obtain the input of internal resources, technical help, financial support, and time commitment. This communication of review and commitment is perhaps the most important, for without it no alliance can survive– *cut off from the mother tree* so to speak. Corporations lose interest in a pet project if it no longer makes money, starts to cause problems, or no longer fits the plan of action. If your deal is up for review, be sure you have all the facts and support of your partner. If there is likely to be a problem with continuation, it is imperative to keep the partner informed if that is appropriate to your working contract. Your ultimate obligation is to the integrity of the relationship with your partner. Often disputes arise between your partner and the organization. It's a dilemma. It's a skillful walk between your obligation to your employer and your relationship with the partner.

We had a highly profitable and active alliance with an insurance broker in Cape Town, South Africa. Annually we met with him in the beautiful Prince Edward Hotel to review our business and to discuss expanding our interests together. Outside the perimeters of the hotel's palm-treed fountain court was a violent regime. My partner and I had had a long and successful working relationship. We were good friends, and we rarely talked politics, but the awful system of apartheid was never far away. My company decided to cease doing business in South Africa, and I was instructed to end the alliance in Cape Town. If this didn't end a good friendship, it would, at the least, severely impact my revenue. I dithered and procrastinated and one day received a phone call.

"Hello Michael. Paul here," said a clipped South African accent. "What's this I hear about you pulling out of South Africa?"

Oh, no!

"Yes, it's true–but I have an alternative for you," I said, thinking on my feet.

Driven to action, I made an arrangement with another

firm who would work with our contracts and give Paul the service he deserved. It worked well, and I was able to keep a friendship and keep my job.

Law 7. Find other things to do with your partner.

A well-constructed and maintained international alliance is a valuable thing. You have invested a great deal of time and effort into the process and have developed a golden relationship with your partner. It is producing the results you all agreed upon, and everyone concerned is working well together. You are eager to talk with this partner about something else you can do together in the future.

For about three years, Texas-based Baylor College of Medicine has been providing education and medical supplies to Tomsk University Medical School in Siberia to combat the ever-growing HIV/AIDS epidemic. Every year a doctor from Baylor visits the school and reviews the program and assists the faculty in the education exercise. The alliance works well; the relationships are excellent, and in 2001 it was felt that more could be developed from the collaboration. Along came Houston Community College System (HCCS) that was introduced by people from Baylor.

Establishing joint ventures with community education organizations throughout the world is a key objective of their international initiatives department. A perfect opportunity lay with Tomsk Polytechnic. Based on the credibility already established between Baylor and the academics of Tomsk, HCCS was able to make a deal with the Polytechnic to provide them with curriculum and graduation standards for trade and artisan courses. Basic business, agriculture, and nursing programs will follow later. Faculty members from HCCS will visit the Polytechnic from time to time, and graduating students desiring higher degrees will be able to obtain better access to U.S. learning institutions. If this program proves successful, officials in Tomsk expect to expand it throughout the whole region of Siberian Russia. Tomsk has a thousand year reputation as a center of study and learning. They see this as a golden opportunity to revive that good standing.

Take your alliances to the next step. Revive their purposes and meanings and constantly pump new blood into their veins. These can be the most valuable products of your cross-culture competence.

9

The Gender Dimension

The societal revolution of the twentieth century, in a century of revolutions, was the beginning of enfranchisement for the western woman. Considering that the opening of the last century provided little hope for the rights of women and the fight was restricted to a few remote and hardy people who were regarded as cranks, it is nothing short of amazing that women have won the rights and positions of responsibility that they have. History may well prove that these denials for the benefit of mankind have been the largest single waste of human ability. However, much of the world disagrees with the west even on the basic tenets of the enfranchisement of women and the consequent freedoms that this brings. Many would say that the west also has a long way to go before prejudice and attitudes are put in order and women can expect a fair and equitable playing field in the business world. It is apparently a cultural thing and each culture has a different way of approaching the issue. Western women are playing an increasing part in world business. Politics and non-government organizations are filled with women working with culture varieties and doing deals across cultures. Their specific needs and requirements, therefore, deserve a chapter in this book. The issues facing women in the global workplace are often very different from those facing men.

Golden Opportunities

The ferocious competition in the global marketplace and the constant need for talent experienced by international companies has provided women with a golden opportunity. Those companies must equip their workforce with the best people, and many women are recognizing that promotion comes to those who are globally savvy and have international experience in their résumés. Overseas governments and business leaders have not missed this social breakthrough. In recent years, many reports well document western woman's role in business management. As well, high profile cases of sexual harassment legal action and legislation in the United States aid women's roles in the international arena. The result is that some non-western cultures–long prejudicial to women's freedoms–are now under pressure to provide opportunities for education, work, and social self-determination. But the road is likely to be long and difficult. We are brutally aware that women's enfranchisement is one of the major issues of cultural disagreement between Islamic fundamentalists and America. It appears that the one common thread between religious fundamentalists from both east and west is the male dominance of women.

Our focus, however, is business and, while we must be aware of the attitudes of highly vocal minorities that prevail in the world at large, we must examine the challenges that women will meet as they negotiate, sell, employ, and manage in the global marketplace.

The Global Woman

Ruth Benedict got a B.A. degree in international business from Northwestern. After six years with Chevron working on a variety of projects, mainly in the U.S. domestic gas production and transmission field, she found herself on the redundancy list at the time of cutbacks and industry recession–something the energy business has experienced for decades. Her financial compensation package would allow her to live without work for six months, and she had *rainy day* savings for a further six. She decided that her savings would be well spent on education that would elevate her employment worth and at the same time make her a rare commodity. She decided to become an *expert* on China. Ruth would go there and learn the culture, the language, and the republic's energy business–absorbing as much as she could for nine months. Parking her eight-year-old with her parents, she checked into the foreign student's language school at Beijing University. It was a giant effort even for someone adept at languages, but Ruth became reasonably fluent in Mandarin. She traveled as far as she was able in the country and did part time intern work for the China Petroleum Corporation. It all paid off. While she was there, she heard of the deal signed by ENI, the Italian National Oil Corporation, through its subsidiary, Agip China, to develop a huge gas find in the Qaidam basin. She was hired as the vice-president for project development. Her nine months immersion had been worth every minute.

The Rule of Three A's

Ruth is not alone. Women in the international workforce

recognize the rule of the three A's: Ability, Attitude, and Adjustment. The global woman must have these three credentials. In fact, it could well turn out that women are more in tune with cross-culture competence than most men for reasons that we shall see.

1. Ability

There is a myth that western-based companies are reluctant to send women overseas. They are concerned that they will be poorly received in male dominated cultures and that they will have difficulty negotiating with male preponderance management in those cultures. This is as much a male dominant misreading in the west as it is a myth in the overseas cultures. The real truth is that in international business conditions and environments, a woman will be judged on her ability–probably more so than a man. In fact, the biggest problem women face in overseas work is not with men overseas but rather with their own colleagues. According to Robert Moran and John Riesenberger in their book, *The Global Challenge: Building the New Worldwide Enterprise*, women returning from abroad report that "the biggest barriers come from within the corporation, rather than from situations encountered during foreign assignments." Once men are convinced of the capabilities of their female colleagues, they will offer the right support and cooperation that is so important to international projects. It is sheer ability, however, that will defeat these culture-based objections as well as establish their credibility with the foreign participants. Experience has shown that if women establish their competence, experience, and authority, they will be taken seriously and treated with professional respect by foreign executives. It is well known by overseas business people that American women play an ever-increasingly important role in business. It is up to the American female manager to *sell* her authority and her ability to the people she must deal with. Understanding the local culture, the perceived role of local women, and their place in society is all part of the cross-culture competence she has to learn. When that is thoroughly understood, it should not be hard to see what women must do to separate themselves from that local perception.

2. Attitude

One of the principal keys to cross-culture competence is not allowing the behavior, practices, and principals of a foreign culture to upset us and get to our emotions.

Recognizing that all cultures are different, the manager has to have a *give and take* attitude when it comes to women's rights in cultures other than her own.

I worked with a highly intelligent woman in London who was a political activist and an advocate for women's rights. She had written articles on the subject and had at one time run for a parliamentary seat as a left-wing candidate. Her department was involved with export credit insurance, and she was well regarded as an expert in the field. One day she was asked to attend a meeting to meet a client from the oil rich Muslim state of Qatar. At the meeting, she came out with criticism about women's rights in the Islamic world that froze the conversation. The client was gracious and understanding, but the damage was done.

We may disagree about practices and our perceptions of a culture may be tainted, but we are there for business and not to change an ancient culture. One has to learn not to take things personally.

3. Adjustment

The fine line we sometimes have to walk when working with another culture may present challenges to the female global manager, particularly when the time comes along for out-of-business hours entertainment. The cultural condition of personal space, for example, is sometimes a problem for data-based women. Data-based people are comfortable standing at arm's length from each other; group-based members position themselves even more apart, particularly with people they don't know; and relationship-based cultures like to stand close together, looking deep into each other's eyes–sometimes almost at *breath* distance. Latins are *touchy/feely* and love to hug perfect strangers. While Arab cultures like to be close, they will avert their eyes and avoid handshakes with women. Social time is an essential part of doing overseas business, and sometimes long drinking sessions are part of the program and the business culture. Maintain your poise. Be sure that you make the right judgment and stick to your time or quantity limit–they are watching you. The Japanese will expect you to remain serene, low-key, and modest; the Latins and Russians will be concerned if you do not join in their boisterous behavior. This is not a time for *"when in Rome, do as the Romans"*: it is more of *"when in Rome, be accommodating, but remember who you are."* The visiting female manager from the United States is still much of a novelty for most overseas executives and upon their judgment will hang their opinion of American women for years to come.

Like many other situations in the cross-culture competency arena, women will have to do better than men. The global woman has to be more aware, more sensitive, and play by a different set of rules than her male counterpart. She has to develop an antennae which alerts her to the appropriate local culture boundaries, perimeters, glass ceilings, and other invisible walls which many western women have long since broken through and no longer have the intuition to notice. It's not that the global woman copies the behavior of the culture she is visiting–far from it. She has a culture all of her own. It's a subtle mixture of her own native culture, colored by the precepts of her host's.

The global woman is a construct of the modern, a rare and valuable breed. She is what Nan Leaptrot describes as *the third sex.* When she visits another culture, she has to step outside her own, enter her host's culture, but not take on its personae. She has to be acceptable, but apart. Data-based women are members of a pluralist society in which they can play an equal part. The culture has not assigned roles. Certainly, there are traditional stereotypes, but there are no cultural rules that, if broken, will threaten the society. Most relationship-and group-based cultures have assigned roles for women–some are stricter than others; nevertheless, they are there. In dealing with these roles, the global woman has to accentuate the differences between herself and those of women from different cultures. In other words, the global businesswoman has to walk this tightrope–not only to bridge the culture gap but also to define her relative gender.

Distinguishing oneself from the local culture, yet adjusting to its nuances and making it quite clear that everyone understands how you want to be treated, is essential for success. As a global woman, it is your responsibility to define yourself in a way that will help everybody to work with you in a comfortable manner. Your purpose is to get the job done, to accomplish your objectives. In order to achieve this, you should define your status, your qualifications, your authority, and your intentions. In most cases, this is all made clear prior to the meetings so that you come into the room well-briefed and accepted.

Before any meeting overseas, any businesswoman would benefit from the following suggestions:

- Obtain and mail letters of introduction and authority from her superiors.

- Obtain other letters of introduction from congressmen and elected officials of standing.

- Make contact with the local U.S. Embassy or Consulate and get them involved.

- Send testimonial letters from other customers and clients, preferably in the target country.

- Write a letter of introduction, giving details of her educational and experience background.

- Define her role and objectives for the meeting and the assignment at large.

- Courteously ask for assistance and help in the achievement of these goals.

The global woman plays by a different set of rules. The guidelines are not difficult, but they are different from the ones played by men. She has an invaluable role in the building of international business and because of her visibility, she can turn these apparent obstacles into substantial advantages and look forward to a highly successful career in the world of international management.

Different Rules

Suppose the global businesswoman is dealing with a male-dominated culture situation. She is traveling into his territory.

The global woman is in charge. She makes the rules of overseas interaction; she decides how she will function and operate. Her rules are different from the normal rules applied to male-to-male engagement. Business is human-to-human interaction the world over, and the following rules are all about human interaction:

1. Define your authority and your objectives before any appointment

2. If men from your company are going to the appointment, you need to understand their role, brief them on yours, and clarify the different roles in the meeting. Be sure that your own people will not *let you down* in the meeting and will, in fact, support you and your definition.

3. Have the first meeting on neutral ground. Select a suitable venue and arrange it. Going to a male contact's office will mean that you have to follow his rules and protocol, speak his language, and immediately be subservient.

4. At the meeting, demonstrate that you are his equal. Do this by showing your self-worth and your professionalism. Refer to the testimonials and referrals you have sent him; mention your business experience, travels, and knowledge of

his country and culture. Do *not* refer to your children, family, friends, vacations, homes, or husband unless he asks you.

5. Some cultures may find it embarrassing to ask why a woman is dealing with them. You should say, "You may be wondering why it is that a woman has been sent over here to deal with this issue. It is because I am the expert in . . ."

6. Control the turf and set the limits. Be sure that the foreign businessman understands that you are not an *asset* of the company sent out to help the negotiations. Remind him that your job is to achieve the objectives of the business between the two of you in an efficient, professional manner and that you carry company authority within certain limits and perimeters and nothing more.

7. Articulate the benefits he will obtain by dealing with you and going along with your plans. Make it quite clear what you personally bring to the table. Show him how he will gain in a manner that is appropriate to his culture. Overcome any objections he might have in dealing with a woman before he has an opportunity to make it an issue.

Self-Worth

The all-important quality of self-worth or self-esteem is such an important criteria for the global woman that it deserves special mention. Not to be confused with over-confidence or immodesty, it conveys sincerity, control, and professionalism. It may be that the foreign businessman will be embarrassed that he has to deal with a woman: he might purposely be late or possibly the meeting will be assigned to a subordinate. Don't worry. Let all that wash over and be persistent. First impressions are very important, and self-confidence can be conveyed through the following:

- The use of good posture and bearing

- A strong visual image of conservative dress and elegant styling with subdued color and accessories

- A well-modulated voice: strong, firm, unemotional, and confident

- Excellent articulation using appropriate vocabulary for the culture. Avoid colloquial language. Use strong factual and technical terminology for data-based people, flowery and descriptive for relationship-based, and formal, flattery wording with group-based cultures.

- Demonstration of loyalty and commitment toward your employer and superior, your company and your country. A small American flag pin is very appropriate at this time without being chauvinistic.

Setting the Limits

The global woman maintains control in her meetings. Men have a tendency to test the *availability* of a woman and the laws of sexual harassment are not applicable in most other countries outside the United States, so she has to make her own laws work. Certain cultures, such as Latin American and north Mediterranean, make a habit of female conquest; so a visiting American businesswoman is seen as fair game and quite an achievement. Americans are warm and friendly people, particularly to strangers. It is one of the most attractive traits of the culture and well-appreciated by other cultures; however, foreigners often misread this approachability. You may have to deal with an approach early in the relationship, or it may come during a social time. Whichever way, it has to be handled with tact, firmness, and with an air of finality. Nothing can turn the clock back from a sexually provoked advance that is allowed to proceed. The relationship will never be professional again. The precautions are as follows:

- Keep the conversation business-like and steer it back to business if it is taking a suspicious direction.

- Hold meetings only in offices, official hotel meeting rooms, hotel lobbies, or on neutral territory such as chamber of commerce offices, consular offices, or in airports.

- Don't negotiate the deal in a social atmosphere. Entertainment time is for professional relationship building.

- Depersonalize by taking on the personae of your company: "Our company would like to entertain you tonight" or "My company would like to pick up the entertainment costs this evening."

- During social time, talk about culture, history, travel, news, general business issues, world politics (even religion)—anything, rather than personal problems or men and women. If the drink, conversation, or entertainment gets off-color, then claim tiredness and leave.

- If the going gets too difficult, you have the final weapon. Leave the region or country and ex-

plain that you cannot do business under the pre-
vailing conditions.

Bringing Something to the Deal

In demonstrating that by dealing with you the foreign
businessman can get some tangible benefit, you have got
to be armed with one.

Jane McIntosh was a human resource professional with
ICI, the chemical conglomerate. The company was working on a joint venture with Aramco in Saudi when disagreements came up regarding employment contracts and conditions of British personnel working in Saudi. When the
problem reached an impasse threatening to quash the whole
deal, Jane was asked by her directors to go over and solve
the issue. "Only if you give me sole authority to solve it,"
she said. She arranged a meeting with representatives of
Aramco and told them that she had already negotiated a
solution with her director back home and that she had the
sole authority, in writing, to execute it. Aramco got the
message loud and clear that Jane was the one and only person authorized to solve the problem. Their initial reserve,
doubts, and cultural instincts were put aside, and she got
the job done. Jane demonstrated at the outset that she had
the authority, capability, and the benefit for handling the
situation.

The Power Is in the Difference

The global woman accentuates the difference between
herself and the culture she is visiting. The global woman
builds in five tactical strategies which become second nature. These are:

- separation from the cultural stereotypes of
  women

- definition of herself through personal image (appropriate business attire and accessories)
- the definition of a strictly business relationship with clear limits
- the use of business conversation and behavior
- an understanding of the local culture and basics of the language

By demonstrating her differences, the global woman has developed a power and advantage few men can achieve. The age of globalization could well be the age of the global woman. Through her active leadership and tenacity, the world could in the future experience a new massive social revolution as the almost four billion women determine their futures based on choice of education, political representation, and freedom from social barriers.

Global Women and Their Power

Some western businesswomen have long realized the power they have in conducting negotiations, selling, and managing. When the message breaks through, they can surge to the top.

My business career started in the late 1950s. In England, it was rare for women to be in any business role other than the typing pool. It wasn't until the late '70s that things started to change. Lloyd's of London admitted women brokers after much doubt, suspicion, and macho comment. Initially it was odd dealing with a woman: I wasn't sure how to handle it. I was confused, uncertain and generally critical. Clearly, the women were in control; it was the men who were disadvantaged. The women I interacted with were remarkably successful at their job and clearly knew how to handle the male confusion. Instinctively, global women seem to know this.

Intuition

Global women also know that their intuitive abilities are far more sensitive to cultural fine-tuning than most men. Their abilities to read body language, voice inflection, and mental attitudes are an awesome weapon in the cross-culture competency race. They can sense subtle shifts in perception and point of view and can discern genuity from fake.

Likewise, the global woman is able to develop information, get support, and achieve progress from men which other men would never be able to obtain. Often men tend to confide in women before they confide in men. Men from a culture unfamiliar to women in business will be charmed, persuaded, and flattered by the global woman. She will be appreciated, protected, and remembered.

Easy Humility

The global woman also recognizes that her easy ability for humility comes in handy in her cross-culture communication with members of the group-based. Far more understanding of this feature than most men, she is able to demonstrate modesty and withdrawal at the appropriate time. But she still has to remember that she is separate and removed from the culture she is visiting. It's all a question of intelligent application of a very useful skill.

Trainer Teacher

The global woman recognizes that her role is one of educator, trainer, and teacher. Most of the world wants to learn her skills and acquire her knowledge but cannot see any way to achieve them. The process of economic globalization is one of the practical roads toward this enlightenment, and the global woman is the message carrier. In the

United States, there are more women in the speaking and training profession than there are men. There are more women members of the National Speakers Association than men. It seems that women take to educating others more naturally than men. The global organization will be dependant on women to educate its work force.

Customer Consciousness

The global economy, like the new economy, is customer led. Customer service and attention has become the *female* profession. Customer-led companies will be led by women in the future even more so than they are now. Women tend to be better listeners and more attuned to customers' needs than men are. Also they are often better than men at co-operating, sharing, and collaborating under pressure. The global woman is an expert at customer service. It is this skill that she will teach and demonstrate to the rest of the world that has scant understanding of the standards of customer service which is, by the way, often taken for granted by Americans.

Keeping Confidence

Global women are trustworthy. Trust is a high quality commodity in the global marketplace. A combination of distance, lack of knowledge, stereotyping, and cross-culture incompetence can add up to lack of trust–whether it be accurate or misplaced–and most businesspeople the world over are reluctant to do business with people they neither know nor trust. Women are trusted more than men, and the global woman knows that. Executives will trust her with confidences and secrets that they would not share with most men. The global woman recognizes this and knows that her reputation is the most valuable asset she has.

Patience

Patience is a virtue anywhere, but in the world of diverse and confusing cultures, it is an outright advantage. The global woman has the patience of Job. We have seen that cross-culture competence includes coping with the differing attitudes toward the importance of time. This is the root of more culture collisions than most issues. The patience to deal with these incongruities and to maintain decorum throughout the process is a quality sorely to be desired. It is considered that women have more patience in their nature than do men. If this is the case, then women have a quality to engage in global business which many men lack.

Empathy

To say that the world understands the existence of culture collision after September 11, 2001, would be an understatement. The realization that there are such deep misunderstandings between humans came as a shock to most people living in the west who thought that the progress of globalization was proceeding nicely–apart from a few hotheads who threw eggs at World Trade delegates and slung cream pies at Bill Gates. "Why do they hate us?" was the question of the hour, still unanswered, basically because there is no understandable answer. In 1882 a Sioux chief was reported to have asked his people the same question about the actions of the U.S. government but got no answer.

The hate that breeds in the rich culture dish of ignorance, prejudice, poverty, and fundamental religion is so distant from the breakfast table of the American home that it cannot be explained by morning show pundits and make any sense. But dad still has to kiss his wife and kids goodbye and go to work in an Indonesian-owned company, and mom has to close the sale of a house to an Indian businessman and his family. Events have a habit of pulling us up short and demonstrating to us that we had better start to learn how to live with one another and understand why some people think and act the way they do.

Empathy is our first lesson and it is defined as the ability to accept the differences between people and build on them in a positive manner. The British may come to accept American directness as honesty rather than rudeness; the Americans may accept British bureaucratic procrastination as sensible caution rather than obstinacy; the silent Finn may be able to accept the talkative Italian for his communication skills; and the exaggerated courtesy of the Japanese may be accepted by the pragmatic German as more acceptable than hostility.

The global woman knows that she has the skills of cultural empathy more than most. She has the ability to imagine herself in the shoes of a person from another culture and can share and understand this individual's feelings and attitudes.

Japanese Change

Change in the lifestyle and traditional role of women is more evident in Japan today than in most cultures. In a country that has had to reckon with extreme self-examination in recent times and take a hard look, if it can, at some of its most ingrained ethnicity, the role of women in society, politics, and business is catching Japanese men off-guard.

The younger, well-educated generation of urban women who now seek careers in major international corporations do not accept the traditional roles of their mothers and grandmothers. Filial obligations still persuade them to go through the matchmaking protocol but on *their* terms. Matchmakers never experienced anything like this in the

old days–young women now say no. They are no longer
the retiring, submissive porcelain-faced dolls of the gei-
shas.

No longer prepared to stay at home cleaning, cooking,
and *being nice* while their salarymen husbands spent all
day and practically all night at the corporate gristmill, they
are seeking divorces and careers. This social revolution led
Prime Minister Koizumi to recently appoint five women
to his cabinet–including the foreign minister.

Senior jobs in corporations are still hard to come by for
women but the revolution is on. Yoshie Kitagawa, for instance, runs a predominantly female equities team at ABN
Amro Bank in Tokyo, flying in the face of traditional attitudes–particularly in the conservative banking and financial services sector.

These profound changes are being driven, not from
outside, but by women themselves. History may show that
Japanese women are the change catalyst which will mold a
new Japanese culture more suitable for working in a global world.

The twenty-first century belongs to women–in particular the western women–just as most past centuries seem to
have belonged to men. Now we see the shifting of family
responsibilities, the changing of educational demographics, and the altering of business and governmental leadership patterns. All of this indicates a rising trend, and we
are only at the cusp of the century. This could be the biggest culture shift of history when it's looked at one thousand years from now. The effect of this massive move will
be dramatically important to most non-western cultures and
possibly a cause for considerable culture collision in years
to come. But the sea change will come from within the
culture and will be led by the women themselves.

10

Global Presentation Skills

Sooner or later (some people like to hope it will be later rather than sooner) the global manager will be expected to make a presentation to a cross-cultured audience or to a group that largely consists of people not belonging to the manager's culture base.

Special skills will be needed if the occasion is to be a success. Careers are made and destroyed every day during public presentations. We all know of examples where speakers could have used the *power of the podium* to enhance their careers, but they didn't–usually because they didn't know how. Even worse, they were unable to motivate and communicate to their audience in an effective manner: this may have resulted in a ruined project or a shattered sale due to the lack of some very basic presentation skills.

Video interaction over Intranet networks is commonplace in the modern global company; video conferencing and network seminars are highly popular for long distance personnel; and customer service demonstrations across committed satellite transmissions are fast becoming the way businesses keep in touch. These presentations are just like standing at the front of the room with a real live audience of warm bodies; however, the *warm bodies* are watching your every move when you are in the same room with them. Your ability to please, influence, and inspire is equal to your ability to displease, deflate, and defuse. With the right questions answered and the right techniques understood, the live presentation experience is not only pleasurable but also business promoting and career enhancing as well.

High quality presentation skills are an enormous attribute to the cross-culture competent manger. Only through capable communication can diverse cultures understand each other, become educated, and feel encouraged. Only through skilled communication can stockholders, customers, and associates receive an effective and accurate corporate message. Thousands of speeches are presented daily throughout the world to culturally diverse audiences. Varying styles and techniques must be adopted when addressing these specific groups.

First you must know what you want to achieve. What's the desired outcome? Many managers fail to ask themselves this question. They just accept the speaking slot at the conference or at the sales briefing as par for the course–part of the job.

Preparation

John Burke was an up-and-coming manager in the international commercial department of Chase Bank. He had the opportunity to address an international meeting of managers in New York about U.S. banking systems–a chance to shine among his peers. He made a professional presentation and was delighted when it was all over. His first question after he stepped down from the platform following the applause was, "How did I do?"

"Fine, Johnnie, just fine," his friends replied. Six hours later few could remember what he spoke about. Twenty-four hours later few could even remember his name. What had John done wrong? Why did his chance to shine and make a reputation fall flat? The answer: John had thought more about himself and the speech than about the people who had to listen to it.

Speaking, presenting, training, educating–it's all about conveying thoughts, ideas, information, and understanding for the benefit of the audience and helping them to make progress in their lives. So, keeping in mind that every speaking engagement is important and having been asked to make a presentation at an important conference, how should we proceed?

- Write down what you want your audience to do as a result of your presentation. What understanding do you want them to have after the event? What action do you want them to take? What do you want them to do differently?

- What do you want them to remember two weeks after the meeting?

- Who does your audience consist of? What is the culture mix? What do you know about their skills, their knowledge, and attitudes? What are their real needs?

See how all these questions are directed to the interests of the audience and what you as presenter need to bear in mind as you prepare your talk. Rodney Chase, Chairman of BP America, prior to addressing a Houston Partnership Conference on U.S./U.K. trade, sat down and wrote out the intention, "I want to tell the audience that BP is more of an American company than a British company." A simple statement and a dramatic revelation–something most people in his audience did not know and probably still remember long after the event.

Action Plan

According to Tony Jeary in his book, *Inspire Any Audience*, there are three basic actions you can aim for in determining what you want your audience to do as a result of your presentation:

1. change of attitude
2. learn something
3. attainment of or improvement of a skill

This is the goal of your presentation, and it should be the most important focus of the preparation process. Once you have written down your main purpose, you are then ready to move into the key technique of *rememberability*.

Memory Chip

Leaving your audience with an item of memorable value is a superb skill. Our problem as presenters is that all too often we drown our people in facts and material. Far better to leave them with one small nugget that they will remember and can take to the bank. Could you explain your concept in one sentence on the telephone to your mother? Can you tell it to a perfect stranger in the time it takes to descend three floors in an elevator? If not, then chances are your audience won't be able to remember what you were trying to tell them.

The memory chip needs to be a carefully constructed, well-honed statement containing strong, emotive words and rounded phrases. Churchill knew how to do this, sometimes in a word but more often in a statement such as: "If you ask what is our aim? I reply that it is victory, victory at all cost, victory no matter how long or hard the road might be. . . ." That is a memorable statement–more than six decades after his presentation!

Audience Participation

Remember that the audience's time is more valuable than yours. There are more of them, so it's important that we realize that they are only in it for what they can get out of it. Everybody, yes, everybody, has the same goal in life that applies to every culture, gender, and age. It's called "What's in it for me?" As presenters, we tend to forget that eternal truth.

Before we can answer that question, we must know the demographics of the audience. The global manager must know the culture base of his audience, their education level, age grouping, job descriptions, and reason for attending the meeting. According to Tony Jeary, if this is a compulsory or training meeting, the attendees can be divided into four types:

- prisoner–doesn't want to be there

- vacationer–goes anywhere to get away from work

- graduate–knows it all, so doesn't need to be there

- student–always wants to learn something new

During the meeting, however, an able presenter can change prisoners, vacationers, and graduates into students and have almost everyone dying for more. It's all a question of presentation skills, preparation, and providing exactly what's needed for the benefit of the audience and for their organization. No company on earth wants to send a group of people into a conference, seminar, or simple management meeting and find that it was a waste of everyone's time.

Label Attached

Within moments of standing up to speak, the audience has you labeled. Right or wrong, they have put you into a category such as interesting, energetic, boring, or unprepared. It may be inaccurate, but it is usually lasting. The key is to decide well before the presentation how you want to come across to the audience. That decision will be largely based on understanding the people you will address. A German engineer speaking to an American work force would be strongly advised not to be rigid, formal, and militaristic. An American salesman addressing an Oriental group of dealers would not want to come over as a *gung-ho, slap-'em-on-the-back type* as the dark-suited Oriental gentlemen look on with blank expressions.

The key is to balance your own personality and core character with sensitivity for the culture of the audience. Under no circumstances should you subvert your true self for something different. Audience members can spot a phony from the back of the room. It is an important measure of cross-culture competence to be audience savvy.

Feature Presentation

Now that we know our audience make-up and what we want to tell them, we can design the presentation. Organizing a speech is simply the ability to verbalize thoughts in a coherent manner so that the individual audience members can understand them. Many speakers find it difficult to make the change from written word to spoken word or alternatively writing down what they say. The reason is that we speak in short plain sentences and we normally write in longer descriptive phrases. Our reading comprehension rate is faster than our listening rate. This is particularly true with audiences who do not have English as a first language or when the services of a translator are required. Reading a speech verbatim from written text is a hopeless nightmare of boredom, waste of time, and misunderstanding for an audience.

A business presentation is normally organized according to one of five structures:

1. Chronological. Tracing events and facts through a time span. The development of a product, market, or concept, for example.

2. Importance. Categorizing material in order of priority.

3. Comparisons. Showing the pros and cons of issues and material.

4. Headings. Categorizing your material into, for example, geographic sections, departments, or products.

5. Bad news, good news. Delivering the painful information and explaining it. Then move into the good news of hope, opportunity, and the future.

We shall see from the culture specific detail later in this chapter that certain culture groups prefer one or more of these structures to other styles. Therefore, we have to take this into account during our preparation.

There are three parts to a presentation: introduction, body, and conclusion.

The introduction is where your reputation is made. Make it brief, attention catching, and interesting. The points or headlines of the body of the speech are the *meat and potatoes*. The conclusion is where the memories of the presentation are made. Finish with a *bang*–like the ending of a classic symphony.

The speech is now ready for putting on paper. Avoid the written speech if you possibly can. Many companies have their media or public relations department prepare written talks. Fine. Read them; understand them; and then throw them away. Please do not read corporate written statements unless you are likely to lose your job by not doing so! Put the information into a structure and language that fits *you and your audience*, not some guy in corporate thousands of miles away. Let your creativity have its way and feel empathy for the audience, and you will prepare a blockbuster presentation that will do both you and your audience credit.

It is also important to recognize that there are a number of practical questions to answer:

- At what time of day is the presentation to take place? After lunch? After dinner?
- How much time is allotted for the presentation?
- Will there be a question-and-answer period?
- What type of facility is the meeting to be held in?
- How many people are expected to attend?
- What types of visuals will be needed and what's available for your use?

- Will handouts be needed or appropriate for clarification and/or to take home?

Great presenters always looks relaxed, poised, and in control. Why is this so? Not only because they are experienced speakers but also because they have 'rehearsed' it–over and over again, usually in their heads!

Patricia Fripp has won every speaking award possible: Toastmasters International Golden Gavel Award; The National Speakers Association Cavat Award; its revered CPAE Speakers Hall of Fame Award; and she was elected the first woman president of that association. Fripp does 100 presentations annually all over the world for associations and Fortune 1000 companies and never fails to rehearse every presentation. Every point, every gesture, every platform movement is a practiced work of art. Fripp, of course, rehearses in front of mirrors, but, more importantly, she rehearses in her head. "As I take my early morning walk, I rehearse my talk. Every detail is in my head so that when the time comes I know instinctively what and when to say and do," she says.

If you are using visual aids and equipment, you should make sure you understand how to operate it–and that it works. Nothing is more frustrating for an audience than to have audio/visual engineers helping presenters with their equipment during valuable presentation time.

Know the room you will present in. Visit it early in the morning or the night before to check it out. Find out where the light controls are, where the podium will be located, and how the audience seating will be arranged. Finally, sit at the back of the room during a prior presentation if possible. It helps to understand the geography of the room layout and get the *feel* of the room, the audience, and the mood of the meeting.

Presentation Protocol

Several years ago an oil executive was giving a presentation in Saudi Arabia. He had never been there and flying long distance was tedious for him. He was an accredited expert geologist and his subject was the future of oil and gas reserve development in the Kingdom. He had not allowed sufficient time to get over jet lag nor acclimatize to the desert conditions. As he entered the exotic surroundings of the convention hall, its rich ambiance and the humid perfumed air took him aback. He was up next on the stage dressed in his dark suit and tie. Launching into his written presentation, he failed to recognize that there was a member of the Saudi royal family sitting on the front row. Feeling the heat, the executive removed his jacket and unbuttoned his top shirt button. He rounded off the disaster by telling a joke about a drunk. Needless to say, none of the audience heard anything he said. They were too concerned about the insult paid to the Saudi royal member to think of anything else.

That, of course, is protocol calamity, an extreme version. Unfortunately, it happens regularly when speakers either do not care or do not think about the local culture rules.

Every culture has protocol, which includes a list of unwritten rules of behavior applying to respect and behavior around public events and public figures. The office of the Head of State or of the Monarchy demands certain protocol, which has been practiced over decades or centuries in order to show respect for the office and the country it represents.

Meetings have protocol. The likelihood that there will be protocol increases if the function is a large, public affair, particularly if dignitaries are present. Dress is important in some instances. In 1973 I was invited to the Lord Mayor of London's Annual Dinner in my capacity as president of London Junior Chamber of Commerce. This grand occasion was held in the historic Mansion House in the City of London. Without checking, I arrived at the dinner in my tuxedo (which the English call a dinner jacket) and black tie. The other 500 guests, apart from one or two dressed as I was, were wearing tail coats and white ties. My formal presentation to the Lord Mayor was an embarrassment for me, and I almost went home. Chancellor of the Exchequer Sir Tony Barber–who arrived late in a dinner jacket–delivered the main speech of the evening. He stood to give his presentation and, after a quick glance around the magnificent room, he said, "Sorry about the fact that I'm in a dinner jacket–no disrespect my Lord Mayor–but, probably like one or two others here, I've just flown in from overseas and haven't had time to go home and change." Imagine my relief and my silent heartfelt thanks to Sir Tony. Now there was a speaker who took care of his audience!

Most audiences are very forgiving about minor lapses in protocol, but the cross-culture competent global manger should always be aware of the needs and requirements in the area. Later in the chapter we address protocol of various culture groups.

Interpreters and Language

You want your presentation to be properly understood and acted upon by everyone in the room. Not an unreasonable intention. But in our multicultural and multilinguistic world not everyone will understand what you say, so even if the majority can speak English tolerably well, it will benefit both you and your listeners to use the services of an interpreter.

Your interpreter will be your partner during the presentation and afterward during any question-and-answer session. Get to know him or her and recognize that the success of the occasion will be dependant on how well you understand each other. Take time to chat and be sociable beforehand if possible. It will be time well spent. Your interpreter will convey your feelings, your emotions, and your passion about your subject and will be your physical extension. It helps therefore to provide interpreters with a copy of your presentation material in advance; this may consist of the full written speech or your notes. You will, hopefully, not be speaking from the full written material (some interpreters find it difficult to follow along with a written speech while listening to the speaker–another reason for a beforehand session with the interpreter) but from your notes along with some considerable free range commentary. Interpreters are quite happy to get into the free range material if they understand the gist of your remarks and where you are heading in the speech. However, always be conscious of your interpreter and realize that he or she needs time to catch up, so speak slower than you normally would and intersperse your presentation with pauses after making specific points.

In the briefing you have with the interpreter, you should provide a glossary of technical terms or company jargon you may use that has limited appreciation to anyone outside the group. Also be sure that your English words meet the standards of the interpreter. Colloquialisms are OK only if they are appropriate and in common use. English is an abused language and professional interpreters are more often than not educated in the correct form, vocabulary, and style of the language.

There are two types of translation as follows:

1. Simultaneous Translation

Used in large conferences and multinational meetings, this works through the audio system with audience members wearing headphones.

The system should be checked and rehearsed before the presentation to be sure all the electronics work properly. In this system, the speaker is translated simultaneously–sometimes into several languages. Translators sit in soundproof booths often with a good view of the speaker who should make eye contact with the translators. This is important so that the speaker can receive cues, such as nods and signs, through the window from the translator and adjust the tempo of the delivery if necessary. If you are on a panel, remember that the translator can only hear you if your microphone is live. If you field questions from persons in the audience not using a microphone, you must repeat the question into your microphone for the benefit of the translation and for the audience audio. Sometimes audience members do not speak into their microphone correctly. In this case, tell them how to do so for the benefit of the translators. Remember it takes time for translators to catch up, particularly if, in your excitement, you speak too rapidly.

I made a short presentation at the World Conference of Junior Chamber International in Toronto in 1967. It was translated into eight languages for the multinational group. When it was over, I thought I had offended 75 percent of the audience. Only the English-speaking groups were clapping. In the longest half minute of the day, there was silence from the others. Then they clapped as the translators caught up with my conclusion.

Tip: The life of simultaneous translators is exacting, sometimes hectic, and they are often underpaid. They really do appreciate a kind remark and a *thank-you* from time to time, particularly during the presentation because they often get forgotten. Your consideration will probably make all the difference to the quality of your delivered message.

2. Consecutive Translation

Smaller meetings use consecutive translators particularly where there is a one-language audience. The speaker delivers one or two sentences, stops talking, and the translator interprets. In these circumstances, your presentation needs to be given in short sound bites. The success of the whole thing depends on the ability of the translator. Don't get an amateur.

Tom Britton worked in the Paris office of a large U.K. insurance broker. He was fairly bilingual in French and English. The firm held a client convention in Versailles and hired an interpreter so that Tom could deliver the technical part of the presentation in English. Not long into his presentation Tom stopped, turned to the interpreter, and said in perfect French, "I would be grateful if you would tell them what I am actually saying instead of giving them your own footnotes."

Check out your translators' credentials; check with someone who has used them before, and, if possible, have a *plant* in the audience who can let you know if the interpreter is not translating correctly or appropriately.

International Language

We can talk about our differences all day but, in the end, we are all human and it doesn't matter where your audience is from. There is a common language that communicates across cultures, nationalities, and genders: it's called *body language*. Your relationship with your audience will be made not only by the words you speak but also by the more subtle communication of movement, gestures, and facial expressions.

We can only exhibit effective body language when we are relaxed and have put the nerves under control where they belong. There is nothing wrong with *controlled* nerves; they add adrenaline to your presentation. Nerves can be controlled in the following ways:

- realizing that your audience wants you to win

- being 100 percent prepared

- looking forward to the benefits your presentation will bring to others

- taking deep breaths and doing other relaxation exercises

- thinking about the audience, not yourself

The international language of impressions kicks in the moment you step on the platform. There is a series of subconscious questions audience members ask themselves about speakers:

- Are they credible?

- Do they relate to me?

- Do they have anything worthwhile for me?

- Am I interested?

Real credibility in front of an audience is gained in the first three minutes. This time is vital for managers presenting to any audience but more so when in front of a multicultural group. They will be suspicious and pessimistic particularly about someone they have never seen nor met before. The very first thing a manager must do is to establish credibility on the platform. Credibility is judged by:

- depth of knowledge

- level of preparedness
- background and experience
- appearance
- enthusiasm
- body language
- control

Audiences respond to a speaker's presence rather than to credentials. They take a lot for granted when they hear about degrees and experience in the introduction, but they make up their minds about credibility when they watch and listen to the first three minutes. So in that all-important period of time, the manager has the opportunity to make a reputation. The keys are:

1. Be totally honest with them.
2. Be yourself.
3. Share personal experiences.
4. Be enthusiastic.
5. Be spontaneous.

Demonstrating that you are in control is vital. Believable people know that they are believable. It comes from being real and honest with oneself. Great people are credible because they are real, flat-out honest, and believable, so tell your audience that you have every right to be in front of them. You have the credentials, the experience, and the know-how. And then you demonstrate it as a skilled presenter.

Empathy is the understanding of how your audience feels, how it perceives your message, and how you find common links with them. We do this by referring to people the audience admires and by addressing the issues that are near to their personal goals. All this is achieved through the audience research we do in the preparation phase.

A Vital Management Skill

Management communication skills are much neglected throughout the world; indeed, communication skills are a dire need if man is to live happily together. The cross-culture competent manager is an expert communicator and can stand in front of any audience at a moments notice and inform and inspire.

Anyone who wishes to improve these vital skills should consider joining Toastmasters International. Located in over 8,500 clubs in seventy countries with a membership in excess of 180,000 members, this organization is a perfect place to hone and develop speaking abilities. Those who need to start right at the beginning quickly make the grade into Competent Toastmasters and the qualification CTM. It provides members with the aptitude to stand on their feet at a moment's notice and give short, coherent, and intelligible talks without the usual gut-wrenching anxiety.

Each culture and country has its own preferred audience and presentations style. Reputations, as we have mentioned, are made and lost on the presentation platform. It would be a wise move for cross-culture competent managers to be familiar with these preferences. Let us look at a cross section.

International Presenters Checklist

–Latin America–

Argentina

This huge beautiful country is the second largest economy in South America. It resembles Europe in its sophistication, particularly in the capital Buenos Aires. Audiences are anxious to learn and understand the business methods of the western nations, but there is a cynicism and negativity in the business population as to whether Argentina can ever take its place as a worthy international economic partner.

Language: Spanish

Dress code: Man–business suit with a tie (dark suits are preferred in the evening). Woman–suit.

Toast: Praise the country, business, and the host.

Speech: Greet important audience members and honored hosts and dignitaries. Audience may talk to each other during the presentation. Humor is enjoyed, providing it is witty and clever. Audience participation is limited. The country's economic successes are popular with audiences.

Avoid: Local politics, the economic downturn, military dictators, Eva Peron.

Body language: Audiences appreciate informality once they get used to the speaker. Direct eye contact.

Brazil

Brazilian audiences are often undisciplined, interrupting, and chaotic, but they are intelligent, educated, and keen to learn. Loquacious and verbose, they use gestures and facial expressions to make their point of view known. Various audience members may want to make their individual opinions heard.

Language: Portuguese

Dress code: Man–well-tailored smart business suit, tie, quality shoes. Woman–conservative attire (very important).

Toast: The success of Brazil, soccer stars, and local teams.

Speech: Pay respects to important guests and audience members. Training seminars will have 100 percent participation, possible heckling, and multiple opinions.

Avoid: Argentina, politics. Do not talk about the U.S.A. as *America*–Brazilians think they live in America.

Body language: Maintain good eye contact. Audiences appreciate energetic movement and gestures. Maintain the image of seniority. Maintain control.

Mexico

Mexico's close proximity to the United States has meant that many meetings of U.S. companies are held in this country. Many meeting facilities, therefore, are familiar with U.S. needs. Mexican business people are suspicious of U.S. companies and the history of broken promises by the U.S. government is their example.

Language: Spanish

Dress code: Man–conservative dark suit and tie. Woman–a dress or skirt and blouse.

Toast: Wish individuals great professional success. Praise the beauty of Mexico and the history of its people.

Speech: Be sure that your introduction includes your credentials. Pay respect to VIPs at the meeting and to audience members who have achievements. Praise Mexican successes. Humor is appreciated if it is subtle and clever.

Avoid: Comments about Mexican problems, jokes about women, U.S./Mexican history, religion, money.

Body language: Eye contact can be made but should

not be intense or too long. Avoid pointing to a person or being too effusive.

–Europe–

France

France is the enigma of Europe, the cradle of western civilization, and the economic powerhouse of the region. The French people live in a world of their own (the center of which is France), and they know very little of the outside world. They believe that most of the fine attributes of modern democracies emanated from France. Some of the best global companies are based in France. The people are creative and well educated.

Language: The French are very proud of their language. Most of the population speaks no other. Increasingly, however, business people speak good English and want to take every opportunity to learn more and practice it. An English-speaking presenter should use a well-qualified translator.

Dress Code: Man–dark business suit and tie. Woman–smart, well-tailored suit, not too overdressed in a business setting (even for weekend meetings, a suit would be expected for the presenter. American style *dressing down* is deplored).

Toast: It is suitable to remark on the beauty of France and the ingenuity of the French people.

Speech: Be cheerful and bright. Unless you can speak business standard French, do not try to give the whole speech in French but use frequent French phrases (practice the pronunciation beforehand). Start off the speech with a welcome in French. Then use the interpreter. Use British/English rather than American/English. Ideas are very important to the French, and you may find them engaged in spirited debate during your session or at question time. Greeting VIPs is not customary. Humor is appreciated if it is light and sophisticated. They would enjoy it if it plays against the British or the Americans.

Avoid: Comments about the government, history since the revolution, Napoleon, ethnic issues, religion, Algeria, Devil's Island, French/American public opinion.

Body language: The French are very effusive: they love to debate and argue, and they respect that in others. Status is more important than sex, so take command of the platform whatever your gender. Gesticulation gets more pronounced the further south the meeting. Eye contact is intense, even to the point of intimidating North Americans. Speakers should be more formal than casual and should be cautious about using some American audience interaction methods.

Germany

The German reunification and reestablishment of its capital city in Berlin makes it the largest member nation by far in the European Union. An industrial powerhouse, its business has developed a considerable global presence. German audiences are formal and respect seniority, qualifications, degrees, doctorates, and evidence of learned approval such as published papers and authorship of technical books. Time is of the essence. All meetings, sessions, and presentations will start and finish exactly on time. German business is hierarchical and consensual. Any participation will be done strictly on a seniority basis. Decisions take time to filter through various inclusive committees.

Language: The bulk of the population only speaks German. Increasingly, business people speak good English, and schools are putting English education at the top of the curriculum. Other European languages are also considered important and vital for executives who wish to make progress in their companies in the European Union. Interpreters should be used to make precise translation of technical data and visuals.

Dress code: Man–dark business suit and tie. Woman–trouser or skirt suit in conservative colors. Men may remove jackets in warm weather. Country resort meetings may also be in suits, but lighter colors are acceptable.

Toast: Make a small speech. Admire the natural beauty of Germany. Raise your glass but do not clink. End by saying "Prost." If you are receiving a toast, give a small speech in reply and also end with "Prost."

Speech: Start with a few words of welcome in German. Check the grammar, vocabulary, and the pronunciation with a translator. When using a translator, speak in full complete sentences, and then pause. In German, the most important word in a sentence is usually the last one. They could get annoyed if it takes time to come through. Pay respects to any VIPs and acknowledge senior management who may be present. Presentations in Germany are like academic lectures: they are packed with information and facts, all of which must be supported by credible backup-source evidence and verification. The audience will appreciate a question-and-answer period during which time you will be asked to verify some of your remarks and how you reached your conclusions. Jokes are inappropriate and humor is normally reserved for social occasions.

Avoid: Reference to Germany's twentieth-century history, ethnic issues, sex, politics, religion.

Body language: Speaking style is formal, clean-cut, and efficient. Stand behind the lectern. Do not lean on the lectern or walk around the podium–you will lose authority. Eye contact is direct.

United Kingdom

The British people are divided as to whether their future is in Europe, on their own, or in close association with the United States. At the moment they are muddling along in typical British fashion–half in and half out of Europe–and taking a leadership role in the allied coalition against terrorism. Europeans, mainly the French and the Germans, are critical and nonplussed about this stance but are not surprised. British audiences are generally pro-American and anti-Europe, but inevitably the tide of events will take Britain into the European Monetary Union. They will probably balk at political union for many years. The United Kingdom is a prosperous country with numerous huge global enterprises. It is the largest foreign investor in the United States. Many American companies regard Britain as the right place to invest their European representation.

Language: Few British people speak any other language except English. If another language is spoken, then it is basic French. There is a major difference between British/English and American/English, and the only people who can translate effectively are English people who have lived in the USA for a few years, or vice versa.

Dress code: Man–well-cut dark suit and tie. Woman–dark skirt suit. Minimum jewelry. Country or weekend meetings can be business casual, particularly in the summer, but it is best to check. The British are not as clothes conscious as other Europeans. However, almost every business male owns a tuxedo. Professional men and women attend a score of formal dinners during the year where men wear dinner jackets and women wear dark business suits or evening gowns.

Toast: Official dinners inevitably have a royal toast: "Ladies and gentlemen, the queen." Everybody stands and replies, "The queen." If you give a toast, make a small speech that can be humorous and personal. The recipient of a toast will reply with a short speech of modesty and thanks.

Speech: After dinner speaking is a ritual in Britain. Formal and filled with protocol, almost every organization, association, club, and business in the country has a dinner function at which speeches are made and toasts proclaimed. Good after dinner speeches are amusing, clever, and articulate, and people can gain a reputation as a good *after dinner speaker*. Most business leaders are expected to do some after dinner speaking. Start by addressing the presence of dignitaries, which in England can sound like this: "My Lords, my Lord Mayor, Lady Mayoress, ladies and gentlemen." Check the list of attendees beforehand and get advice. Business seminars are moving increasingly to the American style, but the average British audience is still more formal, remote, and slightly cynical. Don't expect much response. British audiences are reserved and modest and dislike speakers blowing their own trumpet. Humor is appreciated if it's subtle, amusing, and self-deprecating. The British love understatement and clever, sharp, cutting wit.

Avoid: Critical reference to the monarchy, Europe, mad cow disease, foot and mouth disease, British bureaucracy.

Body language: British audiences prefer reserved speakers who keep good eye contact and use verbal dexterity to keep attention. They become cynical and bored if the presentation is too *American*. Refrain from asking for audience participation: it is not generally appreciated.

–Asia–

Japan

Literacy in Japan is close to 100 percent, and 95 percent of the population has completed high school. The lives of young people are filled with examinations and qualification, so the pressure to study and achieve good grades is intense. Working within the group-based culture type means that all decisions are taken within the group with little or no personal recognition. Dominant in the Japanese culture is the need to save face. There are constant pressures to conform and not let the group down. Ethnocentricity is strong as is male dominance. Age is revered. The Japanese are more subjective than objective and, as a result, depend on their feelings rather than on facts and figures. Audiences in Japan are not receptive to outside opinions of foreigners unless someone they respect introduces them and the information provided will be useful to them.

Language: Few westerners can penetrate the hidden nuances of the Japanese language with its codes and significances. Fortunately for the western presenter, most Japanese are taught English from the age of twelve. Translators must be used, but they can be a problem if the speaker is not familiar with Japanese culture. The western propensity to be blunt will not be interpreted to the group that way. The translator will put the statement into a cloud of vagueness and innuendo so as not to offend the audience; then his or her superior will criticize them for lack of clarity.

Dress code: Man–ubiquitous dark blue suit, white shirt and tie. Woman–conservative dark skirt suit, no trousers, minimum jewelry and perfume.

Toast: A business social event may be an opportunity to make a toast to celebrate and honor a group or an entity, not an individual. A short, formal speech and gift giving are usually acceptable, but check the circumstances and the protocol before doing this. Also inform the recipients beforehand.

Speech: Your introduction is critical for the success of your presentation. If possible, the most senior person present should provide it. It will list all your academic credentials, business experience, and position together with your experience in Japan. Begin by recognizing important guests and attendees in order of seniority. Learn a few phrases in Japanese and start with these. Relate to your introducer and say how much of an honor it is to be invited to speak to such an esteemed audience. Keep sentences short and give time for the translator to think out the ways in which the remarks can be conveyed to the audience. It will rarely be a direct translation–it will be an interpretation. After the translator has finished the sentence, smile or bow your head slightly at the audience. They want to maintain a good relationship with you, and you must convey your relationship with them. They may smile back, although a smile can sometimes indicate disapproval. Never use humor in a formal speech. It may be used lightly in the question-and-answer session.

Avoid: Reference to WWII, the Imperial family, bank failures, a sense of urgency, ethnic issues, fishing, whale catching, and environmental issues.

Body language: Avoid direct eye contact. Women will avert their eyes. Be respectful, formal, and non-emotional. Use gestures with caution and avoid pointing with a finger. Indicate something with your arm extended with the palm up.

China

The Chinese audience is anxious to learn from the best of the west. They have an admiration of European artistic creativity, for American efficiency and ingenuity, and for British and French political systems and technological advances. Where they do feel they have something to teach the west is that, like Muslims, they have a sense of moral righteousness and that their superior values make them a truly great race. It is a culture where individualism is taboo and everyone works for the collective. Subordinates are told what to do and parents, teachers, bosses, and managers must be obeyed. The search for virtue is more important than the search for truth, even between disagreeing parties.

Language: Increasing numbers of rising young managers speak English, but you will still need a translator. The best have spent time in western universities. Make sure the one you choose has a working understanding of business and can relate to your material. Prepare extensive handouts and data sheets in Chinese and go through them during your meeting. All visuals should be in Chinese. Power Point presentations are well-known in China and can be prepared there with little problem.

Dress code: Man–dark suit (avoid black) with tie. Woman–skirt (below knee level) or trouser suit (avoid white). Chinese people tend to be more casual than westerners and will often attend business events in semi-casual attire, but the speaker needs to be formally dressed to convey authority.

Toast: We see television news from China of formal dinners with toasts between heads of state. Toasting is a feature of good relations. Glasses are filled and held toward the group or the individual. No clinking. You are expected to drink all the contents. Propose a toast with a short speech and receive one also with a short reply. Pay compliments to the great economic miracles of China.

Speech: Speaking has a long tradition in China and audiences listen carefully with politeness and patience. It is important to understand the education and background of your audience as this may vary considerably. Start with a welcome in Chinese. Go to a language teacher to educate you in grammar and pronunciation. Pay respect to Chinese VIPs in order of seniority and your colleagues and managers in the same way. Work with the translator to *pace* your talk. Humor is appreciated if it is to the point and appropriate.

Avoid: Jokes about their language, customs and sex; do not refer to human rights issues, politics, crime, religion, Chinese/U.S. relations, Taiwan, Tibet and women's rights; avoid slang or jargon and sports figures of speech.

Body language: Be respectful and courteous. Eye contact is direct, but women will probably look away. Aggressive or emphasized gestures and loud laughing will not be appreciated.

Indonesia

This country has the largest Islamic population in the world, a huge oil economy, and almost impossible geography consisting of over 13,000 islands covering 5,000 kilometers east to west and 2,000 kilometers north to south. Indonesia spans three time zones. Politically volatile yet stable at the present time, this enterprising, active country has an ambitious population of energetic, bright, and well educated young people, most of whom want to take part in the world's economic opportunities as soon as possible. Your speech or even the event will probably not start on time. Relax; any indication of impatience will have a negative effect.

Language: Bahasa Indonesian, a language related to Malay, is not easy for westerners to understand. A few speak Dutch and English. It will be necessary to employ an interpreter.

Dress code: Man–lightly colored lightweight suit and tie. Woman–businesslike skirt below the knee and long-sleeved blouse.

Toast: Alcohol is not permitted in this Islamic nation.

Speech: Pay respect to people in senior public positions. Indonesians are very friendly and wish for harmony and understanding. They are used to hearing long and tiresome speeches from their political leaders that they listen to in a differential mood, so an interesting and informative speech would be light relief. They listen carefully to foreigners but do not always understand the content. Unfortunately, you may never know this as they are unlikely to tell you. Light humor is appreciated–for example, your efforts to learn Bahasa.

Avoid: References to corruption, bribery, military issues, politics, human rights, Muslim problems. Also avoid pointing with the forefinger, patting on the head and standing with your hands on your hips (a symbol of anger).

Body language: Gestures should be kept to a minimum. Be respectful and polite, yet with control and authority. Audience interaction will be negligible. Applause will be polite but not effusive.

India

There are over 250 million people with degrees in India. The bulk of the educated population speaks good English. They have a broad general knowledge as well as a specialty (engineer, doctor, architect). They are articulate, creative, hard working, and entrepreneurial. Innovation is a feature of the culture, and a look at India's past will demonstrate how many modern day sciences sprang from the Aryan mind, such as time keeping, geometry, and astronomy. Although the caste system is illegal, it still dominates the spirit of Indian life. Hierarchy is alive and well, although people of lower castes have risen to the head of government and most western businesses promote from merit.

Language: There are 14 major languages in India with 300 minor ones; however, the official languages are Hindi and English. For a business meeting in a major city, it would probably be unnecessary to use an interpreter; nevertheless, I recommend having one on hand in case a question is asked in a language you don't understand, which could well be the case.

Dress code: Man–business suit and tie. Woman–suit with long sleeves and skirt below the knee; a brightly colored sari or a dress with sleeves may also be worn. Be careful not to use leather accessories: this may offend some people.

Toast: Many Indians do not drink alcohol, but toasts do take place from time to time. A small flowery speech celebrating the individual or the group can be made followed by a wish for continued success.

Speech: Smile. Indian people love to smile, and they always notice it in others. It will relax the audience and break the ice. Your introducer should emphasize your academic qualifications, awards, and business status. Recognize VIPs and senior people in attendance. Most educated Indians know the English language better than the average English or American, and they love to hear (and speak) in long cadences with elaborate vocabulary. Down to earth, *give-me-the-facts* speeches will not go down well. Information has to be incorporated in descriptive passages and stories. Indians are good listeners and love to hear about new business opportunities. Comment on their beautiful country (which hopefully you have had the opportunity to see) and on their rich history. Question time could be an eager occasion when participants will stand and often deliver their own speeches, which the chairman will be reluctant to stop unless it becomes argumentative. Indians do not understand or appreciate slang and colloquialisms.

Avoid: Reference to Muslim/Hindu conflicts, politics, pollution, government bureaucracy, corruption, beggars, poverty, Kashmir, Pakistan.

Body language: A respectful manner is appreciated. Avoid demonstrative gesticulation and pacing on the platform or around the room. Eye contact is direct. Some women may avoid it.

Australia

Australians like to *cut down the tall poppy*, in other words, deflate people with airs. Their culture stems from the days of being a British penal colony and the convicts' attitude toward their overseers. Australian audiences, therefore, tend to have a cynical attitude toward *big shots* and anyone who cannot justify their reason for being a speaker/ presenter. Facts are given the highest validity as Australians reason from an objective point of view. Feelings, emotions, and intuition are not trusted as they are in Asia. As the culture mix of Australia changes, so perhaps will the perceptions. Audiences are similar to those in the United States with a participative, interactive, fun-loving attitude and a willingness to learn something that will enhance their lives and careers.

Language: Most Australians speak English; some call it *strine*. They are proud of their accent and slang which definitely separates them from the English. The American presenter needs to check the numerous books that detail the different meanings of certain words. Some can be embarrassing.

Dress code: Man–dark business suit and tie in a business setting. Woman–suit. Smart casual is also customary for conventions and weekend meetings.

Toast: Toasts are informal and usually humorous.

Speech: Acknowledge guests and the beautiful Australian scenery. They are very proud of their cities, particularly Sydney and Perth. The Olympic Games 2000 showed Australia as a top world-class country. Australians are independent and ethnocentric. They like to be perceived as rugged, individualistic, and open-minded. Their egalitarianism stresses a high minimum standard of well-being for the whole of society. Emphasis is on personal ability. Be friendly, relaxed, modest, and unpretentious. They are not easily impressed. Try and avoid being nervous, overly important, and officious. Humor is very important and a way of life with Australians. They like clever wit, tinged with some sarcasm. They love stories about over-coming adversity and making success out of defeat.

Avoid: Comments about aboriginal land rights, the British monarchy, religion, racism.

Body language: Eye contact is direct. Be easygoing, relaxed, and motivating, but not too *gung-ho.*

All professional managers understand the importance of good communication skills. Global managers, however, must have this ability in multiple proportions–even if only to keep away from trouble.

11

Bribery, Corruption, and Other Jail Time

"Do not mistake bribery for corruption."
Vladimir Rushailo, Russian Minister for the Interior, March 2001

In the Yorkshire city of Huddersfield, the firm of James Sykes and Sons has been in business since 1846. They manufacture carpet looms–huge sophisticated pieces of equipment that can make great lengths of patterned carpet at phenomenal speed. Sykes' agents and customers are located throughout the world from Thailand to Turkey, India to Iran, and New Zealand to New England. In the late '60s they were at the top of the tree in their business. There was hardly a carpet manufacturer anywhere who did not operate a Sykes loom.

One day Roger Sykes, great-grandson of the founder, introduced me to Jim Ross, the firm's international sales director. He told tales of deals with officials in high places and how he gets spare parts through customs in Madras. We sat around the table in awe. This man seemed to know everybody worth knowing in every country worth going to. But that was mild compared to what he told us next. Not only was he making arrangements to ship an Aston Martin automobile to a cabinet minister in Thailand, but he also had engineered a place at Oxford for the son of the governor of Andhra Pradesh. I don't know how much he knew about carpet looms, but he certainly knew how to grease the wheels of commerce in the third world. Had I finally figured out the reason for the U.K.'s global reach?

Show Me the Money

It is probably the second oldest profession. Call it what you like–baksheesh, *mordida*, dash, tea money, spiffs, cadeau, fines, gifts, special fees, access or oil–it's still a bribe. At one time bribery and corruption was ubiquitous in business and trade the world over until civilization realized that this practice has no place in an orderly commercial system that desires to expand and engage in effective competition. However, these practices are inherent and deeply rooted in certain countries and cultures to the point that it is an accepted (and sometimes expected) way of life and sustenance. Second to terrorism, bribery and corruption are regarded by many as the single most important scourge of humanity and, in some cases, the two are inseparable.

The Berlin-based organization, Transparency International, does an annual survey known as the Corruption Perceptions Index (CPI). It ranks countries based on the degree to which corruption is perceived to exist among government officials, public servants, and politicians. According to its 2001 report, bribery and corruption are alive and well in most every country. Even generally clean and pressed Sweden was mentioned in the report because seven Swedish companies and one Swedish individual were blacklisted by the World Bank and disbarred from tendering for its financed contracts when a bribery scandal rocked the institution in April 2001, and several employees were sacked for receiving kickbacks to encourage contracts favoring Swedes.

Then Russian Minister for the Interior, Vladimir Rushailo, lost his job shortly after he made the above quote, but it does demonstrate the utter confusion that exists in some cultures between bribery and corruption. It's as if bribery may be OK when made with policemen, but corruption is not OK if it's made with politicians. Perhaps in some minds it's all a question of the amount of money involved.

Russian Salary

Corruption (or bribery) is splashed across Russia's newspapers every day. Naturally the big numbers associated with the big names are good media fodder. Regional tsars, cabinet ministers and ex-presidents are all part of the racket. There is an old Russian proverb, "I curse you to live on your salary," and another saying is, "Corruption has saved Russia." Who can doubt that the Russian people are punch-drunk on the problem? There exists the tacit acceptance that bribery permeates the Russian way of life, that it is better to pay for free healthcare, free education, and housing services rather than no public services at all. In other words, it's better not to argue for your rights–just pay for them. Western managers working in Russia know that corruption is not restricted to the criminal classes; it is a perverse system of governance. It plagues the country across its eleven time zones and breeds poverty, suspicion, jealousy, and distrust in an already weak public confidence in democratic values. At least the lights are on. In the last twenty-five years, more attention has been paid to this issue than in the past twenty-five hundred years, and Russia now realizes that trade with the rest of the world is its only lifeline and that there is no turning back.

Uphill Fight

As in most world standards of trade, the United States cuts the mustard of regulation and endeavors to enforce agreements by leaning on the worst malfeasance economically. It is a long and arduous process often criticized because of its American or western demonstration of power against the weaker developing nations. More importantly, it is often seen as an attack by western values against deeply and historically held cultural systems–the data-based culture group trying to change the beliefs and processes of the relationship- and group-based culture groups.

For instance, take India. In a country where highwaymen are recognized as a social group and have their own honor system and where stealing crops is as honorable as growing them, it is not difficult to include *access payment* in the same category. It is all a matter of practical creativity to get the job done–something in which the Indian excels. The journey is more important than the destination, particularly if it is colored with innovation, brilliance, and flair. The flamboyant procession filled with bejeweled elephants, princely maharajas, and turbaned fire-eaters is the important part–not the anticlimax–of the final ceremony.

In a society that has looked after each other millennia after millennia, it is reasonable to believe that the systems of baksheesh will die hard. Top politicians cram the jails following high-level convictions in 2000 including Prime Minister P.V.N. Rao for bribing minor members of parliament for their votes. In April 2001, India's chief of the Central Board of Customs and Excise was arrested for *possessing assets disproportionate to his known sources of income*. Even the esteemed sport of cricket, one of the more laudable bequests of the British Raj, is not immune. In December 2000, the Board of Cricket Control imposed a life ban on Mohammad Heussin, former captain of the Indian cricket team, for fixing the results of matches in return for bribes in a global cricket betting racket.

Corruption afflicts South Asia at all levels of state and society. The world looks on in amazement as scarce resources, which should be applied to health, welfare, and education, are applied to massive arms procurement and infrastructure projects that afford political movers and power shakers to line their pockets. The thin line between accountability for corruption and political victimization often appears blurred in this region.

Do Not Pass Go

Bribery, as understood in the west, is jail time. When practiced in certain parts of the south and east, it is considered sensible business. However, in a world gone global, it has no place in free trade and open competition, and those governments who see the future of their countries in the international community are taking far-reaching and dramatic steps to end corruption, starting with their own bureaucracies. They are finding that it takes more effort, tenacity, and patience.

Law and the enforcement thereof is not easy to apply throughout a diverse and culturally different world, but the wish to level the global trade playing field has been so great in the last twenty-five years that giant steps have been taken to get the dirt moving equipment into action.

Moving the Goalposts

As a result of SEC investigations in the mid-1970s, over 400 U.S. companies admitted making questionable or illegal payments in excess of $300 million to foreign government officials, politicians, and political parties. The abuses ran the gamut–from bribery of high foreign officials to secure some type of favorable action by a foreign government to so-called facilitating payments that allegedly were made to ensure that government functionaries discharged certain magisterial or clerical duties.

Congress enacted the Foreign Corrupt Practices Act (FCPA) in 1977 in an effort to curtail the bribery of foreign officials and to restore public confidence in the integrity of the American business system. The FCPA had an enormous impact on the way American firms do business. Several firms that paid bribes to foreign officials have been the subjects of criminal and civil enforcement actions, resulting in large fines and suspension and debarment from federal procurement contracting. Some of their employees and officers have gone to jail. Companies with substantial overseas business found themselves completely cut out of bidding opportunities. Some just pulled out of international business, announcing that they could not compete with foreign competitors who had no such constraints.

Following the passage of the FCPA, Congress became concerned that American companies were operating at a disadvantage compared to foreign companies who routinely paid bribes and, in some countries, were permitted to deduct the cost of such bribes as business expenses on their taxes. Accordingly, in 1988, Congress directed the executive branch to commence negotiations in the Organization of Economic Cooperation and Development (OECD) to obtain the agreement of the United States' major trading partners to enact legislation similar to the FCPA. In 1997, almost ten years later, the United States and thirty-three other countries signed the OECD Convention on Combating Bribery of Foreign Public Officials in International Business Transactions. The United States ratified this convention and enacted legislation in 1998.

The anti-bribery provisions of the FCPA make it unlawful for a U.S. person and certain foreign issuers of securities to make a corrupt payment to a foreign official for the purpose of obtaining or retaining business for or with or directing business to any person. Since 1998, the rules also apply to any persons representing foreign firms who commit any act in furtherance of such a corrupt payment while in the United States.

To avoid such consequences, many firms have implemented detailed compliance programs intended to prevent and to detect any improper payments by or to employees and agents.

It's the Law

The FCPA makes it unlawful to bribe foreign officials to obtain or retain business. There must be five elements that have to be met to constitute a violation. They are as follows:

1. Who or what are you? The law potentially applies to any individual, firm, officer, director, employee or agent of a firm, or any stockholder acting on behalf of the firm. It embraces foreign subsidiaries, foreign nationals, and U.S. residents.

2. What do you intend? There has to be a corrupt intention. In other words, the payment must be intended to induce the recipient to misuse his official position to direct business. The act does not require that a corrupt action succeed in its purpose. The *offer* or *promise* is enough to land you in jail.

3. What are you going to give? The FCPA prohibits paying, offering, promising to pay, authoriz-

ing payment or a promise, any money, or anything of value.

4. Who are you going to give it to? The prohibition extends only to a *foreign official, a foreign political party, party official, or any candidate for political office*. A foreign official means any officer or employee of a foreign government, a public international organization, or any person acting on their behalf. Members of a royal family may come into this category.

5. What's the business purpose? Checking to see whether the payment is made in order to assist the firm in obtaining or retaining business is the final criteria. It doesn't have to be a government contract. You might just have greased the wheels of bureaucracy to find your picture on the post office wall.

Any serious global businessperson in a legitimate enterprise knows that the consequences of bribery are substantial and severe. This overview is not a legal opinion or advice. Any manager who wants to understand the FCPA provisions should consult his or her counsel or utilize the services of the Department of Justice Foreign Corrupt Practices Act Opinion Procedure, U.S. Department of Justice, PO Box 28188, McPherson Square, Washington DC, 20038, Telephone (202) 514-7023.

Egyptian Cadeaus

In June 1994 Lockheed Martin was indicted for allegedly violating the FCPA provisions in connection with an order for three C-130 cargo planes. Lockheed had allegedly given a termination fee to a consultant who had acquired a position with the Egyptian government. Lockheed pleaded guilty to one count of conspiracy in violation of the FCPA and paid a $21.8 million fine plus a $3 million civil settlement. The former regional vice-president of Lockheed was sentenced to eighteen months in prison and assessed a $125,000 fine for bribing an Egyptian member of parliament. Lockheed Aeronautical Systems was temporarily barred from obtaining export licenses for its products.

Indonesian Oil

Triton Energy Corporation was charged in a civil suit brought by the SEC involving the *anti-bribery and books and records provisions* of the FCPA. The SEC alleged in its complaint that officers of Triton Indonesia paid approximately $450,000 to an independent agent for non-existent project goods and services through false invoicing in an effort to influence Indonesian officials. The suit concerned an Indonesian oil field joint venture where Triton Indonesia was the operator. The case was settled when Triton agreed to a permanent injunction and paid a $300,000 civil fine. The officers of the Indonesian subsidiary were also slapped with a permanent injunction and fines of $35,000 and $50,000.

Finger Pointing

There is a plethora of suits brought by firms accusing competitors of bribing officials in order to gain big contracts. No doubt this will continue as long as business competes and as long as jealousy lurks in the heart of man; however, many of these actions fail through lack of proof and unsupporting witnesses where culture is disinclined to *rat* on others in the group. You can, however, rat on your competition anonymously and electronically if so inclined. Government has made it easy for you to spy and report the alleged offender by putting up their bribery hotline on the Trade Compliance Center website. If you want to make a report, go to www.mac.gov/tcc/anti_b/antibribe.

Exporting Anti-Bribery

Following the passing of FCPA, American companies engaged in international business went into free fall. How can we compete? How can we secure those lucrative overseas contracts if we can't compete on a level playing field? Congress was bombarded with demands from *repeal* to *compensation*. Legislators traditionally don't like to repeal anything under one hundred years old, and they certainly don't like to compensate large rich global companies. They passed the buck to the executive branch in 1988 that then commenced working with the OECD to get an international consensus on enacting similar legislation in other countries. The result was a series of agreements, guidelines, and reports incorporated in the OECD Anti-Bribery Convention. The U.S. representatives make annual reports to Congress and these reports make interesting reading.

As of June 2000, twenty-one out of twenty nine members of OECD had taken steps to criminalize the bribery of foreign public officials. However, several significant exporting countries such as Brazil, Italy, and the Netherlands are among the thirteen signatories that have yet to complete their internal processes and formally ratify the convention. Likewise, the U.S. agencies making their report to Congress also have concerns regarding the legislation of certain countries, particularly Japan and the United Kingdom.

They comment that bribery of foreign officials is still a widespread practice in international commerce. From May 1994 through April 2000, indications were that the outcome of 353 foreign contracts valued at approximately $165 billion may have been affected by bribes to public officials. U.S. firms are alleged to have lost 92 of these contracts worth about $26 billion.

Clearly, the combined efforts of the FCPA and the OECD are only scratching the surface of this issue–not surprising for many cultures where fees, tea money, or dash is expected between people who depend on each other's support for survival and where incomes of public officials is at subsistence level.

The Spirit of Giving

You have to be careful these days. Giving will never be the same. The problem: when is a gift not a gift? According to the government guidelines, a gift is a bribe when it is given with strings attached. It's also a bribe if the *gift* is obviously so generous, it's absurd; in other words, it has got to look like a gift such as a Harrods' food hamper, a Cartier Tank watch, a Wine Club selection, that sort of thing. A £100,000 Aston Martin is clearly a bribe.

But there are exceptions as you can imagine. In relationship-based and group-based cultures, gifts come with obligations attached to the recipient. Few Japanese and Chinese would receive a gift from you without a strong sense of return obligation. Reciprocity and a strong attitude of obligation are driving principles in these cultures. To give someone a gift or to extend hospitality requires something in return, so, by certain definitions, such a gift is a bribe. Group-based business people are astonished that westerners can accept hospitality, friendship, assistance, and support and then take their business elsewhere *to get a better deal*. That's the data-based way.

Keeping It in the Family

Relationship-based and group-based cultures are devoted to the survival and well-being of the extended family including–in the case of group-based people–their ancestors and unborn descendants. Family cohesion, health, and prosperity are at the heart of their belief systems and whatever strengths, abilities, connections, and power each individual possesses, it is used for the benefit of the family or group. Doing business with family is a sure way of bringing the resulting benefits to the whole family. The average Chinese restaurant is a family affair; rarely do we see one fail.

When a relationship-based family member gets a powerful and influential government job, this is opportunity–opportunity for family promotion and opportunity for family income through selling influence and connection. Such is the system that has dominated the world of this culture group. Mere law has not often stood in the way of progress!

Such is the jungle of culture confusion, one that the global manager has to cut through every day.

It's the System

Corruption, as we have stated, has been around a long time, but its modern equivalent was given a major boost during the last half of the last century. There is nothing like a centrally planned economy to really get corruption and bribery fired up. After all, it may be the only free enterprise that the entrepreneurs can get into. Therefore, communism, socialism, fascism, and all the other "isms" that keep the people under the heel are a mulch bed for corruption. These decaying bureaucratic composts, where the state licenses and controls everything and encourages nothing, rarely allow for the exigencies of life and the rise and fall of people, power, and popularity. Least of all, they have little tolerance for business, so production of wealth, opportunity for income, or just sheer creativity never crosses their glazed eyes.

Such systems apply to most of Latin America, the Arab world, India, China, Russia, and Eastern Europe. Not that the west is squeaky clean. Corruption scandals rock the foundations of European governments from time to time as they do in the United States. So if we hear of the big-ticket items, it must go without saying that there must be more ice below the water.

* * *

In the summer of 2001, I worked with a group who shipped five 50-gallon containers of medical supplies into Russia to be used in orphanages in Siberia. Our plan was to arrive at the airport of entry late at night (1:30 a.m.) and check our cargo through customs when attention might be at its lowest. Our Russian agent had other ideas. Taking the customs officer into a private room, he *had a discussion*. The goods slid through without so much as an opening. A German engineer told me that he never relies on the system to get his equipment into Russia: he just finds the trucker, gives him a supply of vodka, and *hey, presto*, it arrives. His complaint is that private enterprises have upped the ante, and now his bribes are in big competition from major companies.

Anyone moving around the night life of central Moscow will easily recognize the face of modern bribery: it's usually six-foot-six, thick set, shaved head, no teeth, and a personality that would qualify bin Laden for a beauty pageant. You will come face to face with this charmer if you want to visit your favorite nightclub. He stands outside and demands access money. The club doesn't employ him–they just know that if they object, he and his cronies will be back after hours with a Molatov cocktail. "Where are the police?" you may well ask. Perhaps they are busy; perhaps they have better crooks to fry; and perhaps they just like a share of the spiff. Whatever the reason, it's taking a long time for Russia to abandon old ways. Now at least it's in the open and everybody talks about it.

Lack of faith in the rule of law and its enforcement is another major reason for corruption. If people feel that the police are in on the racket, then whom can you trust? Until a few brave Italian judges and politicians in the 1990s took the war against the Mafia seriously and brought action and law against them in the *Mani Pulite* (clean hands) trials, Italy was slowly turning back into a medieval state. It cost a few of them their lives, but finally the law won, and Italy could stand tall in the international and European community and say the "the people–not the mobsters–are in control." One of the goals of Transparency International is to build local confidence in the rule of law in the realms of business and politics.

Airline Time

Airline insurance accounts are a highly prized and competitive book of business. Most London-based insurance brokers in this field are determined, driven characters who wheel and deal with their clients and with the underwriters of Lloyd's and other aviation insurance markets throughout the world. Charlie Evans was one such broker. With little formal education but with a formidable gift of gab, Charlie could talk his way out of a paper bag. He was invited to quote renewal terms for a Central American national airline–majority owned by the government, minority owned by a company *remotely owned by the president of the country*. Charlie was a dab hand at numbers and sat in front of the airline CEO with his terms.

"Hmm, not as expensive as I thought," said the CEO.

"I worked hard for these terms," said Charlie.

"I have more in my budget than this figure."

"How much more?" asked Charlie.

The CEO told him, and he watched as Charlie altered

the terms to suit the budget.

"All this is on the *QT*," said Charlie, tapping his nose.

"You need paying for your efforts, let's say, 10 percent to you. I have a lot of people to look after," said the CEO.

The paperwork was rigged. Charlie put his money into a Cayman Bank, and everybody was happy until the next year.

"I'm increasing the budget this year," said the CEO, coldly. "I want you to reduce the terms, please."

Charlie had a real problem reducing the terms due to general market hardening, but he finally squeezed a few more bucks from the numbers. The larger dividend was shared out at the previous rate, and Charlie again received compensation from the deal.

Shortly thereafter one of the insured Central American DC10s dropped out of the sky on takeoff.

Loss adjusters are hard matter-of-fact people. They overturn every stone and check every paper trail. Len Smith was one such man. He couldn't make sense of the renewal paperwork. The premium paid by the broker to the insurers was different from the amount billed by the broker to the airline. Why the huge difference? This was way out of line with normal commission.

In a show trial against corruption, the CEO was packed off to prison. Charlie went through nightmares thinking about Central American jails. He was let off with a substantial fine and dismissed from his job back in London. He now runs a beach bar in Costa Rica.

Here Comes the Bribe

Many managers, particularly those who are not involved with global business, feel that international business is driven by bribes, corruption, and unlawful imprisonment. Certainly bribery is widespread and profuse, but it is mostly small, personal, and manageable. Corruption is pretty much the same the world over, and most travelers are put in jail overseas for traffic or drug-related offenses.

If, however, you are involved in a minor altercation involving the police, stand by, for here comes the bribe. This is no happy occasion, but one that can end happily if the right action is taken at the outset. The chances of making a driving error in a bribe conscious culture are considerable: it's as if the two go hand in hand. It seems that the streets are filled with police directing traffic into a massive mix-up which only their ability, with a bribe or two, will untangle. However, be aware that there will be just as many untouchable cops as bribable ones. The settlement conference will last sixty seconds. If the officer is willing to sort out your problem, then the bribe follows. Never discuss money or the amount or the reason for the gift. Typically you will be presented with a problem that can be solved, but it will take money, time, and approval from some superior. You could ask if there is a fee that could solve the problem as you hand over your passport with a single denomination of currency tucked inside. In most countries, a crisp $20 bill will do the trick—but remember, you have just committed an illegal act.

Avoiding the Illegal Act

Fixing a traffic violation may be a minor offence, but bribery of politicians and public officials is potential jail-time. Business people can avoid the possible bribery request from this quarter in a number of ways. Recognize that it is increasingly difficult for a public official to ask for *mordida*. Popular opinion is against him as is the law in twenty-one countries, and he stands a very good chance of being reported to the U.S. Justice Department. Nevertheless, we need to be savvy about this issue and have some idea of how to deal with the problem. There are seven ways to deal with it:

1. Go into your negotiations and the relationship in the belief that you will not have to give a bribe of any sort and that you are totally ignorant of any reason why you should even think about one.

2. Establish a personal relationship with the leader. Become a friend, counselor, supporter and colleague. Give small gifts at Christmas and birthday. Send post cards from distant places and invite him home to meet your family when he visits the country.

3. Study the infrastructure of decision-making. Find out how business is done in the country and in your specific business. If there is a hierarchy of authority or regulation, try to get to know who they are and how the system works. See if a fellow countryman can introduce you to the right people. Use every possible avenue available through the U.S. Department of Commerce and the U.S. consular service.

4. Don't give in to pressure. Once you give in, they will never let you go. Advise your associates not to respond either. Educate them on the issues of bribery. Employ an expert who can give you the specific political, decision process route-map.

5. Never initiate a bribe, for instance, by saying, "Who do I have to look after to get this done?" First, it's an illegal act. Second, you may be bribing the wrong person (or an undercover agent). Third, bribery has a deep cultural nuance in some countries, and you may be making a serious cultural gaff which is likely to wreck the whole deal.

6. Don't be in a hurry. The experienced bribee can

see a bribe coming from beyond the horizon. Lack of detailed planning, lack of study in the local conditions, misunderstanding of the official decision process, constantly changing plans and objectives, and being in too much of a hurry can create more problems. Speed is not a factor in most cultures. It is, therefore, the most sought after feature in the bribery process.

7. You can always say no. The best answer is the easiest. "I am so sorry, but I have two problems dealing with your request. First, if I do what you ask, I am committing a criminal act according to my country's law, and this law applies wherever I am in the world. I would be sent to prison, would have a massive fine against me personally, would lose my job, and my family would be left without support. My company would have a huge fine imposed and would lose its license to export. The worst thing is that it would spoil our friendship, and I wouldn't want that."

If ever an incident comes up where you may be confronted with a major bribery issue, make sure that you do the following:

• Take detailed notes of the names, dates, times, and conversation.

• Keep your superiors informed.

• Report the incident to the U.S. consulate.

It is vital, if involved in these murky waters, to bring the U.S. government in on your side. Believe it or not, they want to help, particularly in the semi-dark conditions of corruption. Remember that criminal minds may be involved and this could lead to coercion and extortion, which are extreme forms of bribery.

Reality Check

Every day business people and their products have to pass through checkpoints, border crossings and customs worldwide. Every day some official brings down the barrier or says, "No."

How do we negotiate these everyday blocks to the blood of commerce?

The reality is that you have got to move forward, get the stuff moved, and do business. The law may be helpful for the serious bribe, but, if confiscated, the company vehicle has to be recovered from the pound; the goods have to be moved out of the customs shed, and you have to get your residency papers processed as quickly as possible.

Who you know, not what you know (that sage advice you heard long ago), now comes into play. Every global manager has dealt with similar issues at some time or another, and they do take time. Phone call after phone call, contact after contact is used up in the process. It takes time, patience, and, yes, often money. So be prepared to be innovative and flexible.

Global cross-culture competent managers are able to appreciate the subtle nuances of officialdom, the way these people think and act, and the consequences of their actions. In such cases, your contacts will literally be worth their weight in gold. Prepare for the inevitable–network, network, network. One day you may really need all the help you can get.

Stand and Deliver

Examples of extortion are scattered throughout the catalogue of human crime. Of course, the extortioner does not see it that way. He views it as changing circumstances or conditions or will invent problems that you haven't thought about. There are examples of what could be described as *soft extortion*. For instance, an engineering project is half complete and before it can proceed further, the officials slap on a regulation or license irregularity that can only be solved by negotiation with the powers that be. Or there is *hard extortion*, which is nearer criminal bribery. An example of hard extortion is being shut out of a country after considerable investment has been made there and only being allowed reentry after substantial bribes are paid to high officials. Extortion is far worse than nationalization, where at least the latter may offer some chance of compensation.

Elf Help

Such arrant highway robbery has become a sophisticated art form. The story of global petroleum giant Elf Aquitaine justifies the adage that "truth is more exciting than fiction." The characters involved could have come right out of a novel. Le Floch-Prigent, the former chairman of the French-headquartered company, and his fix-it man, Alfred Sirven, along with the former French foreign minister Roland Dumas and his mistress, Elf lobbyist Christine Deviers-Joncour, were all accused of massive bribe taking, bribe giving, offshore-money laundering, and slush fund bleaching of global proportions in Africa, Taiwan, France, and Germany. Material information was reported missing from police files, and there were accusations of tampering in digital memory storage. The alleged extortion involved a massive East German scam involving a refinery in Leuna and the privatization of the Minoi chain of gas stations. Elf's dealings with the Treuhandanstalt, the privatization body in former East Germany, and Herr Thyssen, a mysterious Liechtenstein intermediary, led to a web of intrigue, falsification, and use of secret Swiss bank accounts in order to pay off influential German politicians who kept increasing the ante. In the end, the greedy politicos were *wagging the dog*, and Elf soon discovered that its initial *innocent*, simple bribe scheme had turned into a giant backlash nightmare, landing the leading players in a present day version of the Bastille.

Is That the FBI?

If you have nothing to hide, but feel that you may be in danger of extortion, contact a lawyer, the FBI, and a member of Congress in that order and blatantly use the muscles of Uncle Sam. That's what governments do best: lean on other governments, and these days governments easily get embarrassed.

Likewise the media, always anxious for a good story like the Elf Aquitaine fiasco, are only too ready to get into some heavy breathing journalism involving, as this sort of crime so often does, politicians, business, power, sex, money, and greed: a recipe for good steamy stories, selling newspapers, and increased TV ratings.

In Sri Lanka, one of the hot beds of corruption and extortion, the tradition of investigative journalism is kept alive by the private media that regularly exposes official corruption despite draconian censorship regulations.

Open Sesame

Democratization, though weak, incomplete and, in some cases, reversible, has created an opportunity for debate about corruption in South Asia. The debate goes to the heart of the need for culture change. In some cases it creates antipathy toward the ever encroaching tide of globalization, but change is inevitable. Since 1995 governments are increasingly under public pressure to enforce probity in public office. Groups, such as the Center for Media Studies in India, Transparency International in Bangladesh, and

Media Services International in Nepal, are articulating public perceptions through opinion surveys, making it less easy for governments just to dismiss the issue out of hand. Then there is litigation being brought against the perpetrators by non-government organizations, such as Common Cause in India, which, in the face of personal threats and general criticism by politicians, succeeds in bringing legal action to redress public grievances against corrupt officials.

Corruption and bribery are unlikely to decrease much in the near future. The problem, as we have said, is cultural and deep-seated, and every global manager will, sooner or later, have to deal with it. How he or she responds is a matter of character, integrity, cross-culture competency, and expediency—all part of being a world-savvy professional in a dangerous and unpredictable world.

But part of the fun and excitement about being a global manager is the adventure, the challenge, and, yes, the danger. Fortunately for the benefit of the world, some people are prepared to go and face these challenges because the cause is greater than themselves. They choose the global arena rather than sit nine-to-five in a glass cocoon staring at a horizon of what might have been.

12

Dangerous Destinations and Cross-Culture Catastrophe

"Where there's muck, there's money."
An old Yorkshire saying

As soon as you step off the international flight into a foreign country, you are in a very different world from the one you live in. That may be a very obvious statement, but you would be surprised how many people don't think about it. After all, it's not easy to leave your flying cocoon wrapped in soft music, plastic food, and American movies. Maybe you are dropped off early in the morning by the airline you have come to love. Sleepy-eyed, you slouch into the immigration hall and *wham*, face to face with culture shock! Your stomach knots with apprehension. Basic things you took for granted a few short hours ago are no longer in place. Language, culture, money, food, accommodations, and security have all changed. It's a world of difference–an altered state. Here we feel vulnerable, exposed, and somewhat fearful.

We are in business; we have to move on and get the job done. Sometimes we find ourselves in ugly places. After all, business is more often than not done in dirty, over-populated, over-polluted, crime-filled cities. Anybody who thinks it's all tourist resorts and fine restaurants hasn't hustled for international business. As world savvy, cross-culture competent managers, we arrive at our destination having been selected, trained, and properly briefed to face most things and even cope with the extreme situations in a dangerous world the cross-culture catastrophe.

Art of War

Business, Sun Tzu taught, is war. Out-planning, out-maneuvering, and outguessing the competition is all part of the action. Business people abound in war zones. Picking their way between the weapon racks and watching for tanks before they cross the road, they are out there selling everything from drugs to bulldozers, medicines to body bags, and infant food to mobile phones. Of course, what they are banking on is having a foothold in the market when the shooting stops. Traditionally, regions decimated by war experience phenomenal growth when guns are turned into plowshares and people get back to business: just another form of war for some. Recovery often occurs with the help of western aid, just like Germany and Japan after WWII. Wars themselves have never been entirely bad for business. The restaurants and hotels of Islamabad and the Pakistan Telephone Company never had it so good during the Taliban offensive. "Long may this continue," said some

Muslim businessmen as they packed away their rolled rupees.

I Recommend the Pork Chops!

In April 1973, I was having lunch with my client in the venerable Liberal Club, Belfast, Northern Ireland. We had just started the first course when a gigantic explosion rocked the building and rattled the windows and clouds of powdered plaster drifted down from the ancient ceiling into my soup. Through the murk, I was aware of a tall, gaunt figure dressed in a black suit and tie standing beside me. It was the waiter.

"Gentlemen, I recommend the pork chops."

The pork chops! What's he talking about—I've nearly been killed, and he recommends the pork chops, I thought to myself.

It was the best lesson I have learned about getting on with business. Global managers can't worry about war zones or terrorism; they just get on and continue to *recommend the pork chops.*

You've seen those old movies of intrepid, hard-drinking salesmen in war torn banana republics dodging the bullets, being thrown into jail, and doing deals with Che Guevara types—anything to sell mutual funds. I don't think Hollywood understands the *work-a-day* life of the global manager, but what they do understand is human determination to do business and make money. The process does, however, put us into some odd places and strange locations.

What Am I Doing Here?

China Air used to fly ex-WWII Dakotas on its service from Taipei to Taichung, located on the west center of the island. Dressed in my London-tailored striped dark suit and black shiny shoes, I took this flight and climbed aboard the fine old aircraft that sat on the tarmac at an angle of almost 30° tail to nose. When you boarded one of these famous aircraft, you had to climb the 30° incline to your seat, using whatever ropes and grappling irons you could find. The plane was filled with indigenous Taiwanese, their children, and a sampling of livestock. Off we took, all of us looking at the beautiful coastline as we traveled south. Suddenly, the intercom crackled as the pilot delivered a static-filled message in Mandarin and English.

"Sorry, but landing strip at Taichung has been covered by rock fall–we make other arrangements." That was that. My otherwise talkative traveling companions fell silent as we contemplated the *other arrangements*. Ten contemplative minutes later the crackle came on again. "To prove I do not lie I now show you rock fall."

With that he took the plane into a steep WWII dive and banked to starboard. In those days of lax seat belt control, those of us on the port side of the plane left our seats and piled on top of the people and caged chickens to our right. With our noses pressed to the windows, we saw how half a mountain was strewn over the runway. So he did not lie. Good.

Crackle came on again. "Due to the generosity of our magnificent and wonderful government, we are able to land on military airfield."

The Dakota shuddered as we hurtled to earth and landed with a series of backbreaking jolts in what appeared to be a lake but turned out to be a paddy field. Doors were opened, and I finally struggled backside first down into thick black mud. Where did everybody go? As I made my way to the bushes at the edge of the field, I could see no one. Ah, a road. I looked right, then left. No sign of life. But wait, a bus approached, so I did what any Englishman would do under the circumstances and held out my arm to stop it. It is filled with my traveling companions from the Dakota, together with their live property. They all stopped talking at once. The silence was deafening as I climbed aboard. "Taichung?" I asked.

"Taichung," repeated the driver.

I clutched my briefcase as if it were the last vestige of civilization and stared down at my muddy Oxford Street shoes and asked myself, *What am I doing here?* Back came my reply, *Selling insurance!*

In those days, Taiwan was a war zone. Bandits were operating in the mountains, and my client said that they had dynamited the mountain over the runway. These so-called bandits were probably communist groups who were still continuing a guerilla action against the independent republican government of Taiwan. Business was good and profitable, however, and I knew that if I weren't there drumming it up, my competitors certainly would be.

Doing deals in dangerous places can be interesting, exciting, and fun. It definitely comes under the category of *on the job cross-culture training.*

Seriously Savvy

Doing business and traveling in dangerous places requires some serious savvy. This may seem obvious, but scores of people get into difficulties in dangerous places when just a little research, preparation, or even common sense would have avoided it. Just ask the U.S Department of State who bail out, fly out, seek out, find out, and chew out people all the time–people who don't follow a few simple rules. Americans are targets. Period. Now sometimes Brits, Germans, French Canadians, Dutch, and other similars get mistaken for Americans. This happens because most bad guys have no sense of cross-culture recognition. But, in general, it's Americans they are after and, if they can't find any of them, they will take whatever is available if there's money to be made.

Beware of the Blessing

Traveling into dangerous locations is not just the prerogative of business people; believe it or not, some vacationers like doing it as well. They are often called *Adventure Tours*. People flock onto brakeless buses and planes, long past their sell-by date, and into kasbahs and red light districts every day and night. The bad guys lay in wait for credit cards, passports, and crisp new Ben Franklins (which are being counterfeited, by the way, in Russia, Syria, and Lebanon). For them it's almost too easy to pick out the victim, create a diversion, and move in for the pickings, then pay off the cop who was watching it all happen. Vacationers are often snafu at markets, tourist attractions, shows and entertainments, railroad stations, bus stations, airports and hotels, and in any crowd gatherings. It's a known fact that more people get robbed in St. Peter's Square while receiving the Pope's blessing than in any other square mile in the world.

What to Watch For

Thousands of traveling business people mix business with tourism. That's quite acceptable, and we advocate this as part of the cross-culture competency course. What often happens is that in the more relaxed, less attentive tourist mode, the businessperson can lose money, air tickets, and passport, but that's not all. There's also bodily harm. The lowlifes who inhabit our own world also inhabit the rest of the world. They may live in a sexually repressed culture and see an independent western woman as gang rape fodder.

Whether you are on business or vacation or both, you are prone to all the risks that nice people run into when traveling abroad. It isn't that America is necessarily safer (there are thousands of people who won't travel to the

United States because they think it's a dangerous place), but it is all about familiarity–or lack of it.

We should be aware of the following:

- **Nice friendly strangers.** Suspect everyone. Trust no one at first. Certainly, there are many people who just want to be friendly but, sorry, it's rare.

- **Distractions.** Any sudden or unforeseen event that takes your attention is likely to be an opportunity for a crook to move in. Remember you are probably being watched by a criminal mind, and you need to be alert to your environment at all times until you lock the hotel room door.

- **Alcohol, drugs, and just having a good time.** Bars, nightclubs (and any place our mothers would object to) are often joints where trouble starts and sleazy characters love to hang out. It is remarkable how many tourists leave the security of their nice hotel to get a taste of local culture, only to find that they have no money left to pay for the nice hotel.

- **Too many bags, too much stuff.** You know the type–the ones with cameras, binoculars, carry-on bags, souvenir bags, carrier bags (marked Harrods or Heathrow duty free). Plan on minimizing the stuff you bring on the trip. The Rolex you might be wearing could end up in *duty free* in Yemen! It's tough, but travel light and buy essentials at your destination.

- **Avoid the throngs.** If you are with a tour group always keep up with them but stay apart from the throng. (Generally tourists are an attraction in themselves for the wrong types.) Keep away from the busiest tourist attractions at the busiest time; that's when the crooks work overtime.

- **Criminal opportunity.** Ask yourself, "If I was a crook, what would I think about a person doing what I am doing now?" Don't come out of a bank or an American Express office stuffing the large bills into your top pocket. Never pull out your wallet in the bazaar showing everybody all those great credit cards for banks in Delaware. Avoid undoing your shirt to remove your body wallet to pay $9 for museum tickets. Use a safety belt or an ankle strap instead of putting your wallet in your back pocket. Never put your PIN number into an ATM at midnight just off Red Square or any other square and avoid taking more money than you intend to spend into the Amsterdam red light district.

- **Looking neither rich nor poor.** Melding in– that's the secret. Most tourists have more money in their body belt than most individuals abroad make in a year. That's why some of them think that it should be shared. Some tourists dress to impress the group they are with rather than for safety sake. Take a tip from traveling teachers. You can always tell them abroad: they are practical, matter-of-fact, there to learn, and rarely make good targets for crooks. Backpackers who look as if they slept under the Pont Neuf (and probably did) are highly vulnerable.

The Price of Black Gold

Next time you climb into a gas-guzzling SUV and go in search of low price petrol, give a kindly thought to the guy who helped dig it out of the ground.

The oil business takes people to some pretty dangerous places. In fact *The World's Most Dangerous Places* lists many of them as the *most* dangerous places for business travel. They include:

Colombia: According to the national police, 2,600 people were kidnapped there in 1998: they were grabbed at roadblocks, seized at hotels, and driven off in taxis. This hellhole has millions of dollars poured into it to fight the drug thugs. It is still near the top of the State Department's *don't go to* list.

Angola: This is a new popular destination for offshore drillers as it pumps two billion barrels of oil a day. Not only that, it is also one of the world's major alluvial and kimberlite diamond producers. However, Angola has more land mines per square yard than any other country, including Afghanistan, with an estimated 40 percent of the population missing limbs. Experts claim that there are still twenty million explosives buried out there waiting to detonate.

Nigeria: Some oilmen have *Nigeria* written on their hearts. Shell has been there for decades and still persists, while having lost people, equipment, leases, and a good deal of patience. Always politically volatile, Nigerian scams are known throughout the world, and the local economy is run the same way.

Algeria: Algeria was almost the graveyard of the French, and it is the same for business people today if protection precautions are not taken. Terrorists, called GIAs, who continuously fight each other, run the place and everybody else is caught in the crossfire. Expats working for Sonatrach, the Algerian Oil and Natural Gas Company, live in secured compounds and are constantly accompanied by bodyguards.

Russia: Now becoming the foreign oil supplier of choice, Russia has huge reserves ready for devouring by eager Americans devoted to cheap pump prices. Also ready are the gangsters who offer protection and extortion to the oil executives that roam Siberia and the southern independent states. Most of the execs have to pass through Moscow where many of the nice looking new houses and the shiny new cars are owned by criminals–current or reformed. One hundred and twenty foreigners on average are killed in Russia annually.

The above list names some of the worst places the oil industry has to deal with every day, not to mention Saudi, Iran, Iraq, India, and Pakistan.

However, most of us do not have to explore these places for our excitement; there are plenty of other equally dangerous destinations. Gangsters are after money. As far as they are concerned, every businessperson is loaded and ready for picking, but thieves can be foiled before they get their chance if travelers just take a few sensible precautions.

Surviving Business Travel

On Dress:

1. Don't dress *rich*. Dress smart but not expensively in business attire. Dark suits are best when going into a metropolitan area. Otherwise, stick to knit shirts and slacks for both men and women.

2. Keep jewelry to a minimum and do not take anything expensive or anything that even looks expensive. Leave the fancy watch at home. Wear the watch with the face inward and wear it on the right wrist when driving a left-hand drive car.

3. Carry a good but inexpensive briefcase with a shoulder strap. Ladies should carry a briefcase in preference to a purse or handbag.

In Transit:

1. Ask your customer, supplier, or contact to pick you up at the airport. If this is not possible, ask him to arrange for the hotel to do this.

2. If you need a taxi, choose it yourself. Pick the newest one with the oldest driver. Ask what the fare is while in the airport and have the right change. Make friends with the cabbie and keep your luggage in the back seat with you.

3. If you rent a car, acquaint yourself with local traffic laws and procedures beforehand. Rent bigger cars; keep off remote side roads; and do not drive at night, if possible. Understand where you are going and how to get there.

At the hotel:

1. Pick the best available accommodation–one recommended by a reputable travel agency.

2. Never hold meetings with strangers in your room. Either rent a conference room or hold the meeting in the lobby in view of other people.

3. Never give your room number to anyone.

4. Put all your valuables and important papers in the hotel safe.

5. Always talk on the phone as if unfriendly people are overhearing you.

6. If you arrive back at your hotel late, ask hotel security to escort you to your room.

7. Keep the TV or radio on when you are out of the room.

8. If you don't want anybody in your room, hang out the "Do Not Disturb" sign and make the bed yourself.

9. If you have a chair in the room, prop it under the doorknob like they do in the movies. It's probably a better lock than the one built in the door.

At restaurants:

1. Get the hotel to recommend and make your reservation, preferably not at a restaurant used by tourists.

2. Make reservations in a fictitious name.

3. Don't wait outside for your guests; sit at the table.

4. Get into the habit of requesting a table near the emergency exit and in good view of the main door.

Just good common sense:

1. Avoid getting too friendly and talkative with the natives. Don't tell strangers where you are staying, what business you are in, or who your employer is.

2. Make copies of all important papers and put them in the hotel safe.

3. Make three color copies of your passport, put one in your suitcase, one in your wallet, and leave one at home.

4. Vary your schedule. Don't keep to a regular jogging or walking routine. Change your hotel or room without notice and sometimes don't take assigned cabs.

5. Do not carry unmarked prescription drugs and leave questionable reading material at home.

6. If possible, watch your drink being poured.

Extreme Precautions

Travelers have been reported in various parts of the world, such as the Paris Montmartre, the New York subway, and London Soho, wearing jeans, an "I'm from Ohio" tee shirt, and sporting travel *security* belts packed with their most immediate valuable possessions. It's like advertising, "Here is a passport, credit cards and cash. Come and get it."

So far as the bad guys are concerned, the rich takings are so profuse that it's hard to know who to pick off next.

The determined thug knows all about your body belt, even the one strapped to your abdomen, especially when you have to open your shirt to the navel to get out a five-dollar bill. If you intend to go to locations where it would be easy to be mugged or where the bad boys gather, it is wise to take some precautions and learn some tricks for survival and the protection of your return ticket.

When I knew that I had to take $15,000 in new mint twenties and fifties into Russia, I had an inside pocket sewn into my jeans at the front right. It made a slight bulge in a zone not too many men look at, but I got to my destination without molestation. Here then are some of the things you can do to take extreme precaution:

- Keep your expired credit cards, unused rupees, rubles, and drachmas. Put them into an old wallet. Carry the wallet in your inside jacket pocket. When the unshaven yobbo threatens, you say, "OK, OK." Reach inside for your wallet and throw it as far as you can behind the assailant, then run as fast as you can in the opposite direction. Make for crowds, a hotel, or a shop.

- If you must carry a lot of money, spread it around your person. Put some in a wallet, in a money belt, in a neck pouch, in your inside pocket. Better to lose a little than all of it.

- Slit open the lining of your travel case or briefcase and find a place in the lining to squirrel your money away. Shoe linings and soles, pant cuffs and inside pockets on shirts, ankle pouches and added pockets to your boxer shorts also make good hiding places.

- Don't carry a purse. If you must, make sure it's an inexpensive product and don't put anything of value in it. Professional bag grabbers often carry razor knives to slash the shoulder strap. The same can happen to cameras if they are slung around your neck. The best advice is to buy a small camera and carry it in a belt holster.

- Don't fight back. I know that's tough advice. Our natural inclination is to meet violence with violence in self-defense. But these thugs would not let you win without a serious fight. The only sensible thing to do is to give them something and escape.

- Take a self-defense course. Understand the essentials of personal protection: where to jab, punch, or kick an assailant so that it gets his attention if he has bodily harm in his rotten head.

- Totally surprise the bandit by being able to speak a few words to him in his own language, as, "I'm here to do business with your government and you will have bad trouble if you do any harm to me." Who knows? It might work.

The purpose of these paragraphs is not to frighten you into staying at home. The purpose is to develop the cross-culture competent manager into a safety savvy manager as well. There are very few, if any, totally safe venues. Tourists may be able to find them and visit them, but global managers don't have the luxury of choice.

The disparities between rich and poor, between those with opportunity and those living under restriction and between fundamental believers and liberal thinkers, have the effect of setting the world against each other. Jealousy and envy breed discontent and violence. In societies unable to afford good law enforcement and in those having corrupt law enforcement systems, the crooks run riot and some of them have political motives. Raising money for terrorism is big business, and inevitably legitimate business is a target from time to time.

Kidnap and Ransom

According to Robert Young Pelton's *The World's Most Dangerous Places*, "Of the 8,000 known kidnappings worldwide every year, 6,500 were in Latin America with over half occurring in Colombia." The ideal kidnap victim, according to Pelton, "is a mid- to high-ranking executive working for a multinational corporation overseas." The

going rate for foreign managers in Colombia is between
$500,000 and $2 million.

Kidnapping has been reported in the Philippines, Yemen, Chechnya, and Russia, but the vast majority occurs
in Latin America. Apart from Colombia, other hotbeds are
in Brazil, Venezuela, Mexico, Panama, Peru, and Ecuador.
Even Europe has its moments. Italy is always a favorite,
having had fifty-three abductions since 1989; the United
Kingdom and Spain each had nineteen. Because oil and
gas crews get into remote areas of the third world, they
permanently risk running into the banditos at crossroads in
the outback. Now, finally, after many years of hard knock
experiences, energy companies are hiring some big private
armies capable of taking on a small sized country.

Global companies recognized that the lives and continued day-to-day presence of their executives was something they needed to protect and insure. Thus the fertile
trade of Kidnap and Ransom Insurance was developed in
the late 1960s. Today few international managers leave
home without it.

Lloyd's of London is one of the principal markets of K
& R Insurance, along with the American International
Group and the Chubb Group. Policies are offered for
$500,000, $1 million, and additional limits up to $5 mil-
lion for premiums starting at $5,000 per individual, based
on location and length of stay. Lloyd's, as part of its conditions, insists that the information of the insurance be kept
confidential, including the fact that a policy is even in place.
When it comes to getting you out of the clutches, negotiating the ransom, paying for medical expenses, and your loss
of salary, it's a package worth having.

The Participants

The Hiscox syndicate at Lloyd's, a well established and
highly professional specialist in unusual forms of insur-

ance, is the largest kidnap and extortion insurer, having handled over 1100 cases in eighty-seven countries. It insures (not by name, but by coded number) members of wealthy families, actors, musicians, politicians, and business executives against kidnap, bodily harm, extortion, hijack, and malicious detention. (Check it out at hiscox.com.) A firm like the Hiscox organization relies heavily on highly trained specialists to handle the dirty side of the transaction.

The Control Risks Group based in London (crg.com) provides security checks on people who are insured and the company that employs them. They provide advice for managers at risk and offer executives effective methods for dealing with high risk situations as well as providing country and city reports while educating executives on how best to avoid high risk exposure.

CRG are the people who send in negotiators and behind-the-scenes consultants to arrange a kidnapped person's release and settlement of the ransom. They have numerous successes notched up, having handled more than 850 cases in over seventy countries through their offices located in London, Sydney, Moscow, Paris, Singapore, Tokyo, and Washington, D.C. For example, following the kidnapping of a South American businessman, demands were made on his family. The CRG consultant coached the family in the responses. The businessman managed to escape and arrive home while his captors fled on discovering they had lost their prize. The CRG consultant had kept up continual dialogue with the leader, who had no idea his asset had escaped. The police moved in and arrested the perpetrator. On another occasion, an expatriate company in Russia called in CRG after it was threatened with extortion and demands for cash payment that would have put it out of business. The hoodlums had actually visited the company and met with its lawyer. The CRG consultant, working in conjunction with the local crime squad, set up an elaborate entrapment resulting in the arrest and detention of four of the ringleaders who were tried, convicted, and jailed.

Prevention is better than the cure, we are often told. It is the same with kidnap and extortion. Global managers, in their desire to be world savvy, can apply some useful risk management to prevent nasty things happening to them and their colleagues. CRG conducts workshops and seminars to advise companies on their security and will assist in background checks of new hires. However, it remains a primary responsibility of global managers to be sure that their people and families are safe when traveling into other cultures and moving to expatriate locations. A few simple guidelines are important. Kidnapping usually occurs because, for some reason, the news got out that you were in town and you were profiled as an executive with such and such a company ready to do business. You are also at risk if you have a predictable routine and route to work or if your wife plays bridge every Wednesday afternoon at the *expat* club. If the unfortunate happens and you get hustled away, then follow these simple rules that are part of the State Department's advice to travelers (state.gov/ www.about_state/security):

- Try to remain calm and compliant. Nothing will be achieved if you react violently or if you can be easily overpowered.

- Agree with your captors, and do whatever they ask you to do.

- Get your mental state under control. Try to figure out where you are and where you are going.

- Communicate with your captors and develop a rapport if you can.

- Don't try to be a hero. You may endanger yourself and others.

I'm from the Government

The U.S. Department of State issues a regular list on its website *http://travel.state.gov/warnings_list.html* that looks like this:

Current Travel Warnings

Travel Warnings are issued when the State Department recommends that Americans avoid a certain country. The countries listed below are currently on that list. In addition to this list, the State Department issues Consular Information Sheets for every country of the world with information on such matters as the health conditions, crime, unusual currency or entry requirements, any areas of instability, and the location of the nearest U.S. embassy or consulate in the subject country

Afghanistan - 11/23/01

Indonesia - 11/23/01

Kyrgyz Republic - 11/19/01

Central African Republic - 11/8/01

Solomon Islands - 11/8/01

Macedonia - 10/22/01

Sudan - 10/5/01

Tajikistan - 9/26/01

Pakistan - 9/25/01

Yemen - 9/19/01

Iran - 8/24/01

Sierra Leone - 8/20/01

Israel, the West Bank and Gaza - 8/10/01

Iraq - 7/20/01

Libya - 6/6/01

Liberia - 5/31/01

Algeria - 5/31/01

Guinea-Bissau - 4/30/01

Colombia - 4/17/01

Bosnia & Herzegovina - 4/13/01

Democratic Republic of Congo - 4/11/01

Somalia - 2/16/01

Federal Republic of Yugoslavia - 2/13/01

Burundi - 12/7/00

Angola - 9/8/00

Lebanon - 8/28/00

Albania - 6/12/00

Nigeria - 4/7/00

Specific travel warnings are published regularly on the same site, for example:

Angola - Travel Warning
September 8, 2000
The Department of State warns U.S. citizens against travel to Angola because of continued military conflict in interior provinces and increased violent criminal activity,

including kidnapping and the threat by criminals and rebel insurgents to kidnap foreigners. Travel within Angola remains unsafe due to high intensity military actions, bandit and insurgent attacks, undisciplined police and military personnel, and land mines in rural areas. Foreign nationals, especially independent entrepreneurs, are subject to arbitrary detention and/or deportation by immigration and police authorities.

Americans who find travel to Angola necessary are strongly urged to contact the U.S. Embassy for up-to-date information. Travel outside Luanda is inadvisable. American citizens traveling outside Luanda, despite this Warning, should always contact the U.S. Embassy for the latest information on security conditions in the provinces to which visits are planned. For further information on Angola, please see the Department of State's latest Consular Information Sheet on Angola.

This replaces the Angola Travel Warning dated July 27, 1999, to update the security situation and to include information about the threat to kidnap foreigners.

Colombia - Travel Warning
April 17, 2001

The Department of State warns U.S. citizens against travel to Colombia. Violence by narcotraffickers, guerrillas, illegal self-defense (paramilitary) groups and other criminal elements continues to affect all parts of the country, both urban and rural. Citizens of the United States and other countries continue to be the victims of threats, kidnappings, domestic airline hijackings and murders. Threats targeting American citizens are expected to continue and possibly increase in response to U.S. support for Colombian drug eradication programs. Colombian groups have been known to operate in the border areas of neighboring countries, creating similar dangers for travelers in those areas. U.S. citizens of all age groups and occupations, both tourists and residents, have been victimized. Bombings have occurred throughout Colombia, including in urban areas, and some foreign interests have been among the targets.

More than 3,000 people are kidnapped each year throughout Colombia, and there is a greater risk of being kidnapped in Colombia than in any other country in the world. In the past 20 years, nearly 120 American citizens have been kidnapped in both individual incidents and large group hostage situations. At least 14 American kidnapping victims have been murdered. Most kidnappings of U.S. citizens in Colombia have been committed by guerrilla groups, including the Revolutionary Armed Forces of Colombia (FARC) and the National Liberation Army (ELN), which were both designated as Foreign Terrorist Organizations by the Secretary of State in October 1997. Since it is U.S. policy not to pay ransom or make other concessions to terrorists, the U.S. Government's ability to assist kidnapped U.S. citizens is limited.

The State Department also issues Public Announcements to disseminate information quickly about terrorist threats and other relatively short-term conditions that pose significant risks or disruptions to Americans. The Public Announcements list looks like this:

- Turkmenistan: issued - 11/16/01, expires - 3/14/02

- Middle East Update: issued - 11/9/01, expires - 2/10/02

- Rwanda: issued - 11/9/01, expires - 3/18/02

- Bolivia: issued - 11/1/01, expires - 2/2/02

- Nicaragua: issued - 10/30/01, expires - 12/1/01

- Sri Lanka: issued - 10/26/01, expires - 1/22/02

- Bangladesh: issued - 10/26/01, expires - 1/9/02
- Worldwide Caution: issued - 10/23/01, expires - 4/19/02
- East Timor: issued - 10/22/01, expires - 3/31/02
- Philippines: issued - 10/5/01, expires - 4/22/02
- Italy: issued - 10/2/01, expires - 1/6/02
- Niger: issued - 9/28/01, expires - 1/6/02
- Georgia: issued - 9/26/01, expires - 11/30/01
- Uzbekistan: issued - 9/22/01, expires - 1/8/02
- Uganda: issued - 9/7/01, expires - 12/6/01
- Colombia: issued - 9/7/01, expires - 12/3/01
- Malaysia: issued - 6/13/01, expires - 12/6/01
- China: issued - 4/19/01, expires - 12/27/01

In addition to this list, the Department issues Consular Information Sheets for every country of the world with information on such matters as the health conditions, crime, unusual currency or entry requirements, any areas of instability, and the location of the nearest embassy or consulate in the subject country.

Be Prepared

Like the Boy Scout motto, the only way to operate in the global environment is to be prepared. Cross-culture competent managers are equipped mentally and physically for unpredictable events. For them it's all part of the adventure and the interest–but they never take unnecessary or uncalculated risks. The best deal in the world is not worth the loss of life or serious injury. We go into real battle for freedom, not for more business, but safety is a matter of degree and personal decision. Whatever your decision, go into it with as much information as you can gather.

Intellectual Property

Individually, global managers represent one of their company's largest investments so it's worthwhile to be sure that they travel safely. However, the information they carry with them is equally important, and people who look just like your competitors are after it. No street thugs with three-day beards, these thieves look just like the clean-cut guy next to you in the bar of the Ritz Carlton, and he is after your intellectual property.

On every public wall in WWII was posted the warning, "Beware, Walls have Ears," or similar cautionary advice. Spies, it was believed, were everywhere, and even the most casual remark by a sailor about to leave port could send his ship to the bottom. Likewise, a casual, inappropriate remark could send your deal to the bottom.

Security is on everybody's mind today, but sometimes we can get too comfortable and off-guard. Maybe we are tired, jet-lagged, or just want to relax and crave human companionship. Beware, the white-collar or mini-skirted crook has been watching and waiting for this opportunity.

Bibliography

Acuff, Frank L. *How to Negotiate Anything with Anyone Anywhere Around the World*. New York: American Management Association, 1997.

Barnet, Richard J., and John Cavanah. *Global Dreams, Imperial Corporations and the New World Order*. New York: Touchstone, 1994.

Bartlett, Christopher A., and Sumantra Ghosgal. *Managing Across Borders*. Boston: Harvard Business School Press, 1991.

Bishop, Bill. *Global Marketing for the Digital Age*. 1999 NTC Business Books, 1999.

Black, J. Stewart, Allen J. Morrison, and Hal B. Gregerson. *Global Explorers*. London: Routledge, 1999.

Chee, Harold, and Rod Harris. *Global Marketing Strategy*. London: Financial Times Professional Ltd., 1998.

Copeland, Lennie, and Lewis Griggs. *Going International, How to Make Friends and Deal Effectively in the Global Marketplace*. New York: Random House, 1986.

Fisher, Roger, and William Ury. *Getting to Yes–Negotiating Agreement without Giving In*. New York: Penguin Books, 1991.

Hampden-Turner, Charles, and Fons Trompenaars. *Building Cross-Cultural Competence*. New York: Yale University Press, 2000.

Hodge, Sheida. *Global Smarts*. New York: John Wiley & Sons, 2000.

Hopfe, Lewis M. *World Religions*. Nashville: Graded Press, 1987.

Huntington, Samuel P. *The Clash of Civilizations*. New York: Simon & Schuster, 1996.

Jeannet, Jean-Pierre. *Managing with a Global Mindset*. Harlow, U.K.: Pearson Education, 2000.

Kanter, Rosabeth Moss. *World Class, Thriving Locally in the Global Economy*. New York: Simon & Schuster, 1995.

Kaplan, Robert D. *The Ends of the Earth*. New York: Random House, 1997.

Leaptrot, Nan. *Rules of the Game–Global Business Protocol*. Cincinnati: Thomson Executive Press, 1996.

Lewis, Richard D. *When Cultures Collide, Managing Successfully Across Cultures*. London: Nicholas Brealey Publishing, 2000.

Marber, Peter. *From Third Class to World Class*. Reading, MA: Perseus Books, 1998.

Marks, Elisabeth. *Breaking through Culture Shock*. London: Nicholas Brealey, 1999.

Morrison, Terri, Wayne A. Conway, and George A. Borden. *Kiss, Bow or Shake Hands*. Holbrook, MA: Adams Media, 1994.

Morrison, Terri, Wayne A. Conway, and Joseph J. Douress. *Dun &

Bradstreet Guide to Doing Business Around the World. Paramus, NJ: Prentice Hall, 1997.

O'Hara-Devereaux, Mary, and Robert Johansen. *Globalwork: Bridging Distance, Culture and Time*. New York: Jossey-Bass Inc., 1994.

Pells, Richard. *Not Like Us*. New York: Harper Collins Publishers, 1997.

Pelton, Robert Young. *The World's Most Dangerous Places*. New York: Harper Collins Publishers, 2000.

Ricks, David A. *Blunders in International Business*. Oxford: Blackwell Publishers, 1999.

Rosen, Robert. *Global Literacies*. New York: Simon & Schuster, 2000.

Rosenweig, Jeffrey A. *Winning the Global Game*. New York: Simon & Schuster, 1998.

Salacuse, Jeswald W. *Making Global Deals*. Boston: Houghton Mifflin, 1991.

Stanat, Ruth. *Global Gold*. New York: American Management Association, 1998.

Faculty of Thunderbird, The American graduate School of International Management. *Thunderbird on Global Business Strategy*. New York: John Wiley & Sons, Inc., 2000.

Urech, Elizabeth. *Speaking Globally*. Dover, NH: Kogan Page, 1998.

Wilfong, James, and Toni Seger. *Taking Your Business Global*. Franklin Lakes, NJ: Career Press, 1997.

Index